Honesty in
the Workplace

FREDERICK LEONG, PH.D.
THE OHIO STATE UNIVERSITY
DEPARTMENT OF PSYCHOLOGY
142 TOWNSHEND HALL
1885 NEIL AVENUE MALL
COLUMBUS OHIO 43210-1222

D0061170

The Cypress Series in Work and Science
edited by *Frank J. Landy*
Pennsylvania State University

Current Titles

Irwin L. Goldstein:
  Training in Organizations, 3rd edition
Kevin Murphy:
  Honesty in the Workplace

Forthcoming Titles

Robert J. Vance and Scott M. Brooks:
  Performance Management and Appraisal
James L. Farr:
  Performance Feedback

Honesty in
the Workplace

Kevin R. Murphy
Colorado State University

Brooks/Cole Publishing Company
Pacific Grove, California

Consulting Editor: *Frank J. Landy*

Brooks/Cole Publishing Company
A Division of Wadsworth, Inc.

© 1993 by Wadsworth, Inc., Belmont, California 94002. All rights reserved.
No part of this book may be reproduced, stored in a retrieval system, or transcribed,
in any form or by any means—electronic, mechanical, photocopying, recording,
or otherwise—without the prior written permission of the publisher,
Brooks/Cole Publishing Company, Pacific Grove, California 93950,
a division of Wadsworth, Inc.

Printed in the United States of America
10 9 8 7 6 5 4 3 2 1

Library of Congress Cataloging in Publication Data
Murphy, Kevin R., [date]
    Honesty in the workplace / Kevin R. Murphy.
      p. cm.
    Includes bibliographical references and index.
    ISBN 0-534-15492-1
    1. Employee theft. 2. Employee crimes. 3. White collar crimes.
4. Honesty. 5. Corporate culture. 6. Industry–Security measures.
I. Title
HF5549.5.E43M87 1992
658.4′73—dc20   92-13136
                                                              CIP

Sponsoring Editor: *Marianne Taflinger*
Editorial Associate: *Heather L. Graeve*
Production Editor: *Marjorie Z. Sanders*
Manuscript Editor: *Catherine Cambron*
Permissions Editor: *Marie DuBois*
Interior and Cover Design: *Sharon L. Kinghan*
Art Coordinator: *Lisa Torri*
Typesetting: *BookPrep*
Printing and Binding: *Malloy Lithographing, Inc.*

To my daughter Kathleen Ann
who, in the time it took me to write this book,
learned to sit up, feed herself, walk, and talk.

About the Author

Kevin R. Murphy is a professor of psychology at Colorado State University. A former Fulbright scholar at the University of Stockholm, Murphy earned a master's degree at Rensselaer Polytechnic Institute and a doctorate degree from Pennsylvania State University. A published author of three previous books, various book chapters, and numerous articles and reviews, Murphy is a fellow of the American Psychological Association, the American Psychological Society and the Society for Industrial and Organizational Psychology.

Preface

When I first agreed to write a book on honesty in the workplace, I had no idea what I was getting into. The topic is incredibly broad, and I found myself reading a diverse set of sources, ranging from books and trade publications describing surveillance devices and security systems to 19th-century works on handwriting analysis. The purpose of this book is to pull together the thinking of researchers, consultants, educators, and managers on the many facets of honesty in the workplace and to present the material at a level that will allow serious researchers to get a foothold on the field, while at the same time giving students and practitioners an accessible overview of the field of honesty in the workplace.

This book was designed for three distinct purposes. First, it can be used in graduate or undergraduate courses in psychology, sociology, and other social sciences, and in business, either as a supplement or as a core text in courses that focus directly on honesty in the workplace. Second, it provides managers, consultants, and other practitioners with an up-to-date discussion of many approaches to dealing with honesty and dishonesty in the workplace. Third, it provides scholars and researchers a review of recent research in many areas related to honesty in the workplace, together with several suggestions for future study.

The book is organized around two general themes. First, honesty or dishonesty may reflect characteristics of the person, the situation, or both. I review ways of increasing honesty or decreasing dishonesty by changing the person (for example, preemployment screening, education in business ethics), changing the situation (for instance, installing better security), or both (for example, changing people's orientation toward the organization). Second, honesty and dishonesty are not necessarily different poles on the same continuum; the strategies most likely to increase honesty are very different from those most likely to decrease dishonesty, and the two are not necessarily complementary. In this book, I discuss ways of increasing honesty and of decreasing dishonesty by changing people, situations, or both.

I could not have written this book without the help and encouragement of several friends and colleagues. Frank Landy, who serves as series editor of the Cypress Series, convinced me to write this book and helped shape the final product in many ways. This is at least the second time in my career that Frank has convinced me to broaden my interests and expertise and to write a book that I would never, without his encouragement, have considered. He has done a tremendous amount over the years to make my career both more interesting and more successful, and I can't thank him enough.

I also thank one of my students, Becca Anhalt, who spent several months camped out in the library, doing a great deal of the footwork that is needed to cover such a diverse literature. Her input was a tremendous help, together with that of the reviewers: Ann Marie Ryan, Bowling Green State University; Paul Sackett; University of Minnesota–Twin Cities; and Kevin Williams, State University of New York at Albany. A number of colleagues, including Paul Sackett and Scott Martin, read drafts of chapters and provided useful insights, while other colleagues, including Jan Cleveland, Robert Hogan, Joyce Hogan, George Paajanen, Barry Staw, and George Thornton, gave feedback and suggestions that helped shape my thinking.

Many organizations generously provided reprints, test booklets, bibliographies, and reports, including the American Polygraphers Association, the American Psychological Association, the Ethics Resource Center, Hogan Assessment Systems, London House, Personnel Decisions Incorporated, and the Society of Stress Analysts. I could not have completed this book without their help. I finished this book while on sabbatical at the University of California at Berkeley, and I received invaluable assistance from the Institute of Industrial Relations and the School of Business Administration there. I want to particularly thank two colleagues who helped arrange that sabbatical visit, Cris Banks and Shelly Zedeck, both of whom also contributed useful ideas to the book.

Kevin R. Murphy

Contents

CHAPTER SEVEN

Encouraging Honesty in Organizations 171

CHAPTER EIGHT

Pitfalls and Promise in the Pursuit of Honesty in Organizations   199

CHAPTER ONE

Understanding Honesty in the Workplace

According to legend, the philosopher Diogenes wandered the streets of ancient Athens carrying a lantern, which he would shine in each stranger's face in a fruitless search for an honest man. In the search for honesty, things seem to have gone from bad to worse. Hardly a week passes without a new scandal, scam, or scoundrel; sometimes it seems that honesty will soon vanish altogether.

Although public awareness of dishonesty has increased, it is not at all clear whether the actual incidence of dishonesty has gone up. As you will see later in this chapter, accurately measuring dishonesty is extremely difficult, and for all we know people may be about as honest—or dishonest—today as they ever have been. What seems to have changed, at least for the present, is the attention given to honesty and integrity, particularly in the workplace. This attention is hardly surprising; reports of dishonesty in government, business, finance, and on the shop floor have become a staple of the evening news. Scandals such as Watergate and Iran-Contra revealed patterns of deception, leaks, burglaries, and lies at the highest levels of government. Investigations of corruption at state and local levels tell a similar tale. The financial scandals of the 1980s, including the collapse of the savings and loan industry and the downfall of many highly respected (and highly paid) stockbrokers, bankers, brokers, and the like, suggest that dishonesty is a significant concern in this sector of the economy. Finally, there is a new public awareness of the problem of employee theft, and controversial methods, ranging from polygraphs and background investigations to paper-and-pencil tests, are being used to deal with the problem. These events and debates have thrust the topic of honesty in the workplace into center stage.

Honesty and Dishonesty in the Workplace

The purpose of this book is to examine the topic of honesty in the workplace and to discuss the many responses to perceived dishonesty, ranging from polygraphs and integrity tests to courses in business

1

ethics, that have been suggested and put into place in various organizations and institutions. In a very general sense, two themes can be used to organize the vast and varied body of research and practice in the area of honesty in the workplace. First, it is necessary to ask exactly what is meant by honesty and integrity, and whether honest or dishonest behavior is caused primarily by characteristics of the person (some people being simply more honest than others are) or by characteristics of the situation (some situations provoking more dishonest behavior than others do). Second, strategies designed to deal with honesty in the workplace appear to take two very different forms. Some are designed to reduce dishonesty, through increased security, personnel screening, and so on, whereas others are designed to increase honesty, through training, motivational strategies (for instance, giving rewards for honest behavior), and the like. Depending on whether you think of honesty as a characteristic of the person or of the situation, and depending on whether your goal is to discourage dishonesty or to encourage honesty, you might attempt very different strategies and interventions. Throughout this book, I will discuss strategies for encouraging honesty, discouraging dishonesty, or both that rely on changing characteristics of the person (for example, through selection or training), the situation (for instance, security measures), or both (for example, requiring all managers to take courses in business ethics).

In this chapter, I will first discuss a number of definitions of honesty, with particular attention to the question of what standards should be used to define honesty and dishonesty in the workplace. Next, I will discuss research on the frequency and seriousness of various types of workplace dishonesty and point out problems in estimating the extent of workplace dishonesty. I will then discuss conditions under which such behaviors as working slowly and sloppily, taking long breaks, or failing to carry out agreed-upon duties may fall under the umbrella of workplace dishonesty. Finally, I will discuss the debate over whether honesty is a characteristic of the person, the situation, or both.

Standards for Evaluating Honesty

Honesty in the workplace is like Tabasco sauce—more is not always better. A person who is completely honest about everything he or she encounters in an organization will probably not be an effective worker (Saxe, 1990). I started this chapter with the legend of Diogenes's search for an honest man. At first, this pursuit sounds noble, but in fact Diogenes was rightly regarded by many of his contemporaries as a crackpot and a crank, in part because he was honest even in situations where honesty was completely inappropriate. His search for an honest man was not a genuine search at all, but rather was his way of rubbing in his view that ancient Athens was populated by liars.

An example may help to illustrate the point that absolute honesty is often neither helpful nor appropriate. In performance appraisal interviews, it is common for supervisors to give higher ratings and more positive feedback than the subordinate deserves. There is evidence that inflated ratings and overly positive feedback are in fact beneficial. Rating inflation helps supervisors avoid unnecessary conflicts within the work group, and overly positive feedback may have a more positive effect on future performance than feedback that is brutally frank (Murphy & Cleveland, 1991). Although this rating inflation is not precisely honest, it is not clear whether it should be labeled a lie. How rating inflation should be looked at may depend on the intentions of the rater. For example, giving high ratings to boost a subordinate's self-esteem is not the same as giving high ratings so that a problem employee will be promoted into someone else's work group.

Imagine an organization in which everyone was always honest about everything. If your secretary thought your suit was ugly, he or she would tell you. If your presentation was not clear and concise, people would not attempt to hide their boredom, and they might stop the meeting at any point to tell you to stop wasting their time. There would be no need to be polite (for instance, people would say "How are you?" only when they were interested in the answer), or to hold back hurtful or destructive observations (for example, telling someone that you notice he or she has gained weight). This type of an organization would not be a congenial place to work and would probably not survive long.

If you accept the proposition that absolute honesty in all interactions is not a reasonable standard, it becomes necessary to define precisely what *is* meant by honesty in the workplace. Most discussions of workplace honesty include notions about refraining from lying and upholding high ethical standards and high levels of integrity. However, each of these ideas is potentially ambiguous, especially in situations like the workplace that involve complex social interactions. To reach an acceptable definition of honesty in the workplace, you must first examine the relationships between honesty on the one hand and lies, integrity, and ethics on the other.

Lies and honesty.   A lie is commonly defined as an intentionally deceptive, stated message (Lewicki, 1983). Honesty is clearly more than the absence of lies. For example, one might be dishonest by leaving out or covering up relevant information. Such an action does not meet the definition of a lie because it involves an *unstated* deception.

Philosophers have struggled over the definition of a lie, and in particular, over the question of whether lies are ever justified. Ancient and medieval philosophers such as St. Augustine and St. Thomas Aquinas recognized a distinction between lies and falsehoods based primarily on the intention of the speaker (Kirwan, 1989). A statement that is not intended to deceive is not a lie, even if it is false. On the other hand, a statement that is objectively true, but presented in a way that is intended to mislead or deceive, is classified as a lie.

The intention to deceive implies a belief that the audience will probably accept the lie as fact. Thus, any analysis of lies must consider not only the (potential) liar, but also the audience. The reaction of the audience is most important in analyzing the category of untrue statements that Aquinas referred to as "polite lies." These are minor misrepresentations, often complimentary, that are not supposed to be taken literally, and that are designed to flatter or please. The assumption here is that the person you are talking with understands that the flattering phrases and flowery greetings are not meant literally, but are rather simply a way of being polite. Thus, asking "How are you?" when you are not interested in the answer is not a form of lying because both parties understand that the question is usually not meant literally.

Analyzing the audience's potential reaction to a variety of less-than-honest statements may be critical in understanding the ways individuals rationalize lying. Cressy (1970) notes that individuals who commit dishonest acts often rationalize that their behavior is not really dishonest, particularly if the behavior is somewhat common or customary. This rationalizing may reflect the individual's belief that dishonest behavior is expected or tolerated in a particular situation and that he or she is not expected to act with strict regard to the truth. Viewed in this light, if the audience does not expect scrupulously honest behavior, then dishonest behavior that does occur may not fit the philosophers' definition of lying. Saxe (1990) suggests that one of the difficulties in discouraging dishonesty is that liars sometimes believe that they are telling the truth. Therefore, a variety of methods aimed at discouraging deception may be ineffective for the large numbers of dishonest individuals who sincerely believe that they are not violating the usual or reasonable standards for honesty in their work environment.

The position that lies are defined in part by the liar and in part by the audience parallels a debate that has surrounded personality research—that is, whether personality traits refer to characteristics of the actor or to attributions of observers. For example, the statement that a person is honest might refer to his or her behavior, or to others' interpretations of that behavior. Although others' interpretations are important for determining whether the behavior in question constitutes a lie, in this book I will treat honesty as a reflection of the actor's actual behavior rather than an illusion on the part of the observer. As you will see later in this chapter, honesty is not necessarily a trait in the sense that a person is either always honest or always dishonest; situational factors are critically important. Nevertheless, honesty does have some basis in reality rather than being solely based on the actor's perceptions, and the avoidance of lies is one component of honesty.

Integrity and honesty.   The terms *honesty* and *integrity* are sometimes used interchangeably when referring to honesty in the workplace. For example, many of the paper-and-pencil tests that are used to make inferences about which individuals are more or less likely to engage in dishonest behavior at work are referred to as "integrity tests." However, philosophers draw a potentially important distinction between the two (McFall, 1987). Integrity is a broader concept that refers to the extent to which a person lives up to his or her personal ideals or values. Integrity usually implies honesty and fairness, because these are values most people claim to uphold, but an individual with a high level of integrity might, in the service of some higher end, engage in dishonest behavior.

Integrity implies the belief that you are acting correctly, which underscores the importance of understanding the norms, standards, and so on that the individual and work group use to define honest and dishonest behavior. A worker who truly believes that a particular behavior is acceptable, because of custom, norms, and the like, may act with integrity even if the behavior itself involves deception or departures from the truth.

Integrity is closely akin to idealism, in the sense that both involve acting in accordance with your beliefs. A person who claims to believe that honesty is critical but who often lies shows little integrity. A politician who claims to believe in compassion for the weak, but who votes to expel the homeless from shelters because affluent neighbors complain, shows little idealism. Although idealism and integrity are usually portrayed as positive qualities, neither necessarily contributes to honesty or even basic decency. Terrible crimes have been committed by idealists such as Hitler, who carried his deeply held but viciously warped beliefs out to their logical conclusion. Integrity is not enough to guarantee honesty or even decency; to ensure these, you must also subscribe to some ethical standard that encourages honesty and a regard for the truth.

Ethics and honesty.   Ethics is the branch of philosophy concerned with understanding human conduct in light of moral principles. The fundamental problem in ethics is defining those moral principles and determining their source (for example, natural law or social convention). Virtually all ethical systems encourage honesty but also allow for situations in which a strict regard for the truth is not required. In an example cited earlier, Aquinas's ethical philosophy recognized that, in social situations, compliments and flattering phrases were not meant to be taken literally and thus would not constitute lies. Utili-

tarian theories of ethical behavior suggest that dishonesty is acceptable if more good comes from being dishonest than from being
honest.

Ethical theories suggest that honesty has two components. First,
one must avoid lies. Second, there is an affirmative obligation to uphold the truth. For example, a manufacturer cannot, according to
most ethical theories, knowingly omit critical information about the
safety of a product from its advertising campaign. For example, in the
1960s and 1970s, several auto manufacturers were accused of failing
to disclose or act on information indicating that their products were
inherently unsafe. Even in cases where no explicit claim of safety was
made about those products, the failure to disclose critical information
is regarded, in ethical theory, as dishonest.

Business ethics has become a buzzword in the popular press and
especially in business education. As I will note later, many business
schools now devote considerable time and effort to courses and training in business ethics. One of the significant, and largely unresolved,
debates in business ethics concerns when and under what circumstances individuals have an obligation to be honest or, conversely,
have the right to conceal or even misrepresent information in their
dealings with clients, workers, competitors, and so on. Although the
speculations of ethical philosophers are useful and interesting, this
debate is more likely to be settled on the shop floor and in the office
than in the classroom. The ethical theories that seem to guide the
everyday behavior of workers, managers, and executives are probably
best understood by examining the participants' behavior.

The ethical theories that guide the behavior of individuals in work
settings are not theories in any formal sense, but rather individual
definitions of good and bad, or more generally, acceptable and unacceptable behavior in the workplace. In a later section, I will review
evidence suggesting that individuals rarely regard their own behavior
as wrong or dishonest, even when they engage in outrageous falsehoods. As long as the behavior in question is tolerated by custom or
accepted by co-workers, superiors, or both as appropriate and justifiable, that behavior is not likely to be regarded by the individual as
dishonest, wrong, or unethical. This finding suggests that to understand honesty in the workplace, we must examine the norms, customs,
and assumptions of members of the organization, as well as the
messages conveyed by the organization about the range and limits of
acceptable behavior.

Defining acceptable behavior in organizations.   The standards
that define workers' and managers' beliefs about behaviors that are
either acceptable or unacceptable in an organization are conveyed
through both formal and informal channels. In later chapters (especial-

ly Chapters 2 and 6), I will discuss the role played by norms of the work group, managers, executives, and so forth in shaping the honesty of individual members of the organization, and I will review evidence showing that if others who are important to an individual regard acts such as taking home tools and materials, padding expense accounts, doing extensive amounts of personal business on company time, and the like as acceptable (and therefore not dishonest), those acts will no longer seem dishonest or wrong to the individual. In this section, I will comment on formal organizational policies regarding honesty.

Policy statements regarding honesty in the workplace often have an air of unreality because they fail to confront the idea that absolute honesty in all dealings is probably not a sensible standard or expectation. Black-and-white standards that forbid any dishonest behavior, no matter how trivial, are fine in theory but troublesome in practice. A secretary who takes a pencil home has, in the narrowest sense, committed employee theft, but it might be unwise to label it as such or to punish him or her. One reason for the widespread disagreement over the extent of employee theft (discussed in some detail later in this chapter) is that very different definitions of theft are used. More broadly, researchers and organizations often fail to specify what constitutes acceptable and unacceptable behavior.

Buckley (1987) recommends that organizations define explicit standards for acceptable behavior to be used in making a variety of

Box 1-1   *Honesty, Integrity, and Goodness*

By most definitions a good person is, among other things, honest. However, honesty and integrity are no guarantee of goodness. Consider the case described below.

The person in question served as the interior minister in a government that was notorious for its corruption, but he himself always exhibited high standards of personal honesty and integrity in his work. For example, when he took his parents on Sunday drives (he was also a dutiful son) in a company car, he would always carefully calculate the mileage costs and deduct that amount from his salary. He rarely took vacations or sick leave, and he always gave a good day's work for a good day's pay.

This individual may sound like a model employee, except for the fact that he was one of the most sadistic butchers of the 20th century—Reichsführer Heinrich Himmler, leader of Hitler's SS. He was personally honest, almost to a fault, and acted in complete integrity with respect to the racist and totalitarian philosophies of the Nazi party. However, his actions hardly fit most people's conceptions of "good" behavior. His career provides a vivid reminder that honesty and integrity do not necessarily imply goodness.

decisions. For example, an organization that discovers that one cᶠ its employees or job applicants has stolen something from the workplace might be tempted to take quick and decisive action (for example, firing the thief). It might be more realistic to consider a number of factors, including the time span involved, the frequency of dishonest behaviors, the dollar value of losses, and the type of misconduct. An applicant who admits stealing $5 from petty cash 15 years ago is not necessarily a bad risk.

It is likely that both supervisors and subordinates use some minimum threshold in defining theft and that taking smaller amounts is not regarded as stealing or at least is not thought of as unacceptable (Taylor, 1986). As I will note in several later chapters, one critical component of any program designed to reduce this type of workplace dishonesty is a decision about the limits of acceptable and unacceptable behaviors in areas related to honesty. An organization that is determined to eliminate every possible form of property and production deviance might find itself going to great lengths to eliminate trivial thefts. While a "zero tolerance" policy has the advantage of drawing a clear line between acceptable and unacceptable behavior, such a policy may have the disadvantage of putting many employees on the "wrong side of the law" and creating difficulties in enforcement. On the other hand, an organization that decides against a zero tolerance policy puts itself in the uncomfortable position of deciding exactly how much honesty it wants or requires. I know of few organizations that have developed a realistic solution to this dilemma.

Honesty in the workplace: definition.   As the preceding sections suggest, the question of exactly what constitutes honesty in the workplace is more complicated than it at first appears. This book is not devoted to understanding every possible deviation from absolute truthfulness in the workplace. Rather, the central focus of this book is on understanding the circumstances under which members of organizations either abide by or violate widely held ethical standards regarding truthfulness in their behavior and communications. These widely held standards may be easily applied to the most spectacular incidents of workplace dishonesty, such as large-scale theft, embezzlement, fraud, and the like, which are clearly recognized as dishonest; research on these acts is discussed in the section that follows. The more difficult and ultimately more interesting questions in this area deal with behaviors that may or may not be regarded as truly dishonest, depending on the prevailing norms, standards, and beliefs about the circumstances under which untruthful behavior is regarded as appropriate and acceptable. These norms, standards, and beliefs are part of a person's ethical theory for workplace behavior.

Honesty in the workplace is defined here in terms of the extent to which individuals and groups in organizations abide by consistent and rational ethical principles related to obligations to respect the truth. For example, everyday social flattery is not (usually) completely honest, but it is almost universally tolerated, and rarely regarded as dishonest. The limitation that honesty is defined in terms of consistent and rational principles implies that individuals cannot adopt completely fluid principles, which change in each new situation, and still claim to be honest. Neither can individuals adopt principles that would not withstand rational scrutiny (for instance, the moral principle that it is acceptable for a person to lie because it makes him or her happy to do so) and still claim to be honest. However, a wide range of beliefs about honesty might meet both these tests, being both consistent and rational. It is therefore quite possible for different individuals to behave quite differently in the same situation (for instance, either disclosing or failing to disclose a product's minor shortcoming) and still regard their own behavior as honest.

The sections that follow review research on the types of workplace dishonesty that have received the greatest attention in the media. Then the chapter will discuss a broader class of behaviors, perhaps less spectacular but more pervasive than theft and embezzlement, that is referred to as production deviance.

Incidence and Extent of Dishonesty in the Workplace

More is written about the incidence and seriousness of dishonesty in the workplace than is actually known. For example, although virtually every author discussing employee theft agrees that it is a significant problem, it is very difficult to pin down exactly how much is lost per year due to employee theft. Similarly, everyone agrees that corporate crimes, ranging from fraud and price fixing to the knowing sale of unsafe or ineffective products, represent a major drain on the economy, but it is very difficult to arrive at any consensus about the extent or seriousness of white-collar or corporate crime.

To illustrate both what is known about and the difficulties in estimating the extent and seriousness of dishonest behavior in the workplace, I will discuss three types of workplace dishonesty that are thought to be especially common: employee theft, corporate corruption, and resume fraud.

Employee theft. Research suggests that serious wrongdoing on the part of employees, such as theft, fraud, embezzlement, and the like, is widespread. Finney and Lesieur (1982) suggested that such wrongdoing is "extremely common, and much more costly than common crime" (p. 256). While it is clear that employee theft, fraud, and so forth represent a serious problem, there is considerable disagreement about exactly how serious that problem is. For example, estimates of the amount lost per year to employee theft vary widely (for examples, see Bacas, 1987; Cunningham, 1989; Inbau, 1989; White, 1984); Table 1-1 presents estimates that vary by a factor of 50 ($4 billion to $200 billion). In part, this variability may be attributable to inflation; earlier estimates tend to be lower than more recent ones. However, as I will note later, differences in these estimates also reflect fundamental disagreements over the extent and nature of employee theft.

In addition to the amounts noted in Table 1-1, several other statistics related to employee theft are widely cited. For example, employee theft is cited as one of the primary reasons for 30% of all small business failures (Inbau, 1989). Meinsma (1985) claims that 10 to 30% of all bankruptcies are due to employee theft. Bacas (1987) claims that employee theft is rising by 15% per year. Hollinger and Clark (1983) note that over 40% of retail and 36% of manufacturing employees surveyed admit to employee theft, although the thefts are often small and may occur only a few times during the employee's entire career.

Employee theft rates appear to be higher in industries in which there are frequent opportunities or strong inducements to steal, such as retail sales, medicine (where theft of drugs is especially common), and banking. As a result, citing any single figure as an overall estimate of the theft rate may be misleading. An overall theft rate statistic will probably overestimate theft rates in some industries (for instance, cement truck drivers may have few opportunities or incentives to steal cement) and underestimate them in others.

Sackett and Harris (1985) give two reasons for the wide variability in the estimates of total losses due to theft. First, they note that the widely cited American Management Association's estimate of $40 billion actually includes all forms of crime against business, including commercial bribery, securities theft, embezzlement, check fraud, and insurance fraud. Outright theft by employees is thought to represent only $5 to $10 billion of the total. Second, estimates of the total amount lost to various types of crime often turn out to represent little

Table 1-1 *Estimates of the Annual Extent of Employee Theft*

$6–10 billion—White (1984)
$5–10 billion—National Institute of Justice (1986)
$20–40 billion—American Management Association (1977)
$40 billion—U.S. Commerce Department (1987)
$4–50 billion (depending on definition of theft)—Moore (1988)
$50 billion—Business Integrity Institute (1988)
$200 billion—Lary (1988)

more than guesswork. Singer (1971) labels such figures "mythical numbers." He illustrates that widely cited figures, such as the total amount stolen by drug addicts in New York City, are often generated by very imprecise processes and are sometimes plucked out of thin air. He shows, for example, that the most widely cited estimate of the amount annually stolen by heroin addicts in New York City (approximately $2 to $5 billion in 1970) cannot possibly be true; some simple calculations make it is easy to show that it would be physically impossible for the number of individuals involved to move and store all the property necessary to generate that much income, much less to steal and fence it.

Horgan (1990) illustrates the process by which similar mythical numbers have come to dominate the debate over the costs associated with drug abuse in the work force. For example, it is widely believed that $60 to $100 billion per year is lost due to drug-related productivity decreases, accidents, medical claims, and theft. Similarly, it is widely believed that drug abusers are more than three times as likely as nonusers to be involved in workplace accidents involving injury to themselves or others. The figure for accidents can be traced back to a study done in one company that actually had nothing at all to do with illicit drug abuse. Rather, the study made a rough guess of the hazards associated with alcoholism in that one company.

The process by which the $60 to $100 billion figure was estimated is even more bizarre. Horgan (1990) shows how this widely quoted figure can be traced back to a single study that made some very questionable assumptions. In this study, it was found that households in which one or more persons had ever admitted to daily marijuana use (even if in the distant past) had a household income 28% lower than that of other households in the sample. This 28% difference was labeled "loss due to marijuana use," implying that marijuana use was the sole cause of the income loss. Alternative explanations of this difference, such as the hypothesis that low income might lead to drug abuse or the existence of some third variable (for instance, a higher availability of drugs in less affluent neighborhoods), were not considered. This 28% loss in income was then extrapolated to the population as a whole, leading to an estimated loss of $26 billion. Another $21 billion was added on to represent the estimated costs of drug-related crime, health problems, accidents, and so on (this $21 billion is itself another mythical number), and the total of $47 billion was then adjusted for inflation and population growth to arrive at figures in the $60 to $100 billion range.

The term *shrinkage* is often used to refer to unexplained shortages and losses in inventory, cash, tools, and supplies. Some proportion of shrinkage is certainly due to employee theft, but it is very difficult to determine exactly how much is lost per year to theft as opposed to a number of alternative causes of shrinkage (for example, sloppy bookkeeping). While various figures for shrinkage and shrinkage due to theft are cited by both sides in debates over various theft-reduction programs, it is unlikely that any of these figures is completely accurate.

Corporate corruption.   Every year, a number of corporations engage in a wide variety of criminal, corrupt, and unethical acts that all involve some degree of dishonesty. Clinard (1990) documents more than 100 cases that include price fixing; wanton disregard for the safety of the public, the work force, or both; fraudulent warranties; fraudulent cost overruns; bribery; and outright theft. Virtually every one of these cases involves dishonest behavior on the part of executives or upper management. Even where the act itself is not inherently dishonest (for example, potentially unsafe disposal of toxic waste), it is common for corporations to attempt to cover up unethical or unseemly behaviors.

Most discussions of crime and other dishonest behaviors at work focus on situations where the corporation is the victim, as in employee theft. The annual losses suffered by corporations as a result of employee theft are undoubtedly large, although as noted earlier they might fall anywhere in the $5 to $50 billion range. However, these losses probably pale in comparison to those the public suffers as a result of corporate crime and corruption. For example, Meier and Short (1982) estimated that annual losses due to corporate crime exceeded $100 billion (in 1982, when $100 billion could actually buy something!). If technical violations of the law, such as antitrust violations, are added to the total, this figure could easily double.

White-collar crimes are not only large in size, they also appear to be widespread. In 1985, more than 10,000 defendants were convicted of federal white-collar crimes; 30% of the suspects investigated by U.S. attorneys were thought to be involved in white-collar crimes (White Collar Crime, 1987). Many of these crimes such as conterfeiting, occurred outside of the traditional workplace, but even factoring these out, it is clear that dishonest behavior among managers and executives is widespread.

The recent collapse of a significant number of savings and loan (S & L) institutions presents another example of corporate corruption and white-collar crime. The S & L crisis was partly the result of fraud, misrepresentation, and abuse of banking regulations on the part of the directors of those institutions; the U.S. Department of Justice estimates that fraud was a significant factor in one-third to one-half of the cases examined. The estimated cost of the S & L bailout exceeds $250 billion and continues to climb.

Schutt (1982) referred to white-collar crime as the "nation's largest growth industry." It is useful to distinguish between two fundamentally different types of white-collar or corporate crime. The first type includes cases where executives or managers commit crimes or dishonest acts on behalf of the organization. For example, executives involved in price-fixing may receive relatively little direct benefit from their illegal activities; the most direct beneficiary may be the organization.[1] The second type includes many other crimes and dishonest acts committed by executives, managers, and so on that represent crimes against the organization; this type might better be labeled white-collar crime. For example, executives might become involved in embezzlement or stock manipulation, in which the organization is the immediate victim. Other forms of white-collar crime might involve using the organization as a front or vehicle for illegal or fraudulent activities. Although the organization may not be the immediate victim, it certainly may suffer as a result of its perhaps unwitting involvement in the criminal activities.

A second useful distinction is between cases where the activity is carried out by one person or a small number of persons acting alone and without the organization's sanction (often referred to as white-collar crime) and cases where the activity is carried out by a large number of individuals as part of the implicit or explicit policy of the organization (often referred to as corporate corruption). The causes and methods that might be used to control these two types of dishonesty are probably quite different.

As was the case with employee theft, a number of estimates of the extent and seriousness of white-collar and corporate crime have been made, but they all appear to be mythical numbers of one form or other. We simply do not know enough about the frequency or scope of white-collar crime to arrive at an authoritative figure.

Resume fraud. Resume fraud appears common. Buckley (1988) cites a report from a committee of the House of Representatives that estimates that one in three applicants falsifies information concerning their education, job history, job responsibilities, salaries, or criminal history. Goldstein (1971) reported substantial discrepancies between completed applications and reports from applicants' former employers concerning the previous position held, previous salary, duration of employment, and reasons for leaving. McKee and Bayes (1987) report that 44% of the organizations they surveyed had experienced at least one incident of resume fraud. Norton (1988) details a variety of ways in which applicants construct fraudulent resumes, including misleading educational credentials, omitted or incorrect employment dates, exaggerated claims of experience or expertise, fraudulent claims of self-employment, and fraudulent claims of serving as a consultant.

---

[1] However, many executives receive performance bonuses, stock options, and the like, so that activities that benefit the organization might also indirectly benefit the individuals involved in corporate crime.

As with employee theft and white-collar crime, estimates of the extent and seriousness of resume fraud turn out to be imprecise. In part, this imprecision comes about because the term *resume fraud* covers a lot of ground, ranging from minor misrepresentations (and even valid disagreements about how particular experiences or qualifications should be presented on a resume) to major falsifications. Difficulty in developing accurate estimates also reflects difficulties with the ways in which fraud statistics are often reported. For example, knowing that 44% of all organizations encounter some resume fraud does not mean that 44% of all resumes are fraudulent. A large organization might see 1 fraudulent resume in 1000, but such an organization would still be counted as part of the 44% that encounter resume fraud.

Implications of imprecise estimates.   Dishonest behavior is, by its nature, difficult to pin down and estimate with any precision (Rosenbaum & Bauer, 1982). In the three cases described above—employee theft, corporate crime, and resume fraud—experts are ready and willing to quote figures about the extent and seriousness of the particular offense, but it is difficult to find agreement or to accept experts' figures as authoritative. An additional difficulty is that the individuals making and publicizing estimates of different types of crime, dishonesty, and the like often have a vested interest in making sure that the estimate comes out the "right" way. For example, Horgan (1990) notes that companies involved in employee drug testing have aggressively advertised estimates of the seriousness of employee drug use that are almost certainly inflated. Unfortunately, hype and hysteria can be profitable if you are selling a method for reducing drug use, employee theft, corporate crime, and so on, and it appears that many of the organizations involved in the business of dealing with dishonesty in the work force tend to overestimate both the scope of the problem and their product's effectiveness in dealing with that problem (APA Task Force, 1991). On the other hand, some individuals or organizations might have a stake in underestimating the seriousness of some of these problems. A union that is fighting a mandatory drug-testing policy is likely to underestimate rather than overestimate problems with employee drug use. Given all of the difficulties in obtaining accurate estimates of theft, crime, and dishonesty, and all of the reasons to come up with either optimistic or pessimistic figures, making precise statements about the frequency, extent, or seriousness of dishonest behavior in the workplace is an undertaking fraught with uncertainty.

The difficulties in estimating the extent and seriousness of employee theft and other forms of dishonesty in the workplace are formidable, but they must be kept in perspective. The same problems are encountered in estimating the frequency of street crimes, security violations, and other acts that are by their nature usually concealed. The fact that we don't know the precise extent of employee theft and other dishonest acts should not obscure what we do know. Even if the lowest possible estimate of their incidence was accepted, employee theft, resume fraud, corporate crime, and the like would still be serious problems that are well worth our attention. Workplace dishonesty is like a snake in the water—slippery and hard to get a handle on, but dangerous to ignore.

Types of Dishonesty

The preceding section reviewed three specific types of workplace dishonesty. This section reviews a broader class of behaviors that might be considered instances of dishonesty and examines the hypothesis that there is only one type of dishonesty, with different acts of workplace dishonesty varying only in their severity, not in their nature.

Property and Production Deviance

Although much discussion of employee honesty has focused on the specific topic of theft, it is clear that the concept of honesty in the workplace is considerably broader. In particular, it is useful to consider broad constructs such as reliability or deviance in discussing honesty in the workplace (Hogan & Hogan, 1989; Hollinger & Clark, 1983). Workers vary considerably in the extent to which they engage in a variety of undesirable or forbidden behaviors, theft being only one of these; programs designed to detect, prevent, or deter theft may capture only a small part of a broad cluster of behaviors indicative of dishonesty at work.

Employee deviance can be broken down into two categories: property deviance, which involves the misappropriation or misuse of another's property; and production deviance, which involves the willful restriction of production or performance that is normally required by the job. Theft, pilferage, embezzlement, and sabotage are all examples of property deviance. Misuse of discount privileges in the retail industry is also considered a form of property deviance (Hollinger & Clark, 1982b). Doing slow and sloppy work; abuse of sick leave; goldbricking; excessive socializing at work; use of drugs, alcohol, or both at work; coming late and leaving early—all are examples of production deviance.

Both property deviance and production deviance can be thought of as forms of dishonesty at work, but the causes of these two types of deviance may not be the same. For example, Hollinger and Clark (1982b, 1983) present evidence from several studies suggesting that job satisfaction has a significant role in production deviance, but is a less important determinant of property deviance (see also Mangione & Quinn, 1975, and Moretti, 1986). In a later section, I will consider the question whether production and property deviance represent qualitatively different forms of dishonesty, or are merely different forms of the same general phenomenon—that is, dishonest behavior in the workplace.

Production deviance and honesty.   A distinction may be drawn between occasional withdrawals from work (because of personal problems, stress, and so forth) and habitual patterns of carelessness, neglect, or abuse of privilege; only the latter are thought of as deviant. Even in this case, the classification of production deviance as a form of dishonesty may seem strange. If you ask your co-workers whether it is dishonest to take a long lunch break or to spend lots of time socializing at work, they may tell you it is wrong, but they probably will not call it dishonest. Nevertheless, when one examines the rights and obligations of both employers and employees, as well as the sources of those rights, it seems clear that most forms of production deviance can legitimately be considered a type of dishonesty in the workplace.

Both the employer and the employee have obligations regarding honesty in the workplace. One way to understand the source of these obligations is to consider the nature of the working relationship and the explicit and implicit contracts that are made between employers and employees. Handbooks, contracts, and the like often spell out specific obligations, although they usually say more about the obligations of the employee than about those of the employer. For example, an organization's administrative handbook might define the expenses that can legitimately be charged to the organization. These formal documents represent one source of information about the specific behaviors that are accepted or sanctioned at work and thus tell us something about the type and level of honesty expected. The unwritten rules that result from the implicit contract between employers and employees may constitute an even more important consideration in determining employers' and employees' obligations regarding honesty in the workplace.

Many historians, economists, and organizational theorists (for example, Ditton, 1977; Mahoney, 1979; March & Simon, 1958) view employment as an exchange involving an implicit contract between the employer and the employee—that is, employment involves a set of mutual rights and responsibilities on the part of the employer and the employee. The employee promises to carry out certain tasks and duties, and the employer promises to provide reasonable working conditions and equitable rewards. The employee who performs sloppy work, takes long lunch breaks, or spends significant amounts of company time on the phone violates this implicit contract, and therein lies the dishonesty associated with counterproductive behaviors at work. Implicit contract theory assumes that employees know their responsibilities when they take the job and by accepting the job agree to carry them out. Failing to carry these duties out is therefore a violation of the implicit promise the employee makes when he or she takes the job.

One difficulty with the notion of an implicit contract is that different parties may have very different interpretations of the duties, obligations, benefits, and so on that are part of that contract. In Chapter 2, I will discuss in more detail the role of attitudes, beliefs, and norms in employee theft and other forms of dishonesty; at this point, I will simply note that the same behaviors may be viewed as either honest or dishonest, depending on one's point of view. Thus, management may view long lunch breaks as time theft, whereas employees may regard them as a long-standing right that is not in the written contract, but is accepted by all employees.

Deviance and organizational level. Virtually all the studies of property and production deviance I have read deal with labor, not management. Similarly, many programs designed to reduce theft, production deviance, and so on seem to be aimed at labor rather than at management. Examples include polygraphs and written integrity tests, security systems, and employee drug tests. It is somewhat ironic that the Reagan administration proposed extending polygraph examinations to large numbers of lower-level employees, in part to discourage embarrassing leaks, at the same time that many higher-level administrators were engaging in apparently dishonest activities in contexts such as the Iran-Contra scandal.

It might make some sense to concentrate on lower-level employees if dishonesty were in fact more common at lower levels in the organization. As with many questions about the frequency and extent of dishonest behavior, the best answer to questions about how much dishonesty exists at different organizational levels is that nobody really knows. Nevertheless, there are some reasons to believe that both property and production deviance may indeed be concentrated at lower levels of the organization.

There is evidence that individuals with low levels of commitment to the organization and to the job are more likely to engage in theft and perhaps in various forms of production deviance (Hollinger & Clark, 1983); several relevant studies will be discussed in later chapters. There is also evidence that commitment to the job, the career, and the organization increases as one moves up the corporate ladder. This focus on lower-level workers may thus seem reasonably justified.

Marxists are likely to view the above discussion as another example of class discrimination (for an application of Marxist analysis to performance appraisal, see Goldman, 1983). In this case, they probably have a point. Even if dishonesty is less frequent at higher levels of the organization—and this is a big "if"—the seriousness of ethical violations committed by managers and executives probably exceeds the seriousness of ethical violations committed by all the other members of the organization combined. Executives have opportunities to steal or waste millions, and sometimes, as in the S & L scandal, they avail themselves of those opportunities. Lower-level employees, no matter how dishonest, rarely have opportunities to engage in theft of this magnitude. An organization seriously concerned with dishonesty would look first to discouraging dishonest behavior at the very top. The fact that most organizations concentrate on the bottom and ignore the top may say something about their commitment to dealing with dishonesty in the workplace.

The types of dishonest acts an individual undertakes probably vary as a function of his or her level in an organization. For example, it seems unlikely that large numbers of executives intentionally do slow and sloppy work (although credible data regarding the incidence of this type of production deviance at different levels of the organization might be hard to come by). It also seems unlikely that lower-level managers or shop-floor workers would engage in such forms of dishonesty as embezzlement and price-fixing. Their position in the organization simply does not provide meaningful opportunities for these types of dishonesty. As you will see in the next chapter, the characteristics of individuals most likely to become involved in property and production deviance suggest that that type of dishonesty is more frequent at lower levels in the organization. However, the opportunities for serious wrongdoing are so much greater at the top that a handful of dishonest managers or executives could do much more damage than could a large number of dishonest production workers.

Types versus Levels of Deviance and Dishonesty

Dishonest behavior in the workplace takes many forms, ranging from goldbricking or excessive socializing at work to embezzlement of millions. It is not clear whether these different forms are all variations on the same theme (that is, dishonesty at work), differing only in terms of their seriousness, or whether instead they are qualitatively different from one another. For example, if a person takes long lunch breaks, is he or she also more likely to steal?

The question whether meaningfully different types of dishonest behavior in the workplace exist or whether all types amount to the same thing is both interesting and important. If all forms of dishonesty are indeed the same behavior, differing only in level or seriousness, it should be possible to scale virtually all incidents of dishonesty in the workplace on a continuum like the one shown in Figure 1-1.

Hollinger and Clark (1983) suggested that production and property deviance could indeed be scaled in this fashion. Although they did not consider white-collar or corporate crime, there is no reason (according to their arguments) that these acts could not be included in such a continuum.

It is important to keep in mind that the arrangement of dishonest acts on a single scale, as shown in Figure 1-1, represents a hypothesis, not a well-established fact. Nevertheless, the idea that different types of dishonesty are all reflections of the same basic phenomenon is appealing in both theoretical and practical terms. The practical importance of describing different types of dishonesty in terms of a single continuum is best understood in terms of the so-called stepping-stone theories that have been proposed in areas such as adolescent drug use (Kandel, 1975; Swaim, in press) and antisocial behavior in children (Patterson, DeBaryshe, & Ramsey, 1989). All these theories involve the notion that small misdeeds come before large ones, with each misdeed representing a stepping-stone toward the next, more serious one. Thus, in the area of drug abuse, if you can keep adolescents from using alcohol and marijuana, you will also keep them from becoming involved in more serious and deadly drugs, such as cocaine and heroin. In the workplace, if you can select or train workers who will not, as a matter of principle, take long lunch breaks, you may not have to worry about more serious violations. An employee who will not take a long lunch break probably will not raid the cash box either.

The alternative theory is that various forms of workplace dishonesty are qualitatively different, and that a person who would never think of taking $10 out of the cash box might be very willing to inflate his or her resume or to use hundreds of dollars worth of company resources for his or her personal gain or benefit. If this theory is true, removing the small stepping-stones (by discouraging the most minor forms of work-

Figure 1-1   *A Continuum of Workplace Dishonesty*

Level	Acts
Most dishonest	stock manipulation
	large-scale embezzlement
	theft of moderate amount of cash
	hiding a prison record on your resume
	taking home small tools and materials
	purposefully sloppy work
	long-distance phone calls from office
Least dishonest	long lunch breaks

place dishonesty might not help in reducing the more serious forms of dishonesty.

The best support for this latter conception of dishonesty in the workplace comes from research on the perceptions of employees and managers who appear to be engaged in wrongdoing. Individuals engaged in these behaviors often believe that they are doing no wrong and that their behavior simply cannot be compared to other forms of dishonesty in the workplace that they regard as really and truly wrong. Even individuals engaged in clear and obvious theft rarely admit to theft but rather label their acts as "borrowing," or as "taking something they deserve," particularly when the theft is relatively small (Carter, 1987; Cressy, 1970; Hollinger & Clark, 1983; Tatham, 1974).

This phenomenon can be explained in two different ways. First, as Cressy (1970) and others (Snyder, Higgins, & Stucky, 1983; Tatham, 1974) note, this belief may be a rationalization. People like to maintain favorable self-concepts, usually including the perception that they are honest people. Relabeling theft as something else might make it easier to preserve this favorable self-perception. A second possibility is that this relabeling is not a rationalization at all but rather reflects the person's honest belief that a particular act is *not* stealing. Thus, rather than practicing self-deception by labeling the act after the fact as "borrowing," people might know that they are in a strict sense stealing but believe that their acts are in fact entirely justified and correct. Furthermore, the fact that managers often do little or nothing to prevent or prosecute theft cases may be seen as implicit consent—a verification that a particular act really isn't stealing after all (Carter, 1987). The types of behavior that are defined as honest or dishonest in specific settings, such as the workplace, may depend heavily on prevailing norms. For example, if the standard practice in an office is and has always been to pad expense account reports, this behavior might not be regarded by workers as dishonest. Some behaviors that are, by the strictest definition, dishonest might be regarded as perfectly acceptable standard practice and seen as qualitatively different from behaviors that are regarded by the work group as dishonest.

An example of the importance of norms in defining what is seen as honest or dishonest comes from research on absenteeism. Chadwick-Jones, Nicholson, and Brown (1982) document the influence of social and group norms on absenteeism and suggest that efforts to reduce absenteeism will fail unless they address these norms. If the work-group norm is to be absent one day a month, workers who conform to that norm will *not* be seen as engaging in dishonest or forbidden behavior. Workers who deviate from the norm in either direction, however, may be subject to sanctions from the group. A person who is absent more often than the norm might be seen as a goldbricker, and the work group might indeed agree that he or she is committing production deviance. A worker who is rarely or never absent might be seen as a rate-buster, and might be pressured by the group to stay home from time to time (Sherif & Sherif, 1969; Zaleznik, Christensen, & Roethlisberger, 1958).

Although the norms of the work group or unit are an important factor in defining what behaviors might be seen as honest or dishonest, these norms do not apply equally to everyone. First, members of the group who have high status, whether formal or informal, are not as tightly bound by norms as low-status individuals are (Hackman, 1976). Therefore, the same behavior might be seen as unacceptable and dishonest when carried out by one individual and perfectly acceptable when carried out by another. Second, a number of personality characteristics might influence the ways in which norms affect an individual's perceptions of honesty and dishonesty. For example, Goodenough (1976) suggests that some individuals depend heavily on

Box 1-2 *Defining Honesty in Different Cultures: The Case of Software Piracy*

The unauthorized use of computer software is fairly common in this country, but most computer users draw the line at software piracy—the resale of illegally copied software. However, in several Asian cities, notably Hong Kong, Singapore, and Taipei, software piracy is big business, and it is easy to get copies of virtually any piece of copyrighted software for a nominal price. Does this mean that individuals in these countries who engage in software piracy are less honest than U.S. computer users, who tend to avoid outright piracy? Swinyard, Rinne, and Kau (1990) suggest that the answer is no and cite differences between Eastern and Western cultures to explain differing attitudes toward software piracy.

Swinyard, Rinne, and Kau, (1990) note that a copyright gives the individual author or creator exclusive rights of ownership and control, at least for some period. They go on to note that in many Asian cultures, tradition emphasizes the importance of sharing ideas and creations and argues against the notion that authors or creators could withhold or restrict the distribution of their creations. For example, many translated Asian books give the author (who created the book) and translator (who made it possible for the book to be more widely shared) equal standing on the title page. As another example, many Asian paintings are signed with the name of the school that produced them rather than with the name of the individual artist. In light of this tradition, one might conclude that it is more wrong for an author to withhold his or her creations than for a "pirate" to distribute them. Although piracy might be formally recognized as dishonest—most of these countries do have copyright laws or trade regulations to protect copyrights—in traditional Asian cultures, copyright infringement may not be viewed with the same level of disapproval as it is in the United States.

environmental or contextual information to make sense of the behaviors they observe in others (a personality characteristic referred to
as "field dependence"). These individuals may be more attuned to and
more influenced by norms than others are.

The answer to the question whether there are distinct types of
dishonesty in the workplace, or whether all forms of dishonesty are
instead manifestations of the same trait that differ only in their level
or seriousness, may depend on the beliefs and attitudes of the individuals involved rather than on the behaviors themselves. If a specific
behavior is not regarded as dishonest by the individuals engaged in or
affected by that behavior, the causes of that behavior and the methods
most appropriate for controlling it might be very different from those
that would pertain if the behavior is recognized by all involved as
dishonest. For example, if there is a norm that everyone takes an hour
for lunch, even though the contract clearly states that only 30 minutes
are allowed, you might use very different strategies for dealing with
this minor violation than you would use in dealing with outright
theft.

The question whether there are distinct forms of dishonesty or
whether all forms of workplace dishonesty should be scaled on a single
continuum becomes even more complicated when one considers the
class of behaviors that represent the opposite of production deviance—
that is prosocial or organizational citizenship behaviors.

Prosocial behaviors.   Production deviance includes intentionally
slow and sloppy work, unnecessary waste, abuse of sick leave and
break time, running large numbers of personal errands on company
time, and other forms of goldbricking. The category of behaviors
referred to as prosocial behaviors in organizational settings represents,
in many ways, the flip side of production deviance. Prosocial behaviors
include things like expending extra effort, volunteering for difficult
assignments, helping other workers perform their jobs, carrying out
tasks not required in the contract or job description, and other op-
tional behaviors that help the work group and organization function
(Brief & Motowidlo, 1986).

Like deviant behaviors, prosocial behaviors are probably affected by
both personal and situational forces (Staub, 1978). Brief and Motowidlo
(1986) cite personality factors, level of organizational commitment,
and beliefs as potential causes of prosocial acts in organizations.
Situational factors that encourage prosocial behaviors include the
organization's climate, the existence and encouragement of recipro-
city norms, and the opportunity to observe and model prosocial
behaviors in others. Staub (1978) notes that prosocial behaviors are

not entirely altruistic but rather are sometimes motivated by desire for personal gain or for approval from others.

Advocates of the view that all forms of deviance can and should be classified on a single continuum might consider prosocial behaviors as part of that same continuum. That is, it might be possible to treat the entire range of behavior from embezzlement and stock manipulation to volunteering for extra work and helping co-workers as different levels of the same trait. Some people may be highly antisocial (for instance, those who steal from the organization or from co-workers), whereas others might be highly prosocial. Advocates of the view that qualitatively different forms of honesty and dishonesty exist in the workplace might treat prosocial behaviors and various forms of property and production deviance as conceptually distinct. According to this view, it might be possible to find individuals who commit some acts of property and production deviance but who also carry out a range of prosocial behaviors.

Research on prosocial behavior does not provide a firm basis for choosing between the alternatives described above. A negative correlation is likely between, on the one hand, prosocial behavior and, on the other, various forms of deviant behavior that are harmful to the organization, co-workers, or both—in other words, individuals involved in employee theft are probably not going to be involved in a great deal of prosocial behavior. However, too little research has been done on the relationship between prosocial behavior and dishonesty to draw a firm conclusion.

Although it may be possible to construct a continuum that includes the whole range of prosocial behaviors, as well as property and production deviance, I think it is more useful to distinguish between three conceptually distinct classes of behavior. First, there are many behaviors universally regarded as dishonest, such as stealing from a co-worker. Second, there are behaviors regarded as acceptable, even though they deviate from the strictest norms of honesty, such as taking home small amounts of office supplies. The norms of the organization and work group, together with the beliefs and personality of the individual (for instance, his or her susceptibility to normative influence), may determine exactly what is included in this category. Third, there are behaviors that indicate a special level of commitment to the organization, the job, or one's co-workers—that is, prosocial behaviors. Although behaviors in different categories are probably correlated (for example, a person who refuses to take long lunch breaks may be unlikely to embezzle company funds and may be likely to volunteer when extra help is needed), the causes of these three types of behavior may differ, and the strategies most likely to discourage the two types of dishonest behavior and to encourage prosocial behaviors may differ substantially.

Psychological Research
on Dishonesty and Deception

Psychologists and other social scientists have had a long-standing interest in several topics related to honesty in the workplace. For example, many of the earliest psychologists, including Binet (a pioneer in the measurement of intelligence), were interested in the psychology of deception (Hyman, 1989). Research in the late 1800s on deception used the conjurer as a model and investigated the ways in which the audience participates in deception or allows it to occur. Early psychologists, such as Munsterberg, were also involved in debunking seers, clairvoyants, and the like.[2] The topic of deception has also drawn the attention of researchers in animal intelligence (Byrne, 1991); the sometimes elaborate deceptions primates practice on one another constitute one avenue that is being used to study the nature of animal intelligence and cognition.

Applied psychologists have also shown considerable interest in the topic of deception, particularly in the possibility of detecting deception in real-life contexts. As Saxe (1991) notes, "the incentives for psychologists to develop lie detection technologies make it almost irresistible" (p. 411). Ash (1976) documents the development over the years of a wide variety of methods for assessing honesty and predicting theft, including the use of background questionnaires and personality inventories (for instance, the MMPI, CPI, and Rorschach), polygraphs, and paper-and-pencil integrity tests.

Early research on honesty generally viewed it as a stable characteristic of the individual. Thus, the dominant view of early researchers was that some individuals were simply more honest than others. This point of view is still influential, especially in areas such as integrity testing. For example, on the basis of his review of research in clinical and industrial/organizational psychology, as well as research on personnel selection in public safety jobs (for instance, police officer) and jobs that created the potential for serious hazards (for example, nuclear reactor operator), Paajanen (1988) identified a number of individual difference variables that are thought to be related to dishonesty, deviance, or both. These variables can be grouped into ten categories, as shown in Table 1-2.

Paajanen (1988) did not argue that these individual differences were the sole cause of dishonesty or that situational factors were unimportant. He did, however, identify a number of characteristics of the person, his or her experience, or both that were likely to predict dishonest behavior in the workplace. The exact mechanisms that link these variables to honesty are not understood, but Paajanen's study

---

[2] Munsterberg was also heavily involved in developing the notion of the polygraph.

Table 1-2   *Variables Thought to Be Related to Dishonesty or Deviance*

1. *Undependability*: Individuals who are irresponsible, impulsive, careless, and so on are thought to be more likely to be involved in dishonesty or deviance.
2. *Problems in socialization*: Individuals with underdeveloped values or a history of delinquency are thought to be more likely to be involved in dishonesty or deviance.
3. *Attitudes regarding deviance and theft*: Individuals who have more favorable attitudes toward theft and delinquent behavior are thought to be more likely to be involved in dishonesty or deviance.
4. *Problems with authority relationships*: Individuals who have difficulty conforming are thought to be more likely to be involved in dishonesty or deviance.
5. *Excitement seeking*: Individuals who engage in thrill-seeking or daring behaviors are thought to be more likely to be involved in dishonesty or deviance.
6. *Work motivation*: Individuals with low levels of work motivation are thought to be more likely to be involved in dishonesty or deviance.
7. *Social influence*: Individuals who are easily influenced by peers or others are thought to be more likely to be involved in dishonesty or deviance.
8. *Unstable upbringing*: individuals with unstable family lives are thought to be more likely to be involved in dishonesty or deviance.
9. *Drug use*: Individuals with a history of substance abuse are thought to be more likely to be involved in dishonesty or deviance.
10. *Unmet needs*: Individuals with low self-esteem, low job satisfaction, and so on are thought to be more likely to be involved in dishonesty or deviance.

SOURCE: From Paajanen (1988).

does suggest that all of these characteristics may contribute to the tendency to become involved in various types of workplace dishonesty.

The position that honesty is a characteristic of the individual was strongly challenged by Hartshorne and May (1928). Their studies suggested that honesty is not a general trait and that there is little consistency in people's level of honesty. These studies involved placing children in a number of situations where they had opportunities to lie, cheat, or steal. Hartshorne and May's major conclusion was that dishonesty is not a characteristic of the person but rather of the situation. That is, children were not highly consistent from situation to situation and would behave honestly in one situation and dishonestly in another. Furthermore, some situations seemed to provoke dishonest behavior in many children, whereas in other situations, dishonesty seemed rare. Similar findings were reported by other authors (Dudycha, 1936; Newcomb, 1929), leading to the belief that honesty is not a stable trait.

Hartshorne and May's (1928) position led psychologists to view honesty testing in a skeptical light (Sackett, 1985). If one accepts the proposition that honesty is not a characteristic of the person but rather is governed by situational forces, it is unlikely that *any* measure of individual differences would be useful in predicting honesty, so that the whole idea of honesty or integrity testing would be a waste of time. However, several reanalyses and reassessments of Hartshorne and May's own data suggest that there *are* stable individual differences in honesty (for example, Burton, 1963; Sackett, 1985). On the other hand, there is substantial evidence that situational factors influence honesty. As in many other areas of psychology, a great deal of attention has been devoted to the relative importance of personal characteristics, situational characteristics, and various combinations of the two in determining honesty in the workplace.

Influence of People, Situations, and Person × Situation Interactions

For much of this century, personality psychologists have debated the relative importance of personal factors (for instance, personality or character variables) versus situational factors in determining behavior (Kenrick & Funder, 1988; Pervin, 1985). At one extreme, some trait theories appear to explain behavior solely in terms of an individual's characteristics. On the other hand, radical behaviorism (for instance, Skinner's theory) seeks to explain behavior solely in terms of situational factors. In the late 1960s, research by Mischel (1968) on the consistency of behavior reignited this debate, and it occupied the attention of personality researchers for some time to come (Mischel & Peake, 1982; Pervin, 1985).

The relevance of this debate for understanding honesty in the workplace is clear. If personal factors are the most important, it makes sense to identify people who are either honest or dishonest, through testing or some other assessment method, or perhaps to develop methods of turning dishonest individuals into honest ones. On the other hand, if situational factors are most important, it makes sense to reduce features of the situation that induce people to be dishonest—for example, lax security or norms supporting dishonest behavior. Finally, if both personal and situational factors are important, it may be best to adopt a multitrack approach to encouraging honesty and discouraging dishonesty—that is, one that attempts to change both the person and the situation.

Trevino and Youngblood (1990) captured the essential nature of the dichotomy between person-oriented and situation-oriented explanations of dishonesty by labeling it as "bad apples" versus "bad barrels." In other words, dishonest behavior in the workplace can be explained in terms of the people (bad apples) or the atmosphere of the workplace (bad barrel). Trevino and Youngblood suggested that, as is usually the case in debates about personal versus situational causes of specific behaviors, both personal and situational factors affected unethical behaviors in the workplace, a phenomenon they called "bad apples in bad barrels."

The debate and its resolution.   Although the interchange between Mischel and his critics, and the flurry of articles supporting one side or the other, is often referred to as the person versus situation debate, it is clear that neither explanation is sufficient (Carson, 1989; Pervin, 1985, 1989). There is considerable evidence that (1) behavior shows some consistency, (2) situational factors are important determinants of behavior, and (3) both personal and situational factors must be considered together to gain an adequate understanding of behavior (Carson, 1989; Kenrick & Funder, 1988). Most researchers accept some version of an interactional approach (Magnusson & Endler, 1977), although there is considerable disagreement over many of the specifics. According to the interactionist view, personal and situational factors both have their separate effects, but they also interact in such a way that behavior cannot adequately be understood by viewing either the person or the situation in isolation.

The notion of a person × situation interaction is hardly a new one, although the idea has taken many forms over the years. Perhaps the earliest interactionist model of honesty was proposed by Aristotle, who suggested that some people are more likely to be affected by situational variables than others are. He believed that people of good character almost always act according to their character, but that people of poor character act virtuously in some situations (for instance, those in which they know they are being watched) and badly in others.

More recent models (for example, Kenrick & Funder, 1988; Wright & Mischel, 1987) suggest that traits such as honesty are relevant in some situations but not in others and that changes in the situation could either heighten or reduce the effect of personal variables such as conscientiousness or integrity. According to these models, traits can be more easily expressed in some situations than in others. For example, when security is very tight and inventories are carefully watched, it is unlikely that you will observe major behavioral differences between "honest" and "dishonest" individuals. Only when the opportunity for dishonest behavior arises will there be any real noticeable differences in the behavior of people whose personalities do differ in this respect.

Kenrick and Funder (1988) suggest that people can change situations and that situations can change people. For example, an aggressive person can bring out hostility in others, making *them* more aggressive. It is easy to see how changes in people (for example, the introduction of new workers) might affect the frequency of honest and dishonest behaviors. For example, if many workers who believe that employee theft is justified are transferred into a work group, this transfer may lower *everyone's* threshold for theft by creating a norm in the work group that sanctions theft. Long-term exposure to this norm can, in turn, change the attitudes and beliefs of workers who initially did not regard theft as acceptable, so that eventually everyone might come to believe that theft is all right. Research on dishonesty and deception suggests that such interactions between persons and situations do indeed occur. It is well established that some people will act in a dishonest fashion in some situations but not in others (Saxe, 1990). On the other hand, some people are more likely than others to be dishonest, no matter what the situation.

Strong versus weak situations.   At times, a situation provides strong cues about the types of behaviors that are expected or appropriate. For example, most people agree about the type of behavior appropriate at a church wedding or in a courtroom (it is not a good idea to bring your harmonica to either place). Personality researchers refer to these situations as "strong situations" (Bem & Allen, 1974; Bem & Funder, 1978; Mischel, 1968; Monson, Hesley, & Chernick, 1982). A strong situation is one in which there is clear agreement about the type of behavior that is appropriate and strong pressure to conform (Price & Bouffard, 1974; Schutte, Kenrick, & Sadalla, 1985).

In contrast, there are many "weak situations," in which it is not at all clear what type of behavior is appropriate or expected. Researchers suggest that personality variables have their greatest effect in weak situations. In a strong situation, there may not be much room to express one's individual personality; a person who is quiet during a wedding is not necessarily a quiet person.[3] In weak situations, situational cues do not tell you how to behave, and people may have to fall back on their own inclinations, judgments, and preferences to determine their behavior.

In assessing the relative importance of personal versus situational explanations for honesty at work, it is important to determine whether the workplace constitutes a generally strong or weak situation. In their review of research on dispositional effects in organizational research, Davis-Blake and Pfeffer (1989) noted that work settings typically represent strong situations. Most people have strong expectations about the type of dress, behavior, and so forth that is or is not appropriate in the workplace (if you don't believe this, try showing up for

---

[3] However, people who behave contrary to expectations in strong situations might be showing their true personalities. A person who is noisy and obnoxious at a funeral is probably a truly noisy and obnoxious person.

work at IBM in shorts); it is difficult for individual differences to surface in the workplace. They further note that organizational experiences affect a number of variables that are usually thought of as traits (for instance, commitment and satisfaction) (see Blau & Scott, 1962; and Kohn & Schooler, 1978, 1982). On the whole, the search for personal variables that explain a broad range of behaviors in organizations has not been fully successful.

While work probably represents a generally strong situation, it is not clear that the workplace always provides strong and consistent cues regarding honesty, theft, production deviance, and the like. Although official rules and policies always discourage such behaviors, unofficial norms may ignore, accept, or even encourage such behaviors. Furthermore, different parts of the same organization may send out very different messages about honesty. Work may represent a strong situation with regard to some behaviors (for example, norms regarding appropriate dress, language, and so on), but it may not necessarily represent a strong situation with regard to honesty. If there are not clear norms and expectations regarding honesty, personal variables may take over in determining whether a person behaves in an honest fashion.

Broad versus narrow traits.   Hampson (1988) notes that some personality traits are considerably broader than others. Traits such as honesty or conscientiousness are broader than traits such as tidiness, in the sense that the former are potentially relevant in a wide range of situations. There is evidence that the cross-situational consistency of broad traits is considerably lower than that of narrower traits. Thus, a basically dishonest person might be honest in some situations and dishonest in others, whereas a generally tidy person will probably be tidy whenever the situation permits.

The lower consistency of broad traits probably reflects their greater susceptibility to situational controls. Because honesty is potentially relevant in such a wide range of situations, it is more likely that it will be tested in a variety of strong and weak situations; in some situations there may be pressures to behave in an honest fashion, in others pressures to break the rules, and in ambiguous situations there may be no particular pressures to behave honestly or dishonestly (Hampson, 1988). The net result of the lower consistency of broadly defined traits is that it is more difficult to explain the behavior referred to by the trait label in terms of personal characteristics than would be the case with more narrowly defined traits. In terms of the example presented above, it makes more sense to say that a person is either tidy or sloppy (that is, that he or she will exhibit this characteristic in most settings) than to say that a person is honest or dishonest. A very honest person will sometimes be dishonest, and a thoroughly dishonest person will nevertheless often be honest. The broader the trait label, the lower the likelihood that it will apply in any particular situation.

—————————————SUMMARY—————————————

Honesty in the workplace is a compelling topic. Whole industries have grown up to deal with workplace dishonesty, ranging from integrity test publishers to security firms. Ethics has become a buzzword in many business schools and even in some corporate boardrooms. The honesty of U.S. workers is frequently compared, usually unfavorably, with that of our international competitors.

Although there is clear evidence that workplace dishonesty is both serious and widespread, little is known about the precise dollar amounts lost to employee theft, corporate corruption, white-collar crime, and the like. Broader forms of workplace dishonesty, such as production deviance, seem almost universal; up to 75% of all workers are thought to commit some acts of production deviance (Hollinger & Clark, 1983). Even with production deviance, though, it is difficult to obtain precise estimates of the frequency or cost of these behaviors. Organizations in which there was no production deviance whatsoever (no socializing, no unauthorized breaks, no slowing down the pace) would be terrible places to work; nevertheless, organizations probably need to place some limits on these behaviors. At this point, it is difficult to know whether the costs associated with controlling all these behaviors would be offset by the increased productivity of workers.

At first glance, honesty in the workplace seems a simple concept. You might define honesty by simply saying that a person who always tells the truth is honest, and a person who doesn't is not. Upon closer examination, however, many complexities arise. For example, should we consider all forms of production and property deviance as manifestations of the same basic trait, dishonesty, differing only in their seriousness, or should we define and address several qualitatively different types of workplace dishonesty? Should prosocial behaviors, such as organizational citizenship, represent the high end of the honesty-to-dishonesty continuum, or do they constitute a distinct type of behavior? If the individuals involved do not regard the behavior as dishonest (perhaps because things have always been done that way, with the tacit consent of management), is the behavior truly dishonest? Many of these questions have no definite answers, yet we must try to address them in designing strategies for dealing with workplace dishonesty.

One reason that it is difficult to define exactly what is meant by honesty in the workplace is that the definition of honesty depends in part on the ways in which both an individual and the others who are potentially affected by a specific behavior interpret that behavior. The same behavior might be honest in one setting, dishonest in another, and in a gray area in a third. It is critical for members of any organization to encourage some common understanding of exactly what is or is not acceptable behavior. A zero tolerance policy, in which everyone must tell the truth about everything at all times, might sound good, but in practice it would probably be a disaster. Organizations must decide exactly how much and what kinds of dishonesty they are willing to live with.

Personality research suggests that we must consider both the person and the situation in defining and dealing with workplace dishonesty. Strategies that change only one of these elements might do some good, but they will probably have only limited success. As you will see in later chapters, this prediction from personality research seems to have been vindicated. I will review a number of methods of dealing with workplace dishonesty that focus either on the person or on the situation in isolation and will show that the success of these approaches is indeed often modest. In the final chapters of this book, I will discuss methods of encouraging honesty and discouraging dishonesty that involve consideration of both the person and the situation and will show that these have unique promise for affecting the level of honesty in the workplace.

CHAPTER TWO

Honesty and Dishonesty in the Workplace: Who and Why

This chapter examines theory and research dealing with the characteristics and motives of individuals who are thought to commit acts of workplace dishonesty. As you will see, there is a great deal of uncertainty surrounding the questions of who and why; much of the research and writing in this area is speculative, and sometimes sweeping conclusions are drawn on the basis of rather modest data. Nevertheless, it is possible to make some useful observations about who becomes involved in dishonest behavior and why and to use this information to help evaluate various proposals and programs for reducing workplace dishonesty.

As in Chapter 1, a substantial part of this chapter is devoted to employee theft. It is likely that behavioral scientists know more, or at least claim they know more, about employee theft than about other forms of dishonest behavior, and a close examination of research on theft helps to highlight issues relevant in understanding many other forms of workplace dishonesty. I will examine employee theft from a number of perspectives, including those suggested by criminologists, security consultants, and psychologists, and will discuss the advantages and disadvantages of each. Next, I will discuss white-collar crime, with particular attention to the probable motives of the various individuals involved.

The final section in this chapter examines a particular form of honest behavior that is often the subject of formal and informal sanctions—whistle-blowing. A close examination of the reasons that some individuals persist in this type of honest behavior in spite of the stiff resistance often met by whistle-blowers provides several insights into honest behavior in the workplace.

Employee Theft

This section examines research on employee theft that attempts to answer two questions: who steals, and why? The question "Who steals?" has both simple and complicated answers. One simple answer, which comes out of research reviewed below, is that certain types of individuals are more likely than others to steal. A wide range of demographic, sociological, and psychological characteristics go into the definition of "theft proneness" (Ash, 1991), but once these people are identified, organizations can reduce theft and shrinkage substantially by weeding them out. Another simple answer, which is somewhat akin to the view expressed by security specialists (for example, Carson, 1977), is that everyone steals, given the right situation. Whereas security specialists are likely to define the right situation primarily in terms of opportunities for undetected theft, a somewhat broader definition might be warranted. The relevant situational factors might include not only security arrangements, but also the norms and expectations of others. If security is lax and your co-workers regard theft of tools, materials, and the like as justifiable and normal, you might be more likely to steal.

The complicated answer to the question "Who steals?" involves a combination of all three factors described above, usually together with a specific set of motivational factors that lead to dishonest behavior. One way to describe the individual who steals is to note that he or she does not regard the particular act of theft as wrong, works in a setting where opportunities for undetected theft exist and where the prevailing norms tolerate theft, and has a motive to steal from the organization.

Who Steals

Individuals who have few ties to the organization or to the community are more likely to steal than those with more extensive ties. For example, Hollinger and Clark (1983) and others (for example, Frank, 1989) note that individuals who are committed to the organization are less likely to steal from that organization (although they may steal from outside of the organization). There is also evidence that new employees, part-time employees, and unmarried employees are more likely to steal.

Hollinger and Clark (1983) also suggest that both property and production deviance are more common in low-paying, low-status jobs. It is not clear whether this is due to the nature of the jobs themselves (the jobs might not be very satisfying), or to the individuals most likely to hold the jobs (younger workers, part-time workers, and so on). In all likelihood, both factors operate here; these jobs attract individuals who are prone to theft, and the nature of the work plus the working conditions provides individuals with a number of motives for stealing from the organization.

Rather than describing "who steals" in demographic terms, it might be more useful to describe these individuals in behavioral terms. It is well known that individuals involved in employee theft are also often involved in a number of other deviant behaviors. For example, alcohol and substance abuse are reliable predictors of employee theft (Hollinger & Clark, 1983; Terris & Jones, 1983). Individuals who enjoy breaking rules or who enjoy dangerous, forbidden activities (thrill-seeking individuals) are more likely to steal (Hogan & Hogan, 1989; Paajanen,1988). Individuals who closely associate with co-workers who steal may themselves be more likely to steal (Paajanen, 1988).

As you may have noted, most of the studies cited here deal with characteristics of the person, and only secondarily with characteristics of the situation, as explanations for theft. In part, this emphasis is due to the research methods typically employed in research on theft (for instance, surveys, crime statistics, and the like), in which the individual is the normal unit of analysis. However, it may indicate a deeper methodological problem in research on employee theft. Al-

Box 2-1 *Demographic Theories of Employee Theft: Descriptions or Explanations*

In a sense, the demographic theories of crime, delinquency, and employee theft are not theories at all, because they do little to *explain* the phenomenon in question. Consider, for example, the widely cited finding that part-time workers are more likely than full-time workers to engage in employee theft. Several potential explanations for this finding include the following:

1. *Money*—Part-timers receive lower pay and benefits, and may need the money.
2. *Bad company*—Part-timers may spend their non-working hours "hanging-out" with individuals with no stable employment, who commit crimes, etc.
3. *Weak links*—Part-timers may have less identification with or commitment to the organization.
4. *Proxy variable*—Part-time status has no direct influence, but whatever variables account for part-timers' status (for example, low skills or poor motivation) also account for theft.

Although demographic "theories" do not provide an adequate explanation for employee theft, they do play a crucial role in developing other theories. For example, an adequate theory of theft must explain why it occurs more frequently in some demographic groups than in others. A theory that explained theft on the grounds that some people are just born dishonest (a "bad apple" theory) would not be adequate, because such a theory does little to explain the demographics of theft. For example, new employees are more likely to steal, but as they attain tenure and identification with the organization, theft declines. This phenomenon cannot be explained by the notion that some people are just born bad. Although demographic theories do not adequately explain employee theft, they do nevertheless provide crucial tests of the adequacy of theories that do try to explain theft.

though most researchers acknowledge the importance of situational factors, we do not seem to know as much about assessing and measuring situational characteristics as we do about assessing the behavior and psychological characteristics of individuals. The hypothesis that almost everyone steals if the situation is right may very well be true, but it is usually very difficult to determine whether in any particular instance the situation is really right. In Chapter 8, I will note that our slow progress in assessing situations constitutes a major roadblock to understanding and controlling dishonesty in the workplace.

Why People Steal

It is important to understand why individuals engage in dishonest and counterproductive behaviors at work, particularly employee theft. Although there is no definitive answer to the question of why some individuals steal, it is possible to piece together several lines of research that give some insight into the problem.

The obvious, commonsense explanations for employee theft boil down to two possible explanations: (1) people steal because they are bad people, or (2) people steal because they want or need the money. Similarly, the commonsense explanation for counterproductive behavior is a variation on the first explanation above—that is, people come to work late, leave early, take long breaks, or do shoddy work because they are lazy and irresponsible. Public discussions of employee theft, ranging from research reports to speeches and articles in business and security-oriented magazines, suggest a somewhat broader set of explanations for employee theft.

Hollinger and Clark (1983) grouped these explanations into five categories, which are shown (together with four additional explanations, described in later paragraphs) in Table 2-1. First, theft is most often explained in terms of external economic pressure. For example, it is widely believed that individuals steal after getting into serious financial problems (for example, after incurring large gambling losses). Second, there are a number of demographic theories of theft. All of these theories stem from the fact that many thefts appear to be committed by young, inexperienced, part-time employees. It is not clear whether it is youth itself that is responsible for the misdeeds or whether young and inexperienced employees have a different orientation to the organization than more seasoned employees. As I will note in several later sections, people who identify with the organization are less likely to steal from the organization than those who are not really committed to the job or the organization. Perhaps younger employees have not yet had the chance to form meaningful bonds with the organization or its members. Another possibility is that new employees simply have less to lose if they are caught stealing; being fired from a

Table 2-1   *Nine Possible Explanations for Employee Theft*

1. *Economic pressure*: Employees steal because they need the money (for instance, to pay gambling debts).
2. *Demographic theories*: Some groups (for example, young, unmarried people) are less stable and more prone to theft than others.
3. *Opportunity*: Everyone steals, given the opportunity; more opportunities result in more thefts.
4. *Dissatisfaction*: Employees who are dissatisfied with their jobs or the organization are more likely to steal; theft may provide revenge, feelings of equity, and so on.
5. *Norms*: Employees steal in situations where the prevailing norms condone theft.
6. *Attitudes toward theft*: Employees who view theft as normal, acceptable, or common are more likely to steal.
7. *Power through theft*: Employees steal to gain a feeling of power, status, or control.
8. *Theft as a safety valve*: Employees steal as a way of letting off steam or getting back at the organization.
9. *Instability*: Emotionally unstable employees are more likely to commit thefts.

job you held for three months is probably less traumatic than being fired from a job you held for 30 years.

A third explanation for employee theft is in terms of opportunity. Many security systems are constructed with the belief that given the opportunity, most individuals might steal. While this belief might seem pessimistic, there is evidence that the single best predictor of theft is the perceived chance of being caught (Hollinger, 1989; Hollinger & Clark, 1983). Security experts suggest that failure to follow simple measures to deter theft places an unfair temptation in front of employees and could turn basically honest employees into thieves (Carson, 1977).

A fourth explanation for theft is that dissatisfied individuals are most likely to steal. The research supporting this explanation (for example, Mangione & Quinn, 1975; Merriam, 1977; Moretti, 1986) does not clearly indicate whether theft is the indirect result of the way organizations treat individuals (that is, poor treatment leads to dissatisfaction, which leads to theft) or whether people who tend to become dissatisfied with their work (for instance, chronically dissatisfied individuals) also tend to steal. There is some indirect evidence that poor treatment from the organization can be a significant factor in theft. For example, Terris and Jones (1982) cited both low wages and a desire for revenge against the organization as explanations for theft in convenience stores (see also Altheide et al., 1978; Greenberg, 1990). However, it is also possible that the same personality characteristics that lead some individuals to be dissatisfied with their jobs might also contribute to theft. The role of attitudes such as satisfaction and commitment in employee theft is examined in more detail in a later section of this chapter.

A fifth possible explanation for theft is that social norms may either encourage or fail to deter theft (Altheide et al., 1978; for similar research on absenteeism, see Chadwick-Jones, Nicholson, & Brown, 1982). That is, if everyone in a particular organization cheats on his or her expense account, and it is widely believed that it is really acceptable to do so, this norm will certainly encourage new employees to cheat on their expense accounts. There is evidence that informal social norms have a much stronger effect on employee theft and other forms of property deviance than do formal rules and regulations (Altheide et al., 1978; Hollinger & Clark, 1983).

Research by psychologists and sociologists suggests a number of other explanations for theft that are not included in Hollinger and Clark's (1983) list. First, it is likely that actual theft is the result of attitudes toward theft. For example, research on thrill-seeking behavior suggests that some individuals steal because it is exciting (Hogan & Hogan, 1989; Paajanen, 1988; Terris & Jones, 1982). Others steal because they honestly believe or talk themselves into believing that what they are doing is not really theft. Still others steal because they believe that everyone else does. Many integrity tests include items assessing attitudes toward theft, and there is evidence that individuals who believe that theft is common and acceptable and that it is not really wrong to steal from the organization are likely themselves to steal (O'Bannon, Goldinger, & Appleby, 1989).

Second, theft may be a way to assert power and attain status, particularly in low-paying, low-status jobs (Altheide et al., 1978). By stealing from the organization, particularly when the theft is undetected, the individual demonstrates a level of power and mastery that the job does not provide. Third, theft may be a sort of safety valve, in the sense that people work out their frustrations with the organization by occasionally striking back in the form of minor theft (Zeitlin, 1971). This theory suggests that employee theft might not be such a serious problem; if the safety valve effect provided by occasional theft were eliminated, individuals would probably move toward some other means of working out their frustrations that could be far more damaging than theft (for instance, sabotaging an expensive piece of equipment). Fourth, some researchers (for example, Frank, Lindley, & Cohen, 1981) treat both theft and production deviance (for instance, careless work, tardiness and absenteeism, time theft) as indicators of emotional instability. This argument implies that dishonesty at work is a form of pathology and that emotionally stable individuals are not as likely as unstable ones to engage in such behaviors. This view of dishonesty clearly implies that it is a characteristic of the person, although different situations might be more or less conducive to the actual exhibition of this pathology.

On the whole, research on employee theft does not support the most widely cited explanation for theft—the theory that people steal because they need or want the money (Hollinger & Clark, 1983). Certainly, cases exist where economic pressures drive otherwise honest employees to desperate acts, but this explanation does not seem to account for the majority of employee thefts. Demographic explanations are not really explanations at all—they simply narrow the field by focusing on groups known to be most prone to theft. Similarly, instability-based theories may be too circular to provide an adequate explantion of theft: instability is often inferred on the basis of thefts and other behaviors and then used as an explanation for these same acts.

There is evidence that opportunity is an important determinant of theft, but it is also clear that some individuals will not steal despite an opportunity to do so, whereas others will attempt theft at the slightest opportunity. The most promising explanations for employee theft and other counterproductive behaviors appear to be couched in terms of three variables: (1) attitudes toward the job and the organization, (2) attitudes toward theft and counterproductive behavior, and (3) informal workplace norms regarding theft and counterproductive behavior.

Role of attitudes toward the job and the organization. Substantial evidence shows that attitudes such as job satisfaction and organizational commitment are related to employee theft (Hollinger & Clark, 1982b, 1983; Mangione & Quinn, 1975; Moretti, 1986). Individuals who are dissatisfied with their jobs or who feel no real loyalty to or connection with the organization are more likely to steal than satisfied employees with close ties to the organization.

One potential explanation for the relationship between job satisfaction and production deviance is that the relationship is spurious, reflecting nothing more than the fact that both deviance and satisfaction are correlated with age. Recall that younger individuals are more likely to commit acts of property and production deviance (Hollinger & Clark, 1983). There is also evidence that younger individuals are more likely to be dissatisfied with their jobs. To test the hypothesis that the satisfaction-deviance correlation was due to both variables' relationship to age, Hollinger and Clark (1982a) statistically controlled for the effects of age. They found that controlling for age did reduce the satisfaction-deviance correlation to some degree but that a significant correlation still held between these two variables.

Bateman and Organ (1983) examined the relationship between satisfaction and deviance from the opposite perspective—by examining the role of satisfaction in encouraging prosocial or "citizenship" behaviors. These citizenship behaviors are, as was noted in Chapter 1, in many ways the direct opposite of deviant behaviors. Prosocial behaviors include extra effort at work, volunteering for difficult assignments, and other forms of going beyond the call of duty to help the organization function. Bateman and Organ showed that these behaviors are positively correlated with job satisfaction. Once again, the direction of causation is somewhat unclear. However, the research reviewed here does suggest that satisfied individuals tend to exhibit prosocial, citizenship behaviors, whereas unsatisfied individuals tend to commit acts that constitute property and production deviance. If you accept the idea that satisfaction contributes to citizenship, it seems logical to believe that dissatisfaction will contribute to deviant behaviors, such as theft, which represent the flip side of citizenship.

A number of authors have suggested that many types of deviance may be a reaction to perceived inequity (Fisher & Baron, 1982; Greenberg, 1990). Individuals who feel that they have been unfairly treated may steal or engage in other acts of deviance to "even the score." Greenberg's (1990) study presents fascinating evidence of this phenomenon. In this study, workers at two large manufacturing plants suffered a temporary 15% pay cut. Greenberg measured employee theft before, during, and after the pay cut and showed that

Figure 2-1 *Employee Theft Before, During, and After a Pay Cut*

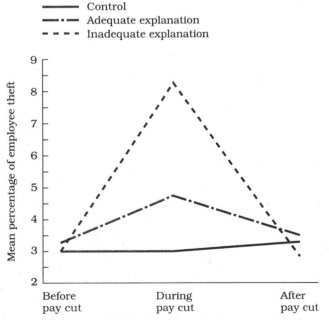

SOURCE: From Greenberg, J. (1990). Employee theft as a reaction to underpayment inequity: The hidden cost of pay cuts. *Journal of Applied Psychology 75*, 561–568. Reprinted by permission of American Psychological Association and author.

Figure 2-2   *Relationships among Equity, Satisfaction, Commitment, and Theft*

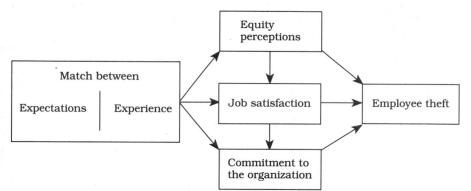

employee theft rose during the period in which pay was cut, then fell back to its baseline level after pay was restored to its normal level. Furthermore, the increase in employee theft was substantial in one plant where an inadequate explanation of the pay cut was offered to employees, but was much smaller in the other plant, where an attempt was made to explain the pay cut to all involved. The results of this study are shown in Figure 2-1.

The results shown in Figure 2-1 suggest that it is the feeling of inequity rather than the absolute loss in pay that is responsible for the increase in employee theft.[1] The pay cut had only a minor effect on employee theft when an attempt was made to explain the pay cut honestly and thoroughly to all involved. When no such effort was made, employees felt that they were being unfairly treated and may have used theft to retaliate against the organization.

The relationships among feelings of inequity, job satisfaction, commitment to the organization, and employee theft are probably complex; Figure 2-2 illustrates one set of hypotheses about the direct and indirect effects of these variables and their antecedents on employee theft. First, the way an individual is treated by the organization, together with the individual's beliefs and expectations, determines that individual's perception of equity or inequity. This perception of equity, in turn, has both direct and indirect effects on employee theft. Individuals who experience inequity may steal to restore a feeling of equity. Inequity may also lead to job dissatisfaction and to a low level of commitment to the organization, both of which may also contribute to employee theft. Second, satisfaction may have both direct and indirect effects. A dissatisfied individual may be more likely to steal (a direct

[1] Greenberg (1990) notes that the research design used makes it impossible to make strong causal statements about the effect of inequity, pay, etc. on subsequent work behaviors.

effect) but may also feel less loyalty and commitment to the organization and may therefore feel less hesitation about engaging in behaviors that are harmful to the organization (an indirect effect).

It should be emphasized that the process illustrated in Figure 2-2 represents a hypothesis, not a set of well-established relationships. Nevertheless, this figure does give an indication of the potentially complex relations between work attitudes and employee theft. In particular, the figure suggests that a single event or condition (here, the match between an individual's expectations and the treatment he or she experiences) can have multiple effects, all of which might in turn affect the likelihood of theft.

Role of attitudes toward theft.   As was noted in Chapter 1, individuals who commit thefts or other dishonest behaviors often claim that they don't view the behavior as wrong or dishonest. This claim is partly the result of after-the-fact rationalization; if you steal something, it is more comfortable to think that your behavior was really acceptable (for example, that you were borrowing, not stealing) than to live with the fact that you are a thief (Carter, 1987; Cressy, 1970, 1986; Tatham, 1974). Although this sort of process might explain what happens after a theft, it doesn't explain why the theft occurred in the first place. Research on the measurement of honesty and integrity provides a clue to understanding why many thefts occur—that is, they are not viewed as thefts, even before the fact.

There is evidence (reviewed in Chapter 5) that many individuals engaged in employee theft believe that their acts are not theft at all, that theft is common, in the sense that most employees do the same thing, and that it is socially acceptable. Indeed, these beliefs form the foundation of many integrity tests (O'Bannon, Goldinger, & Appleby, 1989). The belief that "everyone is doing it" and that taking something from the employer really is not theft is likely to significantly lower the threshold at which an individual will commit acts of employee theft. If security is tight, or if many co-workers make their disapproval obvious, an individual with the beliefs described above might refrain from stealing. However, if the situation is favorable for theft, individuals with these beliefs will probably act upon them.

In addition to attitudes toward theft itself, attitudes toward both the object and the victim of theft may affect the likelihood that an individual will steal a particular object. A person is more likely to steal something if it is considered fair game, in the sense that there are no apparent efforts to control use or theft (for instance, small tools or parts that are not subject to strict inventory control). A person is also more likely to steal if he or she believes that the consequences of not stealing are as bad as or worse than the consequences of stealing. For example, if merchandise is going to be thrown away or will simply spoil if it is left in place, an individual might not regard the act of taking, and arguably saving, that merchandise as theft.

Role of norms.   Although some acts (like stealing a truck) are likely to be viewed as theft by virtually all workers, many acts of workplace dishonesty occupy a gray area, in which they are neither clearly dishonest nor clearly honest—for example, many forms of production deviance and pilferage. The norms of the organization and the work group probably have their maximum effect in these ambiguous cases. As was the case with individual attitudes, group norms probably serve to define what is regarded as honest as opposed to dishonest, theft as opposed to legitimate use of materials and tools, and so on.

The influence of group norms on theft by group members comes from three separate aspects of groups. First, as was noted above, groups help to define what range of behavior is acceptable and what is unacceptable. Second, groups provide rewards for acceptable behaviors and sanctions for unacceptable ones (Hackman, 1976). Third, some groups are highly cohesive, which implies a strong sense of loyalty to and identification with the group, whereas others are loosely defined and not highly important to their members.

The worst-case scenario, from the perspective of a manager trying to control employee theft, may be a work group that is highly cohesive, with the ability and willingness to apply strong sanctions to deviant members, and with norms that tolerate or encourage particular types of employee theft. For example, suppose that all the waiters in a restaurant are close friends, and that most of them feel justified (because they are badly treated by management) in stealing food, turning in false orders, and so forth. There will be strong pressure on the individuals who do not believe this behavior is right to nevertheless go along. Investigations of corruption in police departments (for example, the Serpico case in New York) suggest that honest officers are often pressured to become *actively* involved in corruption; unless everyone is involved, the corrupt officers can never feel completely safe.

On the other hand, norms that discourage theft could be an extremely strong deterrent to theft in the workplace, for two quite distinct reasons. First, it is hard to escape the scrutiny of co-workers, especially when your behavior runs counter to prevailing norms. It is unlikely that the security systems in place in most organizations keep as close a watch on your behavior as that kept by your co-workers, and behavior that violates the norms of the group will attract attention, comment, and pressure to conform. Second, as individuals become socialized into the organization and the work group (as discussed in more detail in Chapters 6 and 7), norms become internalized, in the sense that individuals come to accept them. If your co-workers believe that it is acceptable to take partially worn tools home from the factory, you will tend to develop similar beliefs. This tendency is not universal; some individuals never adopt the norms of the work group. Nevertheless, internalization of work-group norms is a powerful process, and it may help to explain why some individuals who seem honest when they enter an organization later steal or commit other acts of dishonesty.

Three Perspectives on Employee Theft

If you ask why individuals commit crimes and other acts of dishonesty in the workplace, you will probably get different answers, depending on whom you ask. If you ask a criminologist, you will probably get an answer that concentrates on the characteristics of the individual, which are in turn thought to be shaped by a variety of societal and demographic forces. If you ask a security consultant, you will probably get an answer that concentrates on the characteristics of the immediate situation, particularly factors that led to the perception that the risk was either high or minimal. If you ask a social psychologist, you will probably get an answer that concentrates on the broader situation, particularly on the attitudes and norms of the individual and the work group. It is useful to understand more about these three perspectives and the strengths and weaknesses of each.

Criminology is a multidisciplinary field that draws heavily on sociology. It encompasses the study of all aspects of the criminal system, ranging from the characteristics and treatment of offenders to the definition of crime in various societies (for overviews of several aspects of criminology, see Hagan, 1989; Johnson, 1983; and Jones, 1986). Criminologists have for the most part concentrated on crimes that occur outside of normal work environments. Many of the nonviolent crimes studied by criminologists, such as burglary, forgery, or drug sales, represent the criminal's livelihood; one way of describing the distinction between this type of crime and crime in the workplace is to think of the former as crime *as* work and the latter as crime *at* work.

On the whole, criminologists focus on the question of who commits crimes. Research by criminologists often includes assessment of social variables that are relevant in identifying criminals, and although the theories employed by criminologists often include hypotheses about why crimes are committed, these are not usually the central focus of the research. The criminologist's perspective is probably most useful for understanding serious wrongdoing by individuals or small groups in the workplace. Large-scale embezzlement, theft of valuable merchandise, and the like are not easily rationalized, nor are they likely to be accepted as normal practices by the work group. Rather, these acts are likely to be viewed by both the perpetrators and the victims as undeniably criminal acts, and the motivation for these acts and the types of individuals involved may not differ substantially from the motives and individuals involved in similar crimes in non-work settings.

Security experts (for example, Carson, 1977; Curtis, 1973; Fennelly, 1989; Jaspan, 1974; Keogh, 1981; Lipman, 1973) concentrate on the object of theft and on methods of reducing access to that object and the ability to move the object without verification. Their focus is on uncovering and reducing opportunities for dishonest behavior in the workplace. While they are rightly concerned with methods of catching thieves and other violators, they are even more concerned with deterring security violations in the workplace (Carson, 1977). Thus, the security manager in a company that never experiences theft is probably more successful at his or her job than the security manager who catches several thieves a month.

In a sense, the concerns of security consultants mirror those of behavioral psychologists. Both are concerned with controlling behavior by changing the situation. Behavioral psychologists manipulate the frequency and schedule of rewards and punishments, whereas security consultants attempt to make the perceived likelihood of punishment so high as to deter theft and other dishonest acts. Although experts in intelligence and counterintelligence do occasionally draw on the knowledge and findings of psychologists, I know of few substantial interchanges between security consultants and behavioral psychologists. This is a shame, because each group could teach the other a few things.

The weakness in the perspective offered by many security experts is that they do not pay attention to individual and group differences. Although the implicit assumption that everyone might steal in some situations and everyone might be deterred from theft in others might very well be true, the narrow focus on the opportunities offered for theft and dishonesty in various situations ignores the fact that different individuals, placed in the same situation, act in different ways. Even in organizations with essentially no security precautions, many individuals go through their entire career without committing theft or other serious acts of workplace dishonesty. Nevertheless, security experts do offer a set of useful methods for understanding the situational variables that may tempt or deter individuals from committing theft and other forms of workplace dishonesty.

Social psychologists (for example, Baron & Byrne, 1991; Katz & Kahn, 1978; Sherif & Sherif, 1969) concentrate on understanding behavior in its social context. Their principal focus in the area of honesty in the workplace is on the role of attitudes and norms in determining honest and dishonest behavior. This perspective is undoubtedly a useful one; there is clear evidence, discussed in both Chapters 1 and 6, that norms and individual attitudes are important determinants of honesty. However, like the two perspectives discussed above, social psychologists' perspective does not completely account for workplace dishonesty; even where attitudes and norms encourage theft, good security may deter it.

The research of social psychologists probably makes its greatest contribution toward understanding why the individuals involved in workplace dishonesty often regard their acts as perfectly acceptable and normal. The definition of theft, dishonesty, and unacceptable behavior in the workplace is affected substantially by the prevailing norms and attitudes, and a better understanding of these factors could help to explain why there is so much disagreement over the extent and nature of dishonesty in the workplace. This perspective also suggests several avenues for reducing workplace dishonesty by changing the attitudes and norms of individuals and work groups; several suggestions along these lines will be discussed in Chapter 8.

Each of the three perspectives has its strengths and weaknesses. Rather than thinking of a comparison among the three as a horse race, in which the object is to decide which one is best, researchers and practitioners should consider combining all three. The task of understanding and doing something about dishonesty in the workplace is a daunting one and is best attacked from the perspectives of multiple, complementary disciplines. Each perspective encourages you to ask different questions (for example: Who is involved? What is it about the situation that encourages theft?), and each suggests different remedies. As I will note in Chapter 8, the use of multiple strategies, involving efforts to change the people involved (for instance, through selection and training) and the situation (for example, through better security and clarification of norms) to both encourage honesty and discourage dishonesty, offers more promise than any of the specific strategies offered by individual disciplines.

In Chapter 1, I noted that honesty in the workplace was affected by characteristics of the individual, characteristics of the situation, and the interaction between the two, or in other words characteristics of people in situations. Each of the perspectives described here tells us something about one of these three sets of characteristics (security experts for instance, concentrate on the situation), but none of them answers the question of how much influence persons, situations, or the interaction between persons and situations have on honesty in the workplace. This question is a difficult one to answer, in part because persons and situations are not, in reality, completely independent. Rather, there is considerable evidence that "the people make the place" (Schneider, 1987). Thus, you should not expect to find large numbers of honest individuals in work groups whose norms support or encourage dishonesty; they will not be attracted to or comfortable in such groups and will tend to gravitate elsewhere. The separation of personal and situational factors as causes of dishonesty is useful for developing and testing theories, but it obscures the essential links between the characteristics and norms of individual employees and those of the organizations in which they work.

Although persons and situations are not completely distinct, each probably makes *some* independent contribution to workplace dishonesty. First, some people, for whatever reason, are neither trustworthy nor honest, and they will act dishonestly whenever they think they can get away with it. The only sensible way to deal with such individuals is to combine good personnel screening with good security—don't hire them or keep a close eye on them. Second, some situations present an irresistible temptation to most individuals. The only sensible way to deal with these situations is to remove the temptation, which may often involve, once again, tightening your security. However, security is not always the answer; sometimes, the temptation is strong because the act in question is not defined as wrong by the individuals involved. For example, if it is a standard and time-honored practice to pad one's expense account, security may not be the answer; there are ways around almost any security system. Instead, you may have to change the way in which the situation is perceived.

In my opinion, the most common causes of workplace dishonesty are those that involve the joint effects of both persons and situations. Putting a person with a rather broad definition of honesty in a situation where the appropriate standards of behavior are ambiguous is an invitation to disaster. That same person might be completely honest in other situations, where the standards for honest behavior are clear and well accepted, and other persons with different implicit definitions of honesty might be completely honest in that same situation.

If the hypothesis discussed above is essentially correct—that is, if the combination of persons and situations is the most common cause of dishonesty—it is likely that multidisciplinary approaches to workplace dishonesty are the best. Approaches aimed at identifying basically dishonest persons, such as integrity testing, will work for the person component, whereas approaches aimed at removing temptation and making the likelihood of detection substantial, such as better security, will work for the situation component. However, in many instances of workplace dishonesty, neither the personal nor the situational factors are sufficiently strong to suggest dishonesty, but specific combinations of these factors can either lead to trouble or perhaps help you avoid trouble.

Suppose I told you about an organization where workers have easy access to valuable gold objects, where there is virtually no supervision or security, and where inventory control is primitive at best. You might be very concerned about security. If I told you that the organization was a cathedral, and the employees in question were priests and bishops, your concerns about security would seem less pressing; you would expect that these persons might be able to resist the temptation to steal. On the other hand, if the people involved were quite prone to dishonesty, you might still deter theft with situational measures; if the situation changed so that security was tight, and the chances of getting caught were obviously high, you might not expect thefts even if the employees were known felons. The point is, honesty is often determined by the match between the situational and personal forces that impel individuals to either engage in or avoid dishonest behaviors.

Corporate Corruption and White-Collar Crime

The dishonest acts of managers and executives are often treated as being very different from the type of production and property deviance that occurs among lower-level employees. As you will see, this point of view may have some validity. There are, in fact, some good reasons to think of many acts of white-collar crime as qualitatively different from either street crime or employee theft. Some authors object to the use of the term *white-collar crime* because very few of these offenses are ever handled through the criminal justice system, as, conversely, few street crimes are handled via civil suits or administrative penalties (such as loss of a license). Typically, the prosecution of corporate crime is given low priority. In the rare instances where convictions are obtained, penalties are often light; fines are often small enough to be regarded as a normal business cost, and prison sentences are virtually unheard of. However, the term *white-collar crime* is still widely used, and I will use it here, although I will restrict my focus to crimes committed in normal work settings.

Three characteristics seem to distinguish white-collar crimes in organizational settings from other crimes. First, the amount of money involved distinguishes white-collar crimes from virtually all others, except large-scale drug smuggling operations. Hearings before the Senate Judiciary Committee in 1986 dealing with the extent and control of white-collar crime suggested that the average "take" in a white-collar crime was more than ten times the size of the average take in a bank robbery. Second, the individuals who commit these crimes do not fit the profiles for either employee theft or street crime. White-collar crimes are usually committed by well educated, affluent, and highly respectable individuals, although the individuals committing some crimes such as counterfeiting or wire fraud may more closely resemble the stereotypic profile of a criminal. Third, the motives behind white-collar crime sometimes seem different from those behind other crimes.

Some of the reasons cited for employee theft probably do not apply to most cases of corporate corruption or white-collar crime. For example, many employee thefts represent a form of revenge against management or the owners of an organization, whereas white-collar crimes are often committed by the upper managers or owners of the business (Simon & Eitzen, 1986). Similarly, many employee thefts are committed as a way to gain power and status. In contrast, many white-collar crimes are committed by those who already have power and status; indeed, their power and status is often a necessary ingredient to the commission of these crimes.

Demographic theories of employee theft abound, but there is no clear stereotype or pattern for white-collar theft. No obvious cues such as age or marital status can be used to narrow the field in the search for white-collar criminals. As I will note later, our knowledge of white-collar crime lags seriously behind our knowledge of employee theft, even though white-collar crime is almost certainly more costly.

Motivation for White-Collar Crimes

It is important to keep in mind that many white-collar crimes occur outside of traditional work organizations and appear to resemble other crimes in a variety of ways. Examples include counterfeiting operations and a wide range of highly organized frauds, such as using an offer of a phony "free" vacation to get access to your credit card number. Although fascinating and important, these crimes are beyond the scope of this book.

As was the case with employee theft, there are several possible explanations for white-collar crime in organizations. Six of these are set out in Table 2-2. For example, Cressy (1986) discussed several motives for white-collar crimes in work organizations. Some crimes can be explained in terms of fear of failure. Managers and executives are often under substantial pressure to produce results. Even when there is no external pressure, they might become so involved in what they do that a failure is seen as devastating. In these circumstances, the temptation to use dishonest means to ensure success can be substantial.

Second, Cressy notes that managers and executives are affected by norms and by their socialization in much the same way as everyone else is. If they come to believe that particular illegal or dishonest acts are in fact acceptable, they are likely to engage in those acts. Third, he notes that managers and executives often face what he calls unsharable problems—financial problems that can't be solved through normal, legal channels. Managers who face catastrophic losses or

Table 2-2   *Six Possible Explanations for White-Collar Crime and Corporate Corruption*

1. *Fear of failure*: The possibility of failing in a critical project tempts managers to engage in dishonest activities.
2. *Norms*: Managers and executives are most likely to commit dishonest acts if the prevailing norms tolerate or encourage those acts.
3. *Unsharable problems*: Managers face problems that cannot be solved by honest or legal means, and resort to dishonest or drastic solutions (e.g., Jimmy Stewart's character in the film *It's a Wonderful Life* attempts suicide to deal with a shortfall).
4. *Altruism*: White-collar and corporate crimes are committed for the good of the company or the community.
5. *Careless expediency*: A habit of bending the rules may escalate to the point where the violations are major.
6. *Greed*: Lust for money or success leads to crimes of this sort.

problems beyond their capability to solve might be tempted to resort to dishonest means.

Cherrington (1986) suggested a slightly different set of reasons for white-collar crime and corporate corruption. First, he noted that some of these crimes are committed for the good of community or society. For example, a dishonest bid that helps get a vital road or bridge built may be justified in this manner. Second, many crimes are committed for the good of the company. Although there is evidence that dishonest behavior is not in the long-term interest of most organizations (Axline, 1990; Harrington, 1991), managers and executives faced with a looming crisis are not likely to take the long view.

Although the concept of dishonest acts committed for the benefit of the organization may sound almost altruistic, it is important to remember that the individuals involved usually stand to gain from the dishonest act or stand to lose if they refuse to commit the act. For example, executives who falsify test data to attract a large contract, which in turn will ensure the survival of the organization, are not acting in an entirely selfless manner; they are also saving their lucrative and prestigious jobs.

A third motive for many white-collar crimes is what Cherrington (1986) refers to as careless expediency. This attitude allows one to bend the rules to ensure success. Such an attitude can become a substantial problem when small misdeeds become habitual and mushroom into bigger things. Descriptions of a decade-long, multi-million dollar scandal at a major insurance company suggest a process very much like this one. What started out as a few managers bending a few rules grew into an ongoing pattern of fraudulent activity involving fictitious policies and the fraudulent transfer of funds among several departments of the organization.

The final motive Cherrington (1986) cites is simple greed. This is not necessarily confined to a desire for more money, but may also involve an addiction to money-making and success itself. In the late 1980s, several financial scandals were uncovered that involved extremely rich individuals (for example, Boesky, Milliken, and Helmsley). The money itself was probably not the motive. In each case, the individuals involved would have been hard pressed to spend half of the money they had before they committed the illegal acts. Rather, they seemed motivated by a greed for success, which may be as powerful a motive as the simple lust for money.

Employee theft versus white-collar crime.   You probably noticed that the explanations for employee theft on the one hand and white-collar crime and corporate corruption on the other overlap somewhat (for example, organizational norms are cited in Tables 2-1 and 2-2 as possible explanations for both) but that there are also significant differences. To some extent, these differences are a function of the different jobs. Because managers have higher levels of responsibility, along with greater authority to make independent decisions, explanations that involve expediency, unsharable problems, and—perhaps this is stretching matters—fear of failure and altruism might be more applicable to managers and executives. However, some of the differences between Tables 2-1 and 2-2 probably reflect our assumptions about the differences between management and labor rather than actual differences. For example, opportunity is a widely cited factor in employee theft but is not often used to explain white-collar crimes. Similarly, explanations involving instability, deviant attitudes, and a desire for revenge are more frequently applied to employee theft than to white-collar crime. Perhaps these factors really do tell us more about the behavior of lower-level employees, but it is difficult to escape the impression that the explanations for white-collar crime are somehow less damning than those frequently cited for employee theft. When is the last time you heard someone explain employee theft in terms of altruism, or explain white-collar crime in terms of emotional instability? Marxists (if there are still any Marxists left) would explain this difference in terms of class differences. Although you may not feel comfortable siding with the Marxists, in this case, they may have a point.

Honesty in the Face of Consequences: Whistle-Blowing in Organizations

Most of the discussion thus far has been devoted to dishonesty in the workplace. Something can be learned, however, from studying honesty and trying to understand who is honest and why. This task turns out to be difficult for the simple reason that honesty does not attract as much attention as dishonesty. It is no news that 99% of your managers didn't embezzle anything today, but when one does embezzle something, this act becomes the focus of immediate attention. One form of honesty, however, has attracted considerable attention—whistle-blowing. Whistle-blowing is notable for several reasons, the most important of which is that negative consequences often ensue for the whistle-blower. It is important to understand why people are willing to face such consequences to act honestly and honorably.

Although the phenomenon is probably as old as organizations themselves, the emergence of whistle-blowers has received a great deal of public attention in the last several years (Miceli & Near, 1985; Near & Miceli, 1986). Whistle-blowers are defined as "organization members (former or current) who disclose illegal, immoral, or illegitimate practices under the control of their employer to persons or organizations who may be able to effect action" (Miceli & Near, 1985, p. 4). Depending on your point of view, whistle-blowers can be thought of as either

Box 2-2   *Corporate Social Responsibility and the Pursuit of Profit*

Some corporate actions, such as polluting the environment or selling products of dubious value, are legal but are viewed in a negative light because they represent a perceived failure of the corporation to live up to its social responsibilities. On the other hand, socially responsible actions, such as gifts to charity and community service, are often viewed in a very positive light. Organizations often go to considerable lengths to publicize their "socially responsible" actions and to cover up their "socially irresponsible" ones.

In a provocative essay, Milton Friedman (1970) argued that the first responsibility of a corporation is to increase profits and that "socially responsible" acts such as donations to charity are in fact a deviation from the organization's true purpose and responsibility. While this argument might strike you as coldhearted, it cannot be dismissed entirely. A for-profit organization that devoted a sufficiently large percentage of its resources to charity, community service, and other socially responsible causes would soon go bankrupt, which would substantially harm stockholders, workers, and the community.

Tuleja (1985) suggests that involvement in charitable and community organizations is not, in fact, a diversion from the pursuit of profits but rather represents an investment in the organization's long-term survival and profitability. Investments in the community, such as scholarships for needy students, help to ensure that the community will continue to provide a profitable environment for future business, a qualified workforce, and so forth. Viewed in this light, socially responsible actions are often in the long-term interest of the organization and may not be inconsistent with Friedman's insistence that profits are the true responsibility of a corporation.

heroes or rats. Those who regard whistle-blowers as heroic reformers point out that they often risk retaliation and scorn to act in ways that ultimately benefit both the organization and society (Miceli & Near, in press, a). On the other hand, whistle-blowers are often treated with contempt by members of the organization. Drucker's (1981) description of whistle-blowing illustrates this reaction. He claimed that " 'whistle blowing' after all, is simply another word for 'informing.' And perhaps it is not quite irrelevant that the only societies in Western history that encouraged informers were bloody and infamous tyrannies..." (p. 50). Rosendale's (1987) description of his own experience as a whistle-blower provides a vivid example of the potential negative consequences of revealing wrongdoing in organizations; he experienced both informal and formal pressure to keep quiet. What makes his story so compelling is that, in his case, the organization itself was the victim of the wrongdoing. Apparently, the embarrassment and disruption of admitting this fact motivated both his peers and superiors to cover up harm the organization was suffering rather than revealing and correcting past mistakes.

Who Blows the Whistle and Why

Several authors have suggested that whistle-blowing can best be understood as a form of prosocial behavior (Dozier & Miceli, 1985; Miceli & Near, 1988). In other words, whistle-blowing is partly but not entirely altruistic; it often benefits the individual who reveals the wrongdoing, as well as benefiting society and (possibly) the organization. The motives involved in whistle-blowing seem to be complex, but they often involve concern for the long-term good of the organization (Miceli & Near, 1988). Although whistle-blowing often leads to short-term damage to the organization (Dozier & Miceli, 1985), it is likely that organizations that continue to do wrong will eventually be found out and that the consequences of external exposure would be more severe than those that result from whistle-blowing (Miceli & Near, in press, b).

Research on whistle-blowing has addressed a number of questions, such as the sorts of wrongdoing that trigger whistle-blowing (in general, the more serious the act, the greater the likelihood of whistle-blowing) or how organizations respond to whistle-blowing. One particularly interesting question is who blows the whistle. In virtually every instance where whistle-blowing occurs or could occur, a number of individuals are aware of the wrongdoing, but most people choose not to report the wrongdoing. What factors predict the emergence of whistle-blowers? Research on this question can be summarized under four categories: (1) characteristics of the individual, (2) job characteristics, (3) work-group characteristics, and (4) organizational characteristics.

Individual characteristics.   Several individual characteristics increase the likelihood of whistle-blowing, including status, educational level, values, and professional affiliation (Miceli & Near, 1988, in press, a; Near & Miceli, 1987). High-status individuals and individuals with higher levels of education may feel more immune to retaliation, whereas individuals with egalitarian value systems might feel that they have a legitimate right to question the actions of their superiors. Many professions and professional societies require that individuals report wrongdoing that they witness or encounter. On the other hand, individual characteristics such as ambition may decrease the likelihood of whistle-blowing (Hacker, 1978). Individuals who are highly interested in furthering their careers might either identify with the organization and thus regard the wrongdoing as not really wrong, or they may fear jeopardizing their careers by exposing the faults of the organization to others.

Job characteristics.   Job characteristics also affect the likelihood of whistle-blowing. Jobs such as inspector, auditor, or accountant require individuals to be watchful for both wrongdoing and mistakes and to report evidence of either to someone (Loeb & Cory, 1989; Near & Miceli, 1987). These jobs also give individuals unusually high levels of exposure to information, events, and the like that might trigger whistle-blowing. Other jobs do not involve the investigation of wrongdoing as a primary activity but do require that any observed wrongdoing be reported. For example, the Code of Ethics for Government Service requires that individuals report or expose corruption whenever it is encountered in the course of work (Miceli & Near, in press, a).

Another job-related factor that influences whistle-blowing is the impact of the wrongdoing on the individual (Near & Miceli, 1987). Some types of wrongdoing directly involve a number of unwilling participants; many of the stories of whistle-blowing discussed in the media result from product designers, engineers, or inspectors who feel forced to participate in schemes to hide or distort damaging data or test results. An individual who can stop a questionable practice also stops the discomfort or distress that results from his or her involvement in that practice.

Work-group characteristics.   Two characteristics of work groups appear to affect whistle-blowing. First, the norms of the work group may define both the practices that are considered wrong (potential candidates for whistle-blowing) and the acceptability of whistle-blowing itself (Miceli & Near, in press, a; Near & Miceli, 1987). There is usually a strong norm in favor of conformity and against "tattling," but if the work group supports the notion that wrongdoing should be exposed, whistle-blowing might occur, especially in response to acts or practices that are defined as unacceptable by the work group. Second, whistle-blowing is more likely in large work groups (Miceli & Near, 1988). This finding runs counter to a large body of research on diffusion of responsibility (for instance, Latane & Darley, 1968), which shows that individuals are less likely when in large groups than they are in small groups to take action to prevent wrongdoing or to aid others. The effects of group size on whistle-blowing may depend greatly on the norms of the group. It may be easiest to blow the whistle when (1) the triggering act is defined as wrong by the group, (2) the group supports reporting the wrongdoing, (3) the group is cohesive, and (4) the group is large.

Organizational characteristics.   Several organizational factors appear to affect whistle-blowing. For example, whistle-blowing, both internal and external, appears less likely in large organizations than in small ones (Miceli & Near, 1985). This phenomenon has several potential explanations, including diffusion of responsibility,[2] or the difficulty of psychologically identifying with large organizations. Second, the climate of the organization affects whistle-blowing. As we note later in this section, organizations engage in a number of activities that are likely to lead their employees to believe that whistle-blowing will lead either to beneficial changes in the organization or to retaliation and denial.

Internal versus External Whistle-Blowing

Whistle-blowers must choose whether to report wrongdoing to members of the organization (internal whistle-blowing) or to individuals outside of the organization (external whistle-blowing). Internal whistle-blowing gives the organization the opportunity to correct the wrongdoing and to avoid the various negative consequences of external exposure. Thus, organizations might be well advised to encourage internal whistle-blowing. There is evidence that internal whistle-blowing is more likely when the organization is generally fair and consistent in the treatment of its employees (Miceli & Near, 1988) and when employees believe that the organization will take appropriate action in response to the report of wrongdoing (Near & Miceli, 1987). External whistle-blowing is most likely when employees believe that management is unwilling to change (Miceli & Near, 1985). Research on

[2] Earlier, we noted that diffusion of responsibility research may not accurately predict the effects of work-group size on whistle-blowing. This may, however, be due to the effects of group norms and cohesiveness. Large organizations are likely to be less cohesive and to have less well-defined norms than will smaller work groups, and thus diffusion research may be more accurate when applied at the organizational level than when applied to the immediate work group.

whistle-blowing suggests that these beliefs are frequently well founded. Miceli and Near (in press, b) note that nearly all individuals who resort to external whistle-blowing first try internal channels; they go outside the organization only when it appears that the organization will not take appropriate actions without external pressure.

Retaliation against whistle-blowers. Whistle-blowers often experience some form of retaliation, particularly from their immediate supervisors and co-workers (Near & Miceli, 1986, 1987). In part, this retaliation probably results from work norms that define whistle-blowing as tattling, but it may also reflect the fact that the immediate supervisor and co-workers are often involved in the act or practice that triggers the whistle-blowing. Retaliation is more serious for external than for internal whistle-blowing and, interestingly, is more harsh when the offense is serious (Near & Miceli, 1986).

Although the possibility of retaliation probably deters many individuals from blowing the whistle, retaliation may have unexpected effects. In particular, there is evidence that the threat of retaliation may lead to *more* whistle-blowing (Miceli & Near, 1985). One possible explanation for this finding is that the threat of retaliation increases the potential whistle-blower's perception that the organization will not correct the situation unless there is external pressure to do so.

A variety of laws now exists that are designed to protect whistle-blowers. The effects of these laws have been mixed (Miceli & Near, 1989; in press, b; Sculnick, 1986). On the one hand, there is evidence that whistle-blowing has increased. On the other hand, there is evidence that retaliation is just as prevalent now that the laws have been passed as it was prior to passage of the laws. One reason for this prevalence is that retaliation is sometimes difficult to prove, especially if it occurs in relatively subtle ways, such as ostracism by colleagues and supervisors. However, a recent lawsuit against an aircraft manufacturer resulted in a multimillion dollar award to several employees who had experienced retaliation. It is possible that awards such as these will have a greater effect on retaliation than the laws passed to date have had.

Rather than simply providing protection from retaliation, laws are now providing positive incentives for whistle-blowing, often in the form of financial rewards (Miceli & Near, in press, b). In most cases, these financial incentives are so small that they will probably have little effect—with one major exception. Lawsuits brought on behalf of the government under the False Claims Act could yield substantial amounts to individuals who blow the whistle on violations covered by that act (Feliu, 1990). A whistle-blower who initiates such a suit could receive up to 30% of the judgment in a successful suit; the incentive to report substantial violations of this law could be enormous.

While moves to encourage whistle-blowing are in many ways beneficial, they can have negative consequences. Frequent whistle-blowing may create an atmosphere of distrust and paranoia and may encourage the belief that you must avoid mistakes (no matter how trivial) or the whistle will be blown. In the worst case, whistle-blowing might become a form of revenge or harassment, in which disgruntled subordinates and peers use the system to stir up trouble and the appearance of wrongdoing. The financial incentives under the False Claims Act might even encourage whistle-blowing for extremely minor or technical violations that would have been addressed without outside pressure, in the hope of cashing in on any lawsuit or settlement that may result.

Personal versus Situational Variables as Predictors of Whistle-Blowing

The research reviewed above outlines a number of personal and situational variables that are likely to be related to whistle-blowing. Although these studies have concentrated more on situational variables, whistle-blowing may represent a class of behavior where, in the long run, personal variables are more important than situational ones. This conclusion is not based on empirical data; the data simply don't tell us which class of variables is most important. Rather, it is based on two characteristics of whistle-blowing: the small number of individuals typically involved and the normative pressure to keep quiet.

As I noted earlier, in most cases of whistle-blowing, many individuals are fully aware of an organization's apparent dishonesty or violations, but few blow the whistle. Those who do speak up are almost always ostracized by co-workers, supervisors, and other members of the organization. These two facts suggest that situational pressures usually work against whistle-blowing, and it is a rare individual who can or will resist the pressure to keep quiet. In Chapter 1, I discussed strong versus weak situations. In virtually all organizations, situations in which whistle-blowing might occur are strong situations, where the pressure to keep quiet is unmistakable. Nevertheless, some individuals resist that pressure.

It is not clear which individual characteristics determine who blows the whistle and who keeps quiet. Depending on your perspective, you might cite characteristics ranging from integrity, if you admire whistle-blowers, to an inability to adapt to social situations, if you think of them as tattlers. In all likelihood, a mix of admirable and maladaptive characteristics motivates individuals to blow the whistle when others are keeping quiet. More research is needed to determine the exact mix of these characteristics.

SUMMARY

The most important principle that emerges from a survey of the research on who commits acts of workplace dishonesty and why is that our stereotypes are probably not true. First, dishonesty in the workplace is not confined to a few bad people; if the situation is right, almost everyone might become involved in some form of property or production deviance. Second, workplace theft, embezzlement, and the like are usually not committed out of economic need, or even (for the most part) greed. The dollar value of the objects stolen does not seem to be the driving influence in many workplace thefts. Rather, complex motives, ranging from a desire to get revenge or restore equity to a simple enjoyment of the thrill involved in committing and getting away with minor crimes, lie behind many workplace thefts.

In discussing employee theft, this chapter highlighted the possible roles of attitudes toward the job, the organization, and theft itself, as well as work-group norms, as potentially critical determinants of theft. Some of these same variables are also relevant in understanding white-collar crime in organizations. In Chapter 8, I will discuss ways in which organizations might try to change attitudes and norms in an effort to increase honesty and decrease dishonesty.

Three perspectives on theft and dishonesty were contrasted, and potential areas of interchange between criminologists, security experts,

Box 2-3 *Why Whistle-Blower Protection Laws Fail*

A number of state and federal laws exist to protect whistle-blowers from retaliation such as loss of a job or undesirable assignments. The 1978 Civil Service Reform Act created the Merit Systems Protection Board (MSPB); one job of the MSPB is to protect federal employees against retaliation for whistle-blowing. However, research by Miceli and Near (1989, in press, b) suggests that the MSPB has had little impact on the likelihood of retaliation. The percentage of federal whistle-blowers who experience retaliation (approximately 20%) was virtually unchanged after the Civil Service Reform Act took effect and the MSPB assumed responsibility for protecting whistle-blowers.

Miceli and Near (in press, b; see also Near & Miceli, 1986) suggest that the key to protecting whistle-blowers is not legislation, but rather managerial support. As long as managers view whistle-blowing as a form of betrayal (see, for example, Drucker, 1981), it is hard to see how laws could be written that would eliminate retaliation. It is probably possible to provide protection against immediate dismissal, but a person who is regarded as a traitor to the organization can probably kiss his or her career goodbye. Until and unless attitudes toward whistle-blowing change, whistle-blower protection laws are unlikely to be effective.

and social psychologists were suggested. It is likely that each of these three perspectives has something useful and unique to say about dishonesty in the workplace, but a combination of all three is substantially more useful than any one perspective. In this section, I also discussed one hypothesis about the relative importance of persons, situations, and person × situation interactions in explaining dishonesty. This hypothesis represents my best guess and may say more about my own biases in interpreting the research than about the data itself. Nevertheless, it is useful to speculate on the relative importance of these three factors, because different strategies exist for attacking each. Strategies that concentrate on either the person or the situation are described in Chapters 4 through 7.

The final section in this chapter examined whistle-blowing. Research in this area suggests that the reasons for honesty, especially in the face of potentially devastating consequences, are every bit as complex as the reasons for workplace dishonesty. As was the case with dishonesty, the best explanations for whistle-blowing are probably those that consider the person, the situation, and the interaction between persons and situations.

CHAPTER THREE

Problems in Predicting and Detecting Dishonesty and Deception

A number of methods, techniques, and technologies have been developed to detect, infer, or predict dishonesty and deception in the workplace, ranging from automated security devices such as cameras and alarms to polygraphs and paper-and-pencil tests. Several chapters in this book (particularly Chapters 4 through 6) discuss the strengths and weaknesses of specific methods of detecting or deterring dishonesty. Before examining these methods, however, it is useful to understand the problems and difficulties frequently encountered in determining whether a dishonest act has occurred in the workplace and who might be involved in that act. The successful prediction and detection of deception depends on a number of factors, including characteristics of the relevant situation, the strategies and techniques used to identify individuals likely to have been involved in the dishonest act, and the definition of what constitutes honest or dishonest behavior in different settings in a particular organization. The purpose of the present chapter is to outline the range of issues that must be considered in evaluating any method of predicting or detecting dishonesty or deception.

Detecting Dishonesty

As this chapter will show, it can be extremely difficult to detect deception and dishonesty in the workplace, regardless of the method or technique used. For the most part, this chapter will focus on the most widely discussed and most visible form of workplace dishonesty—employee theft. However, many of the problems encountered in attempting to detect employee theft are also encountered when dealing with other forms of property and production deviance.

Deception and dishonesty can be difficult to predict for two reasons. First, nontrivial acts of dishonesty, such as theft and embezzlement, can be relatively rare, and it is difficult to detect any condition when the base rate is low (Murphy, 1987). For example, if a doctor is attempting to diagnose a very rare form of heart disease, the very fact that it is rare increases the likelihood of a misdiagnosis. Second, individuals who commit dishonest acts of this type usually go to some lengths to conceal their behavior. Therefore, evidence or information that might be used to predict deception and dishonesty may be difficult to obtain or, once it has been obtained, difficult to accept at face value.

This chapter begins by describing the various steps involved in detecting workplace dishonesty. Next, research on the effects of situational factors (for example, the frequency of deception in different contexts) on one's ability to accurately predict or detect deception is discussed. The sections that follow cover standards for evaluating the various methods of detecting deception. Finally, situations in which it might be relatively easy or relatively difficult to successfully detect deception are described.

Steps in Detecting Deception and Dishonesty

The successful detection of deception and dishonesty in the workplace involves four basic steps: (1) recognition, (2) localization, (3) investigation, and (4) classification. First, you must recognize that a dishonest act has occurred, something that is often surprisingly difficult to do. Many dishonest acts, including even large-scale thefts, go undiscovered because of inadequate inventory control, accounting procedures, supervision, and so on. Acts of production deviance may be particularly difficult to discover or recognize, in part because many of these, such as long breaks, slow work, or excessive socialization, are not regarded as dishonest or forbidden by individuals in the organization and therefore do not attract attention. Second, you must determine who is most and least likely to be deceptive or dishonest. This may involve identifying individuals, situations, or both that are most likely to be associated with dishonesty. An organization that investigates all employees every time a theft is discovered may catch the thief, but it will probably go broke in the process; usually, some initial screening or localization of the problem is needed before serious investigations can be undertaken. Third, the organization must gather and evaluate information that can be used to help identify the dishonest or deceptive individuals or predict future dishonesty. Finally, the organization must make decisions on the basis of this information, which often involves classifying individuals as either honest or dishonest and deciding what to do about individuals classified as dishonest. As I noted in Chapter 1, organizations must define the range of behaviors that are treated as honest or acceptable as opposed to dishonest or unacceptable, and they must also define the consequences of overstepping the bounds of acceptable behavior. Presumably, some forms of dishonesty or deception, such as embezzlement, will be grounds for immediate dismissal or sanction, but the responses to other forms of workplace dishonesty might not be so straightforward or clear.

Recognition that deception or dishonesty has occurred.   In some cases, where the individual is caught in the act of committing a theft or a serious act of production deviance such as sabotage, it is easy to recognize that a dishonest act has occurred. In most cases, however, it might not be so easy. For example, as was noted in Chapter 1, widespread disagreement exists about the frequency and extent of employee theft. One reason for this disagreement is that in any given organization, it is often difficult to determine whether or when theft has occurred and how much is missing at a particular point in time. For example, suppose you believed that employees were stealing from your inventory. You could only be sure about the existence and extent of employee theft if you knew all of the following: your actual inventory, your expected inventory (that is, the inventory you would have in were there no theft, waste, spoilage, and so on), and the amount of inventory lost to all causes other than theft.

The accurate assessment of inventory, receipts, and the like in even a small business can be surprisingly difficult. The technical literature dealing with methods of inventory control is both broad and complex; for a sampling of the many concepts and methods involved in the assessment and control of inventories see papers by Chapman and Carter (1990), Jordan (1988), Madia (1990), Pyke and Cohen (1990), and Winsdor (1991). These papers make it clear that the accurate assessment of both expected and actual inventory can be both time-consuming and expensive.

The term *shrinkage* is often used to refer to a variety of unexplained shortages and losses in manufacturing, retailing, and other work environments. Employee theft is thought to be a major component of shrinkage, although the precise amount lost to theft is often difficult to determine. Indeed, *shrinkage* seems to mean very different things in different environments. The term is sometimes used as a euphemism for shoplifting (Shoplifting in America, 1991) or internal theft (Conway & Cox, 1987), but it might also include shortages that are due to computational errors on the part of management (Masuda, 1990). Other authors use the term to refer to unexplained differences between expected gross profit and actual profit (Cohen, 1990). Knowing the amount of shrinkage does not guarantee that you will know the amount of employee theft. A quick examination of the processes by which shrinkage is estimated suggests that it may be difficult to accurately determine the total amount of shrinkage, let alone the percentage due to theft.

In the case of dishonest behaviors other than theft, it may be even more difficult to recognize that the behavior has taken place. The literature on business ethics (for example, Axline, 1988, 1990) suggests that careful observation of the behavior of one's subordinates is one key to maintaining high ethical standards. However, several forms of production deviance (for instance, working on personal projects on company time) and white-collar crime (for example, insider trading) involve many behaviors that are not clearly or obviously dishonest. Very close scrutiny might be required to detect these acts and to piece together their meaning or implications.

Localization: narrowing the list of individuals, situations, or both. Investigations of employee theft and other dishonest behaviors range from broad screening assessments, in which all employees or job applicants are assessed for indications of potential dishonesty, to highly focused investigations involving a small number of individuals who, on the basis of available information, appear likely to be involved in specific incidents of dishonest behavior. The decision whether to cast a broad or a narrow net in investigating workplace dishonesty involves a trade-off of potential risks and benefits. If you investigate everyone, you run no risk of overlooking the guilty parties (although your investigation methods may fail to identify them); on the other hand, you must spend time and resources investigating a large number of innocent individuals. If you narrow your focus to a small number of individuals, you save a great deal of time and money but run the risk of overlooking one or more of the guilty parties.

The optimal balance between the benefits and risks of narrow and broad investigations of dishonesty depends in part on the methods used to narrow the field. If highly accurate methods can be used to identify those who are either most or least likely to be involved in workplace dishonesty, substantial benefits and few risks might result from defining your investigation narrowly rather than broadly. For example, if a particular piece of merchandise is missing and only a few individuals had ready access to that merchandise, it is obviously more sensible to concentrate on those individuals than to investigate others who had little or no opportunity to steal the items in question. On the other hand, methods of screening that have limited accuracy or validity may not provide a basis for substantially narrowing your investigation. For example, evidence reviewed in Chapter 2 suggests that employee theft is more frequent among younger, less experienced employees than among employees who have more substantial links with the organization, such as tenure and socialization. This evidence implies that you might want to restrict your investigations of employee theft or dishonesty to this younger group. However, the risks associated with concentrating solely on younger employees and ignoring older ones in all theft investigations may be unacceptably high; the correlation between age, experience, and theft rates is probably too low to justify the use of age or experience as an absolute screening criterion for narrowing investigations of employee theft.

Preemployment testing—drug tests, polygraphs, integrity tests, and the like administered to job applicants—represents the broadest type of investigation, in which the employer attempts to measure a general propensity toward dishonest or forbidden acts rather than investigating a specific incident. As I will note later in this chapter (and also in Chapter 4), preemployment screening involves a variety of special problems, including potentially high error rates when these tests are used to make decisions about job applicants.

Investigating and predicting dishonesty and deception. Once dishonesty is discovered or suspected and an initial decision has been made about the scope of the investigation of the acts in question, the investigation of specific individuals must begin. The investigation of actual or potential dishonesty in the workplace can take many forms. Internal security investigations might sometimes closely parallel criminal investigations, involving the collection and evaluation of eyewitness testimony, forensic evidence, and other forms of evidence similar to that collected by police and other criminal investigation bureaus. Organizations also use a variety of surveillance methods, ranging from internal spies to computer monitoring, to both deter and detect dishonest behavior (Carson, 1977; Cook, 1988; Fennelly, 1989; Keogh, 1981).

Many of the methods used to investigate dishonesty involve assessing individuals, using tests, interviews, behavioral and physiological reactions, and the like to infer or detect dishonesty. These methods may be classified in terms of whether they are used to detect or infer past or present behavior (for instance, to determine who stole a particular piece of merchandise) or instead to predict future behavior. For example, a polygraph examination might be used as part of the interrogation of an individual suspected of a particular incident of theft in the workplace, although, as I note in Chapter 4, the use of the polygraph in the workplace is now strictly limited. Investigations of specific acts or incidents allow you to focus your attention on relevant questions or evidence, whereas in broad investigations of character or propensity to steal, it is difficult to determine exactly what might be relevant or irrelevant. Investigations of specific acts have the added advantage of focusing on something that definitely did happen. In contrast, attempts to predict future performance focus on an indefinite target—something that might happen.

Preemployment testing is used to predict future dishonesty, which in principle is harder to do than detecting past dishonesty. An individual who fails a preemployment drug test or who receives a low score on an integrity test might be regarded as a poor risk and passed over in favor of other job applicants. However, as you saw in Chapter 1, honesty in work situations is determined by a number of personal and situational factors, and you can never be sure that an individual who might be dishonest in most situations will be dishonest in a specific future situation.

The classification of assessment methods into those used to detect present or past dishonesty and those used to predict future dishonesty is not determined by the method itself, but rather by the way in which the method is applied. For example, the great majority of the employment-related polygraph examinations given in the last ten years were given as preemployment tests. Although the questions in the examination might have focused on past behavior (for example, "Have you ever stolen from a previous employer?"), the purpose of the examination was to make an inference about general honesty and future behavior. If an individual admitted to stealing from a previous employer, the inference was usually made that the individual might also steal from future employers, and negative recommendations about future employment were often made on the basis of admissions or inferences about dishonest behavior in the past.

The distinction between detection of past dishonesty and prediction of future dishonesty is important, because a method that is reasonably accurate or valid for one purpose might have little validity for the other. For example, some evidence shows that carefully conducted polygraph examinations have some validity for detecting past misdeeds, particularly when the investigation is focused on a small number of individuals who are suspected of specific acts on the basis of evidence that is independent of the polygraph (Office of Technology Assessment, 1983; Raskin, 1988). The same technique seems to have little validity when it is used to predict future behavior, particularly when it is used in broad screening rather than in narrowly focused investigations (Ben-Shakhar & Furedy, 1990).

Classification and decision making.   On the basis of the information obtained in the preceding step, two distinct decisions must be made. First, you must classify each individual as either honest or dishonest, deceptive or nondeceptive, or the like. Because there is often some level of uncertainty in this classification, the categories might be less sharply defined. For example, you might classify individuals as very likely, somewhat likely, or unlikely to be involved in workplace dishonesty, or you might place them somewhere on a continuum from completely honest to completely dishonest. Second, you must decide what to do about your classifications. For example, if your investigation leads you to believe that an individual is very likely to have been involved in a specific incident of dishonest behavior, you must decide whether to punish or otherwise sanction the individual, and if so, how (for example, through warnings or termination). The course of action chosen will probably depend on the severity of the incident (for example, large-scale thefts will be handled differently from minor types of production deviance), the degree of certainty in your classification (for example, consequences might be harsher if you are certain than they would be if the evidence is equivocal), and the position of the individual in the organization. There is clear evidence, for example, that the treatment of job applicants or new employees who fail a drug test or are involved in specific infractions is harsher than the treatment of more established employees (some of this evidence is reviewed in Chapter 4). It is also likely that the same behavior will have different consequences depending on whether it is carried out by a lower-level employee or by a manager or executive.

Decision Errors

Whenever decisions are made about individuals, some errors will be made. Human behavior in complex situations is not perfectly predictable, and no method for making important decisions about individuals in organizations is completely free from error, whether these decisions relate to honesty or not. Keep in mind, therefore, that although this section focuses on errors in decisions that relate to honesty, many of the issues raised here are relevant to all decisions made in organizations.

In evaluating the methods used to make decisions about the probable honesty or dishonesty of individuals, it is important to consider: (1) the total number of errors that result, (2) the types of errors that are made, and (3) the consequences of those errors for both the organization and the individual being assessed. To understand the different types of decision errors that might be made, consider Figure 3-1. This figure illustrates the four possible outcomes if individuals take some test that classifies them as either relatively honest (if they pass) or relatively dishonest (if they fail). When the classification matches the true state of affairs (for example, a dishonest person fails), this is referred to as a correct or true classification. When the classification is different from the true state of affairs, this is referred to as an incorrect or false classification. True classifications lead to correct decisions, such as punishing an employee engaged in dishonest or illegal acts, whereas false classifications lead to incorrect decisions, such as unjustly firing an employee wrongly suspected of theft.

The labels "positive" and "negative" refer to the outcome of the test. In this example, I will discuss a test that is designed to detect deception, so a test score indicating deception is referred to as "positive." Therefore, when a truly deceptive person fails the test, so that the test successfully detects deception, I refer to this as a true positive outcome—

Figure 3-1   *Four Possible Outcomes of a Classification Decision*

Honesty test

		Pass	Fail
True state	**Deceptive**	**False negative** People who pass the test when they should fail	**True positive** People who fail the test when they should
	Not deceptive	**True negative** People who pass the test when they should	**False positive** People who fail the test when they should pass

the outcome of the test is positive (that is, the test score indicates deception) and true (that is, the person is deceptive). When honest individuals fail the test, this outcome is referred to as a false positive, which represents an error in classification. When a nondeceptive person passes the test, this outcome is called a true negative, and when the test fails to detect deception, this is referred to as a false negative classification.

False positives and false negatives both represent classification errors, but they have different consequences for both the individual and the organization; the consequences of each of the four decision outcomes when a test is used in preemployment screening are shown in Table 3-1. Furthermore, because it is difficult to simultaneously minimize both types of errors, since techniques that reduce one sort of decision error often lead to increases in the other, it is usually necessary to accept some sort of trade-off between these two types of decision errors. For example, if you wanted to avoid false negative errors, you might make the honesty test very difficult to pass, so that only those who show very high levels of honesty receive passing scores. The difficulty of the test would certainly reduce your number of false negatives, but it would also lead to a large number of false positives, because many honest individuals would be likely to fail the test.

Costs associated with decision errors.   False negative errors are thought to be most costly to the organization, because in this example a false negative means a failure to detect deception. For example, if an honesty measure is used in personnel selection, false negative errors mean that you hire individuals who later turn out to commit theft or other acts of workplace dishonesty. False positive errors can also be costly to the organization (for example, when the organization fires or fails to hire an honest person), but in many contexts they seem much less serious than false negatives. For example, if the applicant pool is large and includes many qualified applicants, the organization might be willing to accept a number of false positive errors, such as passing over honest candidates, as long as it can avoid false negatives. Indeed, in many situations, organizations cannot avoid false positives; however, the use of valid methods of measuring integrity helps to minimize these errors (Martin & Terris, 1991).

From the perspective of the individual being assessed, false positive errors are much more serious than false negatives; a false positive error might mean that an honest person is denied a job because of a misleading test score. False negatives could also be seen as costly to the individual—for instance, a person who should have been screened out by the test might later run into trouble with the level of honesty required by the organization—but such errors probably will not seem as serious as false positives.

As you will see later in this chapter, the frequency of different types of classification errors depends on characteristics of both the situation in which you are assessing honesty and the method used to assess each individual. However, even if the frequency and type of different errors are known, you must also consider the consequences of classification errors, both for the organization and the individual, in your evaluation of the system used to detect deception in a given organization. These consequences depend on the type of dishonest behavior being investigated and on the organization's policy for dealing with individuals who are classified as dishonest.

From the organization's perspective, false negative errors become increasingly serious as the behavior under investigation itself becomes more serious. For example, the failure to identify individuals who are

Table 3-1   *Consequences of Various Outcomes of Classification When Test Is Used for Preemployment Screening*

	Consequences for organization	Consequences for individual
Correct Decisions		
True positive	Screen out candidates likely to be dishonest	Lose chance for job in situation where you are likely to be dishonest
True negative	Identify candidates likely to be honest	Have chance for job in a situation where you are likely to be honest
Incorrect Decisions		
False positive	Screen out candidates who are likely to be honest	Lose chance for job in situation where you are likely to be honest
False negative	Hire candidates who are likely to be dishonest	Get job in situation where you are likely to be dishonest

involved in large-scale thefts is a more serious error than the failure to determine who takes long lunch breaks. From the individual's perspective, false positive errors are most serious when the consequences of failing the test are serious. For example, individuals who fail pre-employment drug or integrity tests are often removed from the applicant pool; job incumbents who fail these tests are sometimes dismissed (O'Bannon, Goldinger, & Appleby, 1989). In general, false positive errors are more serious when actions taken pursuant to them are final or irrevocable, such as termination, than when such actions are subject to later correction.

Factors Affecting the Accuracy of Classifications

The accuracy with which you can classify individuals as either honest or dishonest, nondeceptive or deceptive, or the like depends on three related factors: (1) the reliability and validity of the method used to

Box 3-1   *Assigning Values to Decision Outcomes: A Difficult But Necessary Task*

To make sensible decisions, you must know two things: the probability of a correct or incorrect decision and the value you attach to different decision outcomes (such as true positive, false positive, and so on). The probabilities can be determined easily (see Murphy & Davidshofer, 1991, pp. 140–144 for examples), but the values of different outcomes can be difficult to assess. Is a true positive better than a true negative? Is a true positive good to a greater degree than a false positive is bad? These questions seem so difficult and subjective that it is tempting to simply throw up your hands and claim that they can't be answered.

Although these questions are difficult to answer, they are impossible to avoid. Suppose you set up a personnel screening system that results in ten false negative (FN) errors for every false positive (FP) error. This implies that you think that each FP is ten times as bad as each FN. If you can't tell me what your values are, it is still possible to infer them from your actions.

The advantage of formal decision theory in this context is that it helps you to analyze the values that seem to be driving your behavior. It is useful to find out that you are behaving as if FP errors are ten times as bad as FN errors, because this provides you with a concrete starting point for assessing what your actual values are. You simply cannot avoid the fact that different outcomes have different values, and it is better for you to think through the values you want to assign to decision outcomes than to have some decision researcher analyze your actions and tell you what values you are assigning to outcomes.

classify individuals, (2) the context or situation in which individuals are evaluated, and (3) your decision strategy.

Reliability and Validity of Classification Methods

An extensive body of research on the standards and methods used to evaluate psychological tests can be applied to the various methods used in assessing or predicting honesty, even when those methods seem very different from the typical tests (such as ability and achievement tests, and personality inventories) psychologists use. The technical standards that define adequate and inadequate measurement are embodied in the *Standards for Educational and Psychological Testing* (1985), published jointly by the American Psychological Association and several other organizations.

Before examining the technical standards of measurement described in this document, it is first useful to consider why such a document is at all relevant in evaluating methods such as the polygraph, voice stress analyzer, or interviews designed to evaluate integrity, which seem quite different from standardized psychological tests. The key to understanding the relevance of these standards is to consider what is meant by the terms *measurement* and *test*. Each of these words has a much broader meaning than you might think.

Murphy and Davidshofer (1991) defined measurement as "the process of assigning numbers (e.g., test scores) to persons in such a way that some attributes of the persons being measured are faithfully reflected by some properties of the numbers" (p. 34). All methods of categorization and classification constitute a kind of measurement; sorting people into such categories as honest and dishonest (which you could represent by the numbers 1 and 0, 10 and 20, or any other two numbers you choose) is a simple form of measurement. The measurement is good if the assignment of people into those categories reflects real attributes of the individuals measured (for example, if the people classified as dishonest really are dishonest).

A test is a method of measurement that uses a sample of behavior to assign people to categories or to assign scores to people. The behavior measured might range from reactions to questions in a polygraph interview, to answers given in response to items on a standardized test. In every test, a limited sample of behavior is used to make inferences about people. When assessing honesty, the individual's behavior in the testing situation is used to make inferences about his or her present, past, or future level of honesty in the workplace. A test produces good, accurate measurements if the sample of behavior allows you to make correct inferences about the characteristics of the individuals measured.

In assessing the quality of measurement obtained from any test or measure, two related factors must be considered: the reliability of test scores and the validity of inferences made on the basis of those scores. Reliability refers to the consistency and dependability of test scores; tests with high levels of reliability are thought to be relatively free of errors in measurement. Validity refers to the extent to which the test allows you to make correct inferences about and assessments of individuals. In the present context, where various tests and assessment methods are used to evaluate the past, present, or future honesty of specific individuals, validity refers to the extent to which the test provides accurate information about the person's level of honesty.

Reliability.   The first requirement of good measurement is reliability. A useful test or assessment method will provide scores that are reasonably consistent over time, over alternative forms of the test, across different examiners, or across different conditions of measurement. For example, if you take two different forms of a test designed to measure your general intelligence (IQ tests), you should expect to receive similar scores on both. Similarly, if you go to two well-designed job interviews for the same company, you should expect to do about the same in both. Unreliable tests or measures produce inconsistent results and therefore may not provide useful information about the individuals tested.

The results of any test, measurement technique, or assessment are affected by a wide range of factors that are irrelevant to the purpose of measurement and together are labeled "measurement error." For example, an individual applying for a job may be asked to take a paper-and-pencil integrity test. Suppose the individual is tired and preoccupied—for example, he or she is going through a stressful divorce and hasn't been able to concentrate. Suppose furthermore that the room in which the test is taken is hot and noisy and that there are constant interruptions. Being tired and preoccupied in a hot, noisy room with constant interruptions will probably affect the answers given to the test (or the errors made in filling out the answer sheet), but such conditions probably have nothing to do with the individual's honesty or integrity. These sources of irrelevant variation in test scores constitute measurement error.

Large amounts of measurement error can undermine the usefulness of any measurement procedure. If factors completely irrelevant to the purpose of measurement (in this case, the assessment of an individual's integrity) have a substantial influence on test scores or on the classifications that result from using the test, the test cannot provide much useful information about the integrity of the individuals tested. Because measurement error is by definition irrelevant to the purpose of measurement, tests that are highly susceptible to measurement error will not, in the end, provide a good basis for classifying individuals. A high level of reliability is the first and most basic requirement of any test or assessment procedure.

The most common definition of reliability breaks down the score each person receives on a test (symbolized by X) into two components: (1) e: errors of measurement and (2) T: true scores, or scores that are free of measurement error. This definition is summarized by the equation:

$$X = T + e \qquad\qquad (1)$$

On the basis of some very simple and reasonable assumptions about the nature of measurement error (for example, that e is completely unrelated to T), it is possible to develop both elaborate theories of test reliability and practical procedures for estimating the reliability of tests and measures. (For an introduction to the theory and procedures for estimating reliability, see Murphy & Davidshofer, 1991; for more advanced discussions, see Cronbach, Gleser, Nanda, & Rajaratnam, 1972; Lord & Novick, 1968; and Nunnally, 1982). The most common measure of test reliability is the reliability coefficient, which represents the relative influence of true scores and measurement errors on test scores.[1] A high reliability coefficient indicates that measurement errors are not a major influence on the scores produced by a test or measurement procedure.

There are several methods of estimating reliability; the choice among methods depends on both practical and theoretical considerations. Depending on your definition of measurement error, different methods of estimating reliability might be more or less appropriate (Standards for Educational and Psychological Testing, 1985). For example, suppose you were using an interview to evaluate each job applicant's level of integrity. The outcome of the interview might depend on the interviewer or on the questions being asked, and even with the same interviewer and set of questions, outcomes might vary over time. Each of these factors (interviewer, questions asked, and time) might represent a source of measurement error, depending on the specific purpose of testing and the definition of the characteristic being measured. This can best be illustrated by considering the different definitions of measurement error shown in Table 3-2 that apply when the interview just described is used to assess either present levels of honesty or future levels of honesty. This table does not exhaust the list of factors that might contribute to errors in measurement (see Thorndike, 1949, for a more complete list); rather, it illustrates the fact that the precise definition of measurement error in any particular testing situation may depend in part on the purpose of testing.

[1] The reliability coefficient can be interpreted as the proportion of the total variability in test scores that can be attributed to true scores. Thus, if a reliability coefficient equals .90, this indicates that 90% of the variability in test scores is due to true scores and 10% is due to errors in measurement.

Table 3-2   *Different Definitions of Measurement Error When an Interview Is Used to Assess Present and Future Levels of Integrity*

	Test is used to measure	
POTENTIAL SOURCES OF MEASUREMENT ERROR	PRESENT INTEGRITY	FUTURE INTEGRITY
Interviewer differences	Error	Error
Differences in questions	Error	Error
Differences over time	True score	Error

Suppose two separate interviews are done at three-month intervals to assess one's level of honesty in the workplace, and the outcomes of the two interviews differ (one classifies you as honest and the other classifies you as dishonest). When the interview is used to assess one's current level of integrity, variability in the outcome of the interview over time might represent true changes in a person's level of integrity, and therefore cannot automatically be regarded as measurement error. However, if the interview is used to make inferences about your integrity over the next several years in the company, differences in interview outcomes over time are more likely to be regarded as measurement errors.

Generalizability theory (Cronbach et al., 1972) offers the most comprehensive framework for studying the reliability of tests and measurement techniques. This theory encourages test users to define carefully exactly what constitutes true scores and measurement error in different situations (as was done in Table 3-1) and provides methods of estimating the reliability of test scores for each of the possible uses of the test (for example, to infer present and future levels of integrity). One of the most important contributions of generalizability theory is that a test or measurement technique might have many different reliability coefficients, each of which corresponds with one particular use of the test. Therefore, a statement such as "the XYZ Integrity Scale is highly reliable" is incomplete; the same test might be reliable for some purposes and unreliable for others.

There is no magic number that represents an "acceptable" level of reliability. It is, however, possible to draw on our experience with different types of tests to provide some rough guidelines for evaluating the reliability of various methods of assessing honesty or integrity. Carefully developed standardized tests of intelligence, ability, and achievement typically demonstrate reliability coefficients in the .85 to .95 range, meaning that measurement errors typically account for 5 to 15% of the test score. Reliability coefficients closer to .80 are typical for many other psychological tests, and reliability coefficients higher than .70 are often regarded as adequate, especially if the test is not the sole basis for an important decision (Murphy & Davidshofer, 1991).

Reliability coefficients substantially lower than .70—that is, tests or measurement devices in which more than 30% of the total score is accounted for by measurement error—often indicate unacceptably poor measurement.

You can do two things to increase the reliability of measurement. First, base your measure on a large number of observations rather than a small number. Standardized tests of intelligence and scholastic ability typically include large numbers of items (often, several hundred). One reason is that a larger set of items yields more reliable measurement. Similarly, an interview that includes many questions will usually yield more reliable measurement than one that includes only a few. The use of many questions, observations, and so on helps to guard against the possibility that a small number of unrepresentative responses will seriously bias test scores. Second, standardize the conditions of measurement to whatever extent possible. One reason for the superior reliability of paper-and-pencil tests as opposed to, for example, unstructured interviews is that the questions asked, the order of questions, and the like are exactly the same for all examinees. If you can keep the setting, the questions, the examiner's style and demeanor, and so forth constant over all applications of the test or measurement technique, you can eliminate these variables as sources of measurement error.

Reasonable levels of reliability are absolutely necessary. Consider, for example, a test with a reliability coefficient of .10. Here, 90% of the variability in test scores would be due to irrelevant factors, and even though the test might tell you something useful about the individuals being examined, the potentially useful information would be buried under and hopelessly confounded with the irrelevant factors that, taken together, represent measurement error. A measurement device that does not demonstrate an acceptable level of reliability is essentially useless.

Validity.   Reliability is necessary but not sufficient to guarantee good measurement. A test that is completely unreliable is completely worthless, but high levels of reliability do not necessarily mean that the test or assessment method is any good. The second requirement of good measurement is validity.

All of the various tests, measures, and assessment methods used in evaluating honesty are used to make inferences about the person. Some are used to make inferences about his or her present or past behavior, attitudes, and the like (for example, measures of personality characteristics related to honesty), whereas others are used to make inferences about future honesty (for instance, tests designed to predict employee theft). The most important question in psychological testing and other similar measurement applications is whether the test leads to correct or valid inferences. For example, if I am using a test to predict someone's future level of honesty and integrity, it is important to determine whether my predictions turn out to be right.

Although there are a number of specific validation strategies, all methods of validation are fundamentally concerned with whether the information provided by test scores is sufficient to allow you to make valid inferences about the individuals who took the test (Angoff, 1988; Cronbach, 1988; Landy, 1987). As is true of reliability, there is no single number you can cite as *the* validity of a particular test. Rather, the level of validity depends in part on the specific inferences you hope to make on the basis of test scores. For example, suppose you used a polygraph examination in which you asked questions about thefts from previous employers. As was noted earlier in this chapter, this examination might be used for detection (that is, making inferences about past behavior) or for prediction (making inferences about future behavior), and the same examination might have different levels of validity for these two purposes.

Validation research typically involves an examination of the test itself and of the relationship between test scores (or other test outcomes, such as a classification of individuals as honest or dishonest) and other measures. The most comprehensive strategy for validation, often referred to as "construct validation," is a process for accumulating evidence about the validity of the inferences made on the basis of test scores. The purpose of construct validation is to understand the meaning of test scores. For example, construct validity research tells us whether a test developed to measure a construct such as integrity actually provides useful information about a person's integrity and whether it provides a basis for predicting his or her future behavior (for example, predicting theft). This method of validation involves two basic steps, construct explication and empirical testing. Construct explication is the process of defining precisely what it is you want to measure and its relationship to other measures, behaviors, and so on. Construct explication leads to a set of predictions or hypotheses about your measure, which can then be subjected to empirical testing. This process can be illustrated by describing some of the steps that would be involved in investigating the construct validity of a new paper-and-pencil integrity scale.

Construct explication begins with a definition of the characteristics that a good measure of integrity should exhibit. As is shown in Table 3-3, scores from a good integrity scale should be (1) related to scores on other, well-validated measures of integrity, (2) higher for apparently honest individuals than for individuals known to be dishonest, (3) unrelated to irrelevant personality traits such as need for achievement, and (4) related to employee theft rates. Each one of these statements represents a hypothesis; if the test you have developed is indeed a good measure of integrity, most or all of these hypotheses should turn out to be true.

As is also shown in Table 3-3, each hypothesis leads to one or more empirical tests. As these tests are carried out, evidence begins to accumulate regarding the degree to which the test allows you to make valid inferences about the construct of integrity. If many or most of the empirical tests support your hypothesis, you may have some confidence that the test will provide useful information about the integrity of the individuals who take the test.

In evaluating the validity of tests and assessment methods used to detect deception and dishonesty, you should look for several things. First, validation should always involve multiple sources of evidence. A test that claims a high level of validity on the basis of a single study or a single coefficient is therefore suspect. Second, a test cannot be valid in the abstract but rather must be validated for specific purposes. Such statements as, "The polygraph is valid," or "The polygraph is invalid," are potentially meaningless. Most tests are more valid for some purposes than for others, and it is necessary to answer the question, "Valid for what?" before you can make any sense of a validity study. Third, validity is a continuum; calling a test either valid or not valid obscures the fact that the level of validity of different tests for specific purposes may vary considerably.

As was noted earlier, any test or measurement procedure that is used to make inferences about honesty, deception, theft, and the like must first demonstrate evidence of reliability. Furthermore, the method of defining and estimating reliability must be appropriate for the intended use of the test (Standards for Educational and Psychological Testing, 1985). Thus, a test that is used to make predictions about job applicants' long-term honesty in the workplace must, at a minimum, show some stability over time. A test that yielded highly discrepant

Table 3-3 *Investigating the Construct Validity of an Integrity Scale*

Hypotheses	Empirical tests
Scores on the test are related to scores on other, well-validated measures of integrity.	Correlate test scores with other integrity tests.
Scores on the test are higher for apparently honest individuals than for individuals known to be dishonest.	Compare the mean score in a random sample from the population to the mean score of convicted felons.
Scores on the test are unrelated to irrelevant personality traits such as the need for achievement.	Correlate test scores with measures of these traits.
Scores on the test are related to employee theft rates.	Compare the average test scores in retail stores with high theft rates and stores with low theft rates.

scores at different points in time would hardly provide a basis for reliable predictions about future levels of honesty. Next, the test publisher or test user must present evidence that the test is valid for its intended uses. If you intend to use a test to screen out potential thieves, you must present evidence that test scores are indeed related to the likelihood of future thefts.

Matching validity evidence to the purpose of testing.   At one time, it was thought that there were several different types of validity and that construct validation was one of many approaches to investigating test validity (Cronbach, 1988). It is now clear that all methods of validation tell us something about test scores and therefore fit under the general umbrella of construct validation. Nevertheless, different uses of tests might make specific types of validity evidence more or less relevant.

Murphy and Davidshofer (1991) distinguish between validity in measurement and validity in prediction. For example, a personality test might measure traits such as conscientiousness or dependability, which are thought to be highly relevant in work settings (Murphy & Lee, 1991). The question whether the test really measures conscientiousness is somewhat distinct from the question whether it will predict specific types of honesty in the workplace.[2] If the ultimate purpose of the test is to predict theft, evidence that it measures personality traits that appear relevant to theft is not enough to justify its use. What is required is evidence of the validity of the test for the specific purpose you have in mind (Standards for Educational and Psychological Testing, 1985).

Situational Factors

Even if you can develop a good test or method of measuring honesty and integrity, the successful detection and prediction of deception and dishonesty in the workplace can be difficult. A number of situational factors can affect your ability to successfully detect dishonesty, independent of any potential shortcomings in your test or assessment methods.

One of the most important variables involved in attempts to detect deception is the base rate, or the relative frequency, of deception. Suppose you are using a test, a polygraph, or a voice stress analyzer to detect which job applicants have stolen from their previous employers or are likely to steal from you. The problem of detecting dishonesty is fundamentally different if half of all applicants are attempting to

[2] However, Binning and Barrett (1989) argue that validity of measurement is usually a critical component of validity of prediction. In other words, if a test does not measure the appropriate construct, it is unlikely that it will nevertheless be correlated with the same criteria that are known to be related to the construct in question.

conceal damaging information than if only 1 applicant in 100 is attempting to deceive (Murphy, 1987). If the base rate is very low, it is extremely difficult to accurately detect deception, and any method that attempts to distinguish between the small number of deceptive individuals and the large number of honest individuals is highly likely to make false positive errors—that is, to falsely accuse a large number of innocent suspects. As I noted earlier, it is difficult to detect any condition when the base rate is low, and the following problem is in no way unique to the detection of dishonesty. Suppose you had a very good method of measuring integrity (for example, a paper-and-pencil test). All methods result in some decision errors, but a good test might result in relatively few. Your test is so good that a dishonest person is ten times more likely to fail the test than an honest one. Suppose further that you have 100 employees, and 4 of them are stealing large amounts from you. If you pick a person at random from this group, the odds that he or she is one of the thieves are 24 to 1 (because there are 96 honest individuals to 4 thieves). Now suppose you give the integrity test to that person, and the person fails. What should you conclude?

Because of the low base rate, you would have to conclude that even the people who fail the test are, in fact, more likely to be honest than dishonest. This conclusion is necessary because in this situation almost everyone is honest; the odds of picking a dishonest person by chance alone are 1 in 24. A good test improves your probability of detecting deception, in this example by a factor of ten. When you put these two facts together, you end up concluding that a person who fails the test is still more than twice as likely to be honest than dishonest.

Murphy (1987) demonstrated analytically the difficulty in detecting deception when the base rate is low. His conclusion was that when the base rate is much below .10 (in other words, when there are 10 deceptive people in a sample of 100), no existing test may be sufficiently sensitive to successfully detect deception. Several critics of Murphy's (1987) analysis (for example, Manhardt, 1989; Martin & Terris, 1991; see also Murphy, 1989) pointed out that the base rate is more critical for some decisions than for others. In the example just given, a test is used to pick a handful of thieves from a large number of honest employees. If the same test is used to rank-order job applicants (for instance, in terms of the probability that they will engage in employee theft), base rates have very different implications. As you will see in a later section, the influence of base rates depends in part on the type of decision in question.

Estimates of base rates.   There is some disagreement about the proportion of employees involved in various types of property and production deviance; different figures are cited for different patterns or types of deviance. Most studies of property deviance have concentrated on employee theft. The base rate for detected theft is quite low. Depending on the industry, approximately 2 to 10% of the employees hired are later found to commit theft (Office of Technology Assessment, 1990). Most thefts, however, are not detected, and the proportion of employees who engage in some sort of theft is certainly higher than 10%. Reviews of research in employee theft suggest that theft levels vary considerably in different jobs, industries, and so on, but that the overall base rate for employee theft is thought to be in the neighborhood of 30 to 35% (Hollinger & Clark, 1983; Jones, Joy, & Rospenda, 1990), although figures as high as 75% have been suggested (Zeitlin, 1971).

Substantial care must be taken in interpreting these base rate figures, because the meaning of the base rate depends very much on factors such as the definition of precisely what constitutes theft (is it theft to take home pencils from work?), the time period involved (do questions about theft cover a specific period or one's whole career?), and the frequency of theft (Office of Technology Assessment, 1990). For example, a person who once stole merchandise worth $10 but never stole again might or might not be included in your calculations of the base rate evidence. If you included cases like this and concluded that the base rate for theft was 30%, this would mean that 70% of your employees never steal anything, no matter how trivial, and that the other 30% might steal once or twice in their careers or every day.

Hollinger and Clark (1983) noted that although a large number of employees commit some thefts, most of these thefts are small and infrequent. Thus, many of the individuals included in the base rate estimates for employee theft are truly petty thieves. The number of employees who steal frequently or who steal large amounts is certainly smaller than the overall base rate, but it is not clear how much smaller. Murphy (1987) suggested that the base rate for nontrivial thefts (frequent or large thefts) might be less than 5% in many industries.

Production deviance appears to be much more common than property deviance. Base rates of 65 to 75% have been cited by several authors (for example, Inbau, 1989; Jones, Joy, & Rospenda, 1990). That is, as many as three-quarters of all employees are thought to engage in some form of production deviance. Although this figure suggests that production deviance is rampant, it cannot be taken at face value. The interpretation of base rate figures for production deviance poses the same set of problems as for property deviance. Does a figure of 75% mean that three-quarters of all workers are constantly or usually engaged in this form of behavior? It is possible that this figure indicates that three-quarters of all employees have engaged in this type of behavior at some point in their careers—it is hard to think of anyone who never took a long lunch break or called in sick when they should not have—but this doesn't mean that production deviance is a common occurrence.

Other situational factors.   The base rate imposes statistical limits on your ability to accurately detect or predict specific forms of dishonesty and deception. Other situational factors have substantive rather than statistical effects. In particular, the norms and beliefs of organization members can make it difficult to detect many types of dishonest behavior. First, work-group norms, the culture of the organization, and so on define the range of behaviors that is regarded as either acceptable or unacceptable. Many forms of production deviance (and perhaps some forms of property deviance) will be hard to detect because they are generally regarded as normal and acceptable, and thus they will not be reported and will not be the subject of special attention or scrutiny. Second, these same norms often define the responses that are likely to be viewed as acceptable when dishonest behavior occurs. If the norms encourage the informal resolution of conflicts over workplace dishonesty, it may be very difficult to obtain information about these behaviors.

Box 3-2   *Base Rates and Expertise in Detecting Deception*

Research on attempts to detect deception on the basis of nonverbal behavior, voice inflections, and other cues obtained by observing the potentially deceptive individual might overestimate the difficulty of the task, since many of the studies on this topic have used students or other potentially naive individuals as subjects. To provide a fairer test of the ability to detect deception, Ekman and O'Sullivan (1991) conducted several studies using subjects who presumably have some expertise with the task. In particular, they assessed the ability of U.S. Secret Service agents, federal polygraphers (from, for example, the FBI and the CIA), judges, police, and psychiatrists to detect deception in a series of realistic videotaped statements. Only Secret Service agents scored better than chance in this task; none of the other expert groups was able to reliably detect deception.

In explaining why Secret Service agents were able to detect deception at a better than chance level, Ekman and O'Sullivan noted that the base rates for deception are probably quite different for Secret Service agents than for police, polygraph operators, or judges. All four of these groups spend significant amounts of their time interrogating individuals who routinely deny their guilt. In the case of Secret Service agents, many of these denials are truthful; most of the individuals who mutter threats against public officials in a bar or similar setting probably have no real intention of doing actual harm. Police, judges, and polygraphers, on the other hand, frequently listen to denials from guilty individuals. Ekman and O'Sullivan suggested that having to detect deception in contexts where it is rare may lead to the development of different skills than does having to detect deception in contexts where it is common.

As I will note in later chapters, the expectations, norms, and beliefs of workers and managers are a major determinant of honesty in the workplace. Behavior that is expected or tolerated, even though it does not meet the strictest definition of honesty, will be difficult to detect or deter. In contrast, if the behavior in question is not accepted as honest, reasonable, or tolerable, it is likely that the work group will impose sanctions on the offending individual that will make the behavior itself both easier to detect or infer and less likely to recur in the future.

Decision Strategies

Two aspects of the decision strategy employed in determining whether deception or dishonesty has occurred (and if it has, what to do about it) substantially affect the overall quality of your decisions: (1) whether the decision is relative or absolute and (2) your tolerance for different types of decision errors. Earlier in this chapter, I discussed the trade-offs between false positive and false negative decision errors and noted that strategies designed to minimize one type of error tend to inflate the other. For example, if you are greatly concerned with false positive decision errors (for example, situations where honest individuals fail an integrity test), you could set the cutoff score for failing at such a low level that practically everyone who takes the test will pass it. This will indeed minimize the number of false positives, but at the cost of multiplying false negatives (for example, cases where dishonest individuals pass). Rather than designing a strategy to reduce only one type of decision error, you need to consider the optimal balance between the different types of errors you might make. How you strike this balance may depend in part on whether the decision in question is an absolute or a comparative one (Martin & Terris, 1991; Sackett, Burris, & Callahan, 1989).

Absolute versus comparative decisions.   Decisions made about specific individuals, considered in isolation, are referred to as absolute. For example, you might give an integrity test to a current employee and use the test score to decide whether he or she is likely to have committed dishonest acts (and if so, what you are going to do about it). The most common absolute decision related to honesty in the workplace is whether or not to terminate an employee suspected of theft.

Comparative decisions involve relative rather than absolute evaluation. For example, in personnel selection, your decision might concern which of two job candidates is more or less likely to commit employee theft; all other things being equal, you should hire the individual who is least likely to engage in theft. Note here that you do not have to decide whether any specific individual will commit a theft. Rather, your task is simply to compare individuals to determine who is more likely to become involved in employee theft.

On the whole, comparative decisions are easier and less subject to a variety of sources of error than are absolute decisions (Cronbach et al., 1972). Furthermore, the amount of evidence needed to make good comparative decisions is considerably less than that required to make good absolute decisions. For example, Murphy (1987) showed that when the base rate for employee theft is sufficiently low, no existing test is sufficiently sensitive or accurate to allow you to make a confident statement that a specific individual is or is not a thief. Statements about specific individuals are absolute in nature, and the level of validity needed to make absolute decisions in cases like this is prohibitively high. In contrast, existing integrity tests may have sufficient validity and sensitivity for comparative decisions; research on this class of tests is reviewed in Chapter 5. Even if you cannot marshal enough evidence to determine with confidence whether or not a specific individual is a thief, it is often possible to be quite confident that one individual is more likely than another to steal.

In making an absolute decision, it is probably better to err on the conservative side and not terminate or otherwise discipline an individual unless you have compelling evidence that he or she is indeed dishonest or deceptive. The presumption of individual innocence is built into our basic system of justice (Murphy, 1987, describes decision strategies that incorporate reasonable doubt), and you are probably better off risking false negative decisions (failing to fire a thief) than false positive ones (firing an innocent individual). Comparative decisions may involve fewer concerns about false positive errors, in part because such errors are inevitable in many situations such as personnel selection, where the number of qualified applicants often far exceeds the number of openings (Martin & Terris, 1991).

Consider the case where 100 people apply for 30 jobs. Assume that the base rate for theft in this group is 40%, meaning that there are 60 individuals in this pool who would not steal given the chance. No matter how you make decisions, you must make at least 30 false positive errors (that is, failing to hire an honest individual), because there are only 30 jobs for 60 honest applicants. The existence of these false positives is not a symptom of poor decision making but rather stems from the fact that the supply of good candidates exceeds the number of jobs that need to be filled.

Balancing the costs of decision errors. As I noted earlier, anytime important decisions must be made about individuals in organizations (such as selecting among job applicants or deciding whether to fire a suspected thief), it is virtually impossible to avoid some decision errors.

The best you can do is to minimize both the number and the cost of the errors you make.

Well-validated measures of dishonesty, integrity, and the like allow you to minimize the total number of decision errors in decisions related to workplace dishonesty (Martin & Terris, 1991). In other words, the better the test (in terms of its validity for predicting or detecting dishonesty), the better the decisions. However, as Table 3-1 showed, both false positive and false negative decision errors have a variety of consequences that differ in value or importance for individuals and organizations. A testing program that produces ten false positives is not equivalent to one that produces ten false negatives; to fully evaluate the consequences of various programs for detecting, inferring, or predicting dishonesty, it is necessary to consider the types of decision errors and their relative importance as well as the total number of decision errors. Earlier, I noted that organizations are likely to be more concerned about false negatives (for example, hiring applicants who later steal) than about false positives (for instance, failing to hire honest individuals). From the organization's point of view, testing programs that are biased in favor of false positives and against false negatives are likely to be preferable. For example, one decision you need to make when using integrity tests is where to set the cutoff score for a passing grade. If you are very conservative and set a very stringent standard for passing the test, you will tend to have fewer false negatives and more false positives.

As this example suggests, it is not the test itself that produces false positives or false negatives (see Martin & Terris, 1991, for a forceful statement of this point), but rather the way in which tests are used. If you want to avoid false negatives at all costs, you can do so by setting a very stringent passing score—which will lead to more false positives. People who are very concerned about false positive decision errors (such as job applicants and advocacy groups) can create decision strategies that will virtually eliminate these types of errors (for example, by setting the passing score so low that virtually everyone passes), but this will be done at the cost of many false negatives. The best strategy is probably one that recognizes that both false positive and false negative errors will occur and that attempts to balance their costs. For example, if the managers of an organization decide that false negatives are four times as costly to the organization as false positives, they should design decision strategies that make false negatives four times less likely than false positives. Decisions about the relative value or importance of different decision errors are by definition subjective; job candidates may have very different ideas about the importance of false positives than will managers. Nevertheless, these decisions have to be faced, and it is better to decide these issues through careful consideration of the relative costs of errors than simply to design a system with no clear awareness of the types of decision errors it is likely to produce.

Optimal Situations for Detecting Deception

As I noted earlier, in some situations it will be relatively easy to detect deception, and in others it might be very difficult to successfully predict or detect deception and dishonesty. This final section describes situations in which you are most and least likely to successfully detect or predict dishonesty in the workplace.

Who, What, and Why

Situations in which dishonesty might be relatively easy or relatively difficult to detect can be described in terms of three dimensions: who, what, and why.

Who.   Dishonesty is easiest to detect when it is either widespread or highly concentrated. Widespread dishonesty means that there will be a high base rate, which removes one of the major statistical impediments to detecting dishonesty. Of course, if the base rate is too high, it might be difficult to detect honesty; the problem of sorting a few honest individuals from a large number of dishonest ones is, if anything, more difficult than the problem of detecting dishonesty when the base rate is low.

Although widespread dishonesty may be relatively easy to detect, it may be quite difficult to deal with. Suppose you found that 80% of your work force was stealing materials, supplies, and merchandise. It would be very difficult to fire or otherwise discipline this number of workers. You could probably accomplish something by tightening up on your security, but as I will suggest in Chapters 6 and 8, the strategy most likely to work here is one that attempts to change workers' norms and attitudes regarding workplace theft. Unfortunately, accomplishing such a change can be quite difficult.

Dishonesty and theft are probably easiest to recognize and deal with when they are concentrated in relatively small groups or types of individuals. For example, as I noted earlier, if you can identify the individuals who had access to material that was stolen, your ability to successfully identify the thief increases substantially. Similarly, if you know that specific groups of workers (such as new employees) are most likely to steal, this fact can help to focus your investigation. Again, you have to be careful about concentrating on specific groups of employees solely on the basis of relatively modest correlations between variables such as age, experience, and gender in investigating dishonesty and theft in the workplace.

What.   Some types of dishonesty are easier to detect than others. Dishonesty that is either very serious or rather trivial (for example, embezzlement or long lunch breaks) may be difficult to detect, for somewhat different reasons. In cases such as embezzlement, the individuals involved are likely to make careful efforts to conceal their activities. In cases of relatively minor production deviance, you may find that nobody (including the individual who commits the act) pays much attention to the act. Even though, when averaged over thousands of employees, long breaks and lunch hours can cost large sums in terms of lost productivity, it is often difficult to convince the individuals involved that it is worthwhile to pay attention to minor forms of workplace dishonesty.

Dishonest activities that are moderately serious might be easiest to detect, because there will be some recognition that these activities are not really right but few elaborate attempts to conceal these acts. Once again, it may not always be clear what to do about these activities. If an individual is caught committing a serious crime at work, you would be well justified in firing him or her. If an individual is caught committing some relatively trivial act of production deviance, you might either ignore it or deal with it simply and informally. Individuals who are caught in moderately serious forms of dishonesty are likely to encounter a wide range of responses from the organization, ranging from a simple verbal comment to termination. Policies for dealing with these moderately serious forms of dishonesty and deception probably require more thought and care than policies for dealing with either very serious or completely trivial offenses.

Why.   In Chapter 2, I reviewed research on why individuals steal and commit other forms of dishonest behavior in the workplace. Sometimes, people steal because they need the money, but in most cases, the reasons for employee theft are more complex, ranging from thrill-seeking to restoring one's sense of power and equity in the organization. Theft and other forms of dishonesty will be easiest to detect when the reasons are obvious and hardest to detect when the reasons for these acts are highly idiosyncratic. For example, some retail stores pay very low wages and treat their employees quite badly. It is no mystery why these stores experience employee theft, and it is likely that they experience the greatest amount of theft from employees who are most angry about their treatment. On the other hand, thefts that are committed for strange or uncommon reasons might be the hardest to predict and detect.

Organizations that experience substantial amounts of property and production deviance might benefit substantially from investigation into the reasons for these behaviors. Clearly theft rates and the incidence and severity of other forms of property and production deviance vary across organizations, and it might be more useful to develop a better understanding of the reasons for this variance than to identify and deal with the individuals involved. If the conditions that foster dishonesty persist, you will accomplish little by firing some current employees and then putting new individuals into that same environment. Unless you address the conditions that encourage dishonesty in the workplace, you might find yourself in a cycle where you continually fire some individuals, replace them, and then fire the replacements. This is hardly an effective strategy for dealing with dishonesty in the workplace.

SUMMARY

It can be very difficult to determine whether workplace dishonesty has occurred or is occurring, much less to identify the individuals involved. How well deception can be predicted and detected depends on the methods used to identify and investigate suspects, on the situation in which dishonesty has occurred, and on the decision strategies used to distinguish individuals labeled as "honest" from those labeled as "dishonest."

The basic requirements for success in detecting deception are a favorable situation (for example, a high base rate or widespread disapproval of the acts in question), a reliable and valid method for detecting or predicting dishonesty, and an appropriate decision strategy. A favorable situation is one where there are no statistical barriers to detecting deception (such as a low base rate) and where the prevailing norms discourage the type of dishonest behavior under investigation. The reliability and validity of methods of inferring honesty or dishonesty refer to their freedom from measurement error and their usefulness in helping to identify individuals who are either highly likely or highly unlikely to become involved in workplace dishonesty. The decision strategy employed is important because all methods of evaluating others are prone to error, and a strategy must be developed that strikes a balance between the different types of decision errors you might make.

Probably the most common situation in which assessments of honesty are used to make decisions about individuals is in preemployment testing. Unfortunately, preemployment testing does not always constitute a favorable situation for detecting dishonesty, because the probable base rates for nontrivial deception and dishonesty are often low among job applicants (Murphy, 1987). Preemployment testing also represents a relatively difficult decision—the prediction of future dishonesty rather than the simple assessment of past behavior. As a result, it may be difficult to successfully predict theft, no matter how good the test. The same may be true for other forms of workplace dishonesty. The task of distinguishing honest from dishonest individuals is never an easy one, but as you will see from several of the chapters that follow, it is not necessarily an impossible task.

CHAPTER FOUR

Physiological, Behavioral, and Other Indirect Methods of Detection

Two approaches might be followed in detecting or inferring dishonesty. First, you might ask individuals a number of questions and infer honesty or dishonesty on the basis of their answers. I refer to these as direct methods, and several of them will be reviewed in Chapter 5. Second, you might collect information by observing behavior or taking physiological measures and infer honesty or dishonesty on the basis of this information. For example, it is often assumed that deception is stressful and that a number of physiological and behavioral cues might indicate that the individual is attempting to deceive. The use of such methods to detect deception has a long and varied history, going back almost 3000 years. Ben-Shakhar and Furedy (1990), Kleinmuntz and Szucko (1984), and Lykken (1981) all describe the ancient use of physical signs such as blushing, accelerated heartbeat, and dryness of the mouth as indicators of deception. For example, suspected liars in ancient China were required to chew rice powder, which is extremely dry. Individuals who were suffering from dryness of the mouth would find this impossible to do.

Using Physiological and Behavioral Measures to Detect Deception

This chapter discusses several indirect methods that have been applied to detect deception in the workplace, including the polygraph, the voice stress analyzer, and handwriting analysis or graphology, as well as methods that involve inferring deception from subtle behavioral cues. I will also discuss drug testing, which is used to detect a specific type of behavior, drug use, that might be counterproductive. All these methods rely on indirect indicators of stress or deception, ranging from physiological and biochemical indicators to subtle behavioral cues. The polygraph has been the focus of the greatest amount of controversy and will be discussed first.

The Polygraph

Sometimes referred to as a lie detector, the polygraph is an apparatus used to measure and record physiological responses of an individual under interrogation. Typically, this apparatus includes sensors or devices that measure heart rate, respiration rate, blood pressure, and palmar sweating. The use of a polygraph typically requires the attachment of electrodes, blood pressure cuffs, and sensors to measure respiration rate to the examinee; physiological reactions accompanying answers to various questions are then recorded. The theory behind this technique is that the physiological data provide information that helps the examiner determine whether or not the subject is deceptive in his or her answers to specific questions.

It is important to distinguish between the polygraph examination and the polygraph itself. As O'Toole (1988) notes, the lie detector is the polygraph examiner, not the machine. In other words, the machine does not tell whether or not you are lying (although proponents of this technique suggest that it it provides critical information about deception); rather, it is one component of a complex examination and inference process. In fact, as I will note later, the machine itself and the physiological data recorded by the machine may play a surprisingly minor role in determining the outcome of many polygraph examinations. In the sections below, I will describe the ways in which the polygraph has been used and the methods used in polygraph examinations.

History of polygraph use.   The modern era of inferring deception by measuring individuals' physiological reactions as they respond to questions began at the turn of the century with the introduction of the polygraph. Originally developed by the criminologist Lombroso, this technique was introduced to the United States by Hugo Munsterberg and popularized by one of his students, Marston (Barland, 1988; Ben-Shakhar & Furedy, 1990; Lykken, 1981). During the 1960s, methods of quantitatively scoring the polygraph examination, including computerized scoring, started to develop, and this development continued into the 1980s.

The polygraph was originally confined to criminal investigations and later to investigations of security risks and leaks. However, the polygraph quickly moved into the workplace, where two very different types of applications were developed. First, it was used in investigations that closely paralleled criminal investigations, in which some specific act or event being investigated and a small number of individuals were believed, on the basis of some reasonable evidence, to be involved in the event. Second, the polygraph was used in what Ben-Shakhar and Furedy (1990) refer to as event-free investigations. For example, if the polygraph is used in preemployment screening, no single event or issue is being investigated; rather, the polygraph is being used to conduct a very general inquiry into the character of the individual. A preemployment polygraph examination might be used, for instance, to determine whether an individual had stolen from previous employers or had been involved in other forms of counter-productive behavior. As I will note later, the use of the polygraph in this sort of a general screening, where no specific event or issue is being investigated, is especially problematic.

Although the polygraph is used in criminal and security-related investigations in a number of countries, its use in organizations (particularly for preemployment inquiries) is a phenomenon unique to the United States (Ben-Shakhar & Furedy, 1990; Lykken, 1981). The use of the polygraph in organizations declined dramatically after 1988, when a federal law severely restricted the use of the polygraph in employment settings. However, prior to that law use of the polygraph was widespread; some organizations are still pressing for legislation to overturn existing restrictions on its use.

In the early 1980s, approximately 1 million polygraph examinations were given per year, with nearly three-quarters of those in employment settings (Lykken, 1981). In 1982, the federal government conducted 23,000 polygraph examinations, most in conjunction with criminal investigations (Office of Technology Assessment, 1983). Proposals by the Reagan administration to greatly expand the use of the polygraph in federal settings, particularly for personnel selection and screening in jobs that gave access to classified material, led to a number of investigations of the validity and utility of the polygraph in organizations. Ironically, the administration's proposal to increase the use of the polygraph eventually led to the downfall of the polygraph as a method of detecting honesty at work. Proposals to greatly increase the use of the polygraph in employment settings heightened public awareness of and concern over the shortcomings of the polygraph examination as a method of evaluating the honesty, integrity, or trustworthiness of an individual as an employee.

Critics of the polygraph, particularly in employment settings, include the American and the British Psychological Associations, the Office of Technology Assessment, and even the Pope.[1] However, there is widespread agreement that the polygraph examination can yield reliable and sometimes valid judgments regarding an examinee's deceptiveness. It is useful, then, to examine the nature of the evidence regarding polygraph examinations and in particular the problems with applying this technique in the workplace. Given the fact that poly-

---

[1] The use of the polygraph was condemned by Pope Pius XII as an intrusion on an individual's inner domain (Lykken, 1981).

graph examiners often agree, and given the fact that they sometimes come to the right conclusions, what are the problems that have effectively removed the polygraph from the scene? To understand some of the problems with the use of polygraph examinations in work settings, you must first understand the examination process itself.

The polygraph examination. Polygraph examinations vary depending on the purpose of the examination (for example, preemployment versus criminal investigation) and the training of the examiner. However, it is possible to describe in a general way the major components of a polygraph examination; detailed descriptions of the polygraph examination can be found in Ben-Shakhar and Furedy (1990), Lykken (1981), the report of the Office of Technology Assessment (1983), and especially Reid and Inbau (1977). In general, polygraph examinations consist of four steps: (1) a preexamination interview, (2) a demonstration, often referred to as a stim test, designed to con-

Box 4-1   *Hugo Munsterberg and the Detection of Deception*

In the early 1900s, Hugo Munsterberg wrote a series of popular essays on ways that psychology could be applied in legal settings, culminating in a widely read book, *On the Witness Stand.* He believed that the research of psychologists could be applied to problems such as eyewitness suggestibility and the detection of deception. In the spring of 1907, he was commissioned by *McClure's* magazine to write an essay on the trial of labor leader Big Bill Haywood, who had been accused of complicity in the assassination of a former governor of Idaho. Munsterberg traveled to Idaho, briefly observed the accuser's testimony, and conducted seven hours of psychological testing (including perceptual and word association tests). In an ill-considered interview, which was published while the trial was still going on, he was quoted as concluding that the accusations were completely true. As Hale (1980) notes, this interview was a pivotal event in the decline of Munsterberg's reputation as a spokesperson for applied psychology in America.

In addition to using psychological tests to detect deception, Munsterberg was an early advocate of using physiological measures. One of his students, Marston, was instrumental in introducing the polygraph to the United States. Ironically, Munsterberg's motivation for using psychological and physiological methods was partially humanitarian. He believed that these methods could replace the frequently brutal, third-degree methods used by police at that time to induce confessions. Today, however, critics of the polygraph (for example, Furedy & Liss, 1985) suggest that it represents a "psychological fourth degree," in which psychological rather than physical intimidation is used to wring confessions from individuals under interrogation.

vince the examinee that the machine can detect deception, (3) questioning of the examinee and noting the various physiological reactions that accompany each answer, and (4) a postexamination interview.

The preexamination interview is designed to collect information from the examinee, to familiarize the examinee with the procedure, and to go over the questions that will be covered in the actual examination. Usually, polygraph examinations do not include surprise questions. Rather, the subject is informed of the questions before the examination and presumably will have a chance to think over his or her answers. Preexamination interviews often include very general questions about the examinee, together with questions about whether he or she has ever done anything wrong; they are designed in part to put the examinee ill at ease (Lykken, 1981). As you will see, efforts to subject the examinee to a variety of forms of stress are an integral part of a polygraph examination.

The preexamination interview is the first of several points at which the examiner will encourage the examinee to make potentially damaging admissions. Although the actual interview protocol varies over interviewers and over types of examinations (for instance, preemployment screening is quite different from a criminal investigation), the preexamination interview will often include the suggestion that the examinee should make admissions now, so that he or she will be able to be truthful during the examination.

Before the actual examination, the polygraph examiner will often carry out a demonstration designed to convince the examinee that the polygraph can detect attempts at deception. This demonstration, sometimes referred to as a stim test, can take a number of forms. Surprisingly, this demonstration often involves some form of trickery, such as the use of a stacked deck of cards (Ben-Shakhar & Furedy, 1990; Office of Technology Assessment, 1983). For example, if I want to "demonstrate" to you that the machine is foolproof, I might hand you a deck of cards that includes 52 queens of spades and ask you to pick a card. I could then go through an elaborate questioning procedure and in the end tell you that the machine says that you picked the queen of spades!

At first glance, a demonstration of this sort, particularly one that relies on trickery, hardly seems appropriate for a procedure designed to get at the truth. The demonstration, however, is absolutely essential. In part because they believe that the machine can detect deception, many individuals admit wrongdoing in polygraph interviews. For example, polygraph examiners report that 75% of the job applicants they interview make damaging admissions; 90 to 95% of the adverse reports in preemployment polygraph examinations are based on the respondents' own admissions, not on unsubstantiated analyses of the polygraph charts (Lykken, 1981). If examinees were not convinced that the polygraph worked, they probably would not feel a great deal of anxiety when trying to defeat the machine (proponents of the polygraph claim that the stress of attempted deception is what the machine measures). More important, if examinees were not convinced that the polygraph worked, they would be much less likely to make damaging admissions. Therefore, it is critical to convince the examinee that the procedure works.

After the stim test, the actual polygraph examination is carried out. This usually involves going through the entire set of questions covered in the preexamination interview several times and recording the physiological reaction that accompanies the answer to each question. There are a number of questioning techniques (described in a later section), but regardless of the technique, this phase of the examination is generally short (for example, 30 minutes). It is common to leave the individual alone for a substantial period (for instance, 20 minutes) after the examination while the examiner scores the polygraph report (Ben-Shakhar & Furedy, 1990). One purpose for leaving the subject alone is to provide him or her an opportunity to mull over the answers given during the exam itself.

After the exam is scored, the postexamination interview is conducted. This interview is possibly the most important part of the examination process. It can be used to clarify inconsistencies, but its main purpose is usually to induce confessions (Office of Technology Assessment, 1983). This interview can last as long as several hours, particularly if the examiner is convinced that the examinee is deceptive, and it can be highly stressful. Some researchers (for example, Furedy & Liss, 1985) refer to the polygraph examination as a psychological fourth degree or a psychological rubber hose, in which examinees are browbeaten and coerced into making confessions; the postexamination interview is the time when psychological coercion is most likely to take place.

The outcome of a polygraph examination can take many forms. First, many individuals admit to wrongdoing under interrogation; in these cases, it may not be necessary to conduct any further analysis of the polygraph charts themselves. When individuals do not confess, the examiner must make a decision about the probable truthfulness or deceptiveness of the subject. Many polygraph examinations end in a stalemate, where the examiner does not have sufficiently clear evidence to be comfortable with a verdict in either direction. In other cases, the examiner may feel that he or she has obtained enough information from observations of the subject, answers to various questions, or the polygraph charts (or any combination of these) to render an opinion about the truthfulness of the examinee. Whatever the outcome of this procedure, its results might be compared with other information the organization has regarding the examinee in order to reach a final assessment. However, in applications such as preemployment screening, a negative report from a polygraph examination, especially where direct admissions of past wrongdoings have been made, may be enough to screen out the job applicant.

Techniques in polygraph examination. All polygraph examinations require examinees to respond to a number of questions that are either relevant or irrelevant to the issue under investigation. In describing the various techniques used to construct a polygraph examination to investigate an incident such as the theft of an expensive tool, it is useful to distinguish between three types of questions: (1) relevant questions—questions that are directly relevant to the incident in question (for example, "Did you steal the tool?"); (2) control questions—questions that are irrelevant to the investigation but would probably prove stressful to examinees (for instance, "Did you steal anything from your last employer?"); and (3) irrelevant questions (for example, "Do you own a foreign car?").

In general, three methods are used in constructing a set of questions for a polygraph examination;[2] these, together with criticisms of each method as applied to work settings, are shown in Table 4-1. First is the *relevant/irrelevant* technique. In this method, each relevant question is preceded and followed by both irrelevant and control questions. In theory, it should be possible to determine whether the relevant question is a source of stress—which would indicate deception—and further whether the reaction to that question is substantially different from the reaction to control questions. If an examinee shows substantially more stress in responding to relevant than to irrelevant questions, this is taken as evidence of possible deception.

Table 4-1 *Questioning Techniques in Polygraph Examinations*

	Relevant/irrelevant	**Control question**	**Guilty knowledge**
Features	Compare responses to relevant and irrelevant questions	Compare responses to relevant and control questions (questions designed to be stressful or arousing)	Compare responses to questions that reflect or fail to reflect knowledge that only the guilty party will have
Criticisms	Difficult to define relevant or irrelevant questions if no specific incident is being investigated	Difficult to develop true control questions	Cannot be applied in screening, where no specific incident is being investigated

[2] Lykken (1981) and Reid and Inbau (1977) describe a number of variations on the techniques presented here.

Second, there are a variety of *control question* techniques. For example, Lykken (1981) describes (1) the lie control technique, in which questions designed to elicit deceptive answers (for instance, "Have you ever done anything illegal?") serve as controls; (2) the truth control technique, in which answers regarding a fictitious incident serve as controls; (3) the positive control technique, in which each relevant question is used as its own control, and subjects are instructed to answer twice to each question, once telling the truth and once telling a lie (presumably, stress is higher when the subject lies); and (4) the relevant control technique, in which both irrelevant and potentially relevant questions are asked. This last technique is often used in preemployment screening, where relevant questions cannot be unambiguously identified because no specific incident is under investigation.

Third is the *guilty knowledge* technique, which is used to determine whether the examinee has knowledge of the event that would be available only to the guilty party. Using as an example an investigation of a stabbing incident, the examiner might ask "Was the victim's shirt brown?" "Was the victim's shirt blue?" and so forth and instruct the individual to answer all questions negatively. Presumably, the individual who has guilty knowledge will react to the question that actually taps that guilty knowledge differently from the way he or she will react to other questions.

Distinct methods are used in different contexts. For example, in preemployment screening, it is impossible to use the guilty knowledge technique because no specific incident has taken place about which the individual could have guilty knowledge. Similarly, the definition of a relevant question as opposed to a control question is somewhat arbitrary in preemployment screening. Once again, if no specific event is under investigation, there is no way to determine what is or is not relevant.

In general, research on the polygraph suggests that the guilty knowledge technique is both the most valid and the least commonly used method of polygraph investigation (Ben-Shakhar & Furedy, 1990; Office of Technology Assessment, 1983). One reason for the rather infrequent use of this method is the fact that, until recently, many polygraph examinations were conducted as part of a preemployment screening. Because the polygraph was often used for making general inquiries about job applicants' trustworthiness rather than for investigating specific incidents, the guilty knowledge technique often could not be applied. As I have noted earlier, if no specific event is under investigation, there is nothing in particular about which the examinee could have guilty knowledge. Control question techniques are still the most common, although this method has come under increasing criticism because of the limited validity of comparisons between relevant and control questions (Ben-Shakhar & Furedy, 1990).

Reliability evidence.   Evidence for the reliability of polygraph examinations is often presented in terms of the percentage of agreement between independent examiners. Many studies of polygraph examinations in criminal contexts have yielded impressive levels of agreement, often in the 80 to 90% range. However, Lykken (1981) points out that the level of agreement is substantially affected by the base rate. If both examiners fail 80% of the individuals they evaluate, they must show at least 64% agreement, even if their pass/fail decisions are made at random. Similarly, if two examiners are asked to identify 1 culprit out of 52 examinees, they will show 96% agreement even if they both pick the wrong person.

The effects of high base rates for failure, which are typical in criminal investigations and in some employment-related applications, can best be appreciated through a simple classroom demonstration. Take ten index cards and mark nine of them "deceptive," marking the tenth "not deceptive." Take another set of ten index cards and do the same thing. Shuffle each set, and then have two students in your class act as interrogators, with ten classmates acting as examinees. Have each interrogator give a card to each examinee. You will find that no matter how many times you reshuffle the cards and repeat the procedure, you will achieve at least 80% agreement! If you come up with *any* systematic method of handing out the "deceptive" and "not deceptive" cards (say you give the "deceptive" cards to the people who look as if they might be guilty of something), you will do even better than that. As long as both interrogators fail the great majority of examinees, they will almost always agree.

A second problem in evaluating the percentage of agreement between independent polygraph investigations is the influence of confessions on the outcome of the examination. If a suspect confesses to two examiners, they will indeed agree. You might cite this as evidence for the reliability of the overall polygraph examination (you can coerce confessions out of some of the people all of the time), but it hardly provides evidence for the reliability or validity of the information obtained from the physiological reactions shown by examinees in response to different questions.

On the whole, there is evidence that skilled polygraph examiners can make reliable judgments in criminal investigations, even after adjusting for the potential effects of extreme base rates and induced confessions. It is less clear whether the same can be said in employment settings; not enough methodologically sound research on the reliability of employment-related polygraph examinations exists to draw firm conclusions. More important, evidence concerning the validity of polygraph examinations, especially in employment settings, is far from encouraging. However, a number of methodological problems make the interpretation of this evidence difficult.

Difficulties in validating the polygraph.   Although many studies have dealt with or commented on the validity of polygraph examinations in both criminal and employment settings, the question whether assessments based on the polygraph have sufficient validity to justify the use of this technique has been difficult to settle to everyone's satisfaction. Assessing the validity of judgments based on the polygraph is troublesome for a number of reasons, not the least of which is the difficulty in determining exactly what is being validated (Ben-Shakhar & Furedy, 1990). The polygraph interview is a complex process, which involves interviews prior to the use of the machine, the development of an appropriate list of questions, the polygraph examination itself, the reading of the polygraph chart, the examiner's observation of the subject, and finally the examiner's overall evaluation of the subject's truthfulness. Suppose you concluded that a particular polygraph examiner did no better than chance in detecting deception. Would this mean that he or she was an unskilled examiner, that the machine was no good, that the particular subjects examined were good at fooling the examiner or the machine, or some combination of all of these possibilities? O'Toole (1988) suggested that too much attention is paid to the machine and not enough to the examiner, noting that "attempts to quantify the effectiveness or accuracy of the polygraph tend to foster the myth that the instrument, and not the investigator, is the 'lie detector' " (p. 276).

Similar problems have been noted in research on the employment interview (Landy, 1985). Studies of the validity of the employment interview reflect in part the skill of the particular interviewers, but are also affected by the design of the interview (for example, interviews might be either unstructured or highly structured), by the job in question, by the types of applicants, and so on. Like the employment interview, the polygraph interview is a complex process, and statements about the validity (or lack thereof) of polygraph examination outcomes do not necessarily tell us which parts of the process are or are not worthwhile.

A second methodological problem in interpreting research on polygraph validity involves the role of admissions and confessions made during the examination itself. It is important to note that many studies supporting the validity of the polygraph examination in criminal investigations use the subject's confession or admissions as a criterion for establishing guilt or innocence (Patrick & Iacono, 1991). Because the polygraph is often used to induce confessions, the possibility of criterion contamination—where the polygraph is used to induce a confession, and the confession is then used as evidence of polygraph validity—must be considered. Even when the confession is not used as a direct criterion, the confession certainly will affect the examiner's readings of the polygraph charts. If the examinee has admitted to some wrongdoing, it is unlikely that the examiner will insist that the charts show that the examinee is not guilty. Examinations of polygraph tests in which no direct admissions are made are more credible than those that involve confessions.

Validity evidence. In general, polygraph examinations have shown some evidence of validity in criminal investigations (Office of Technology Assessment, 1983; Raskin, 1988), but the validity of this technique varies substantially, depending on the questioning method. Validity is highest when the guilty knowledge technique is used and substantially lower when the more common control question techniques are used (Ben-Shakhar & Furedy, 1990; Lykken, 1981; Office of Technology Assessment, 1983). The major conclusion of the report prepared by the Office of Technology Assessment (1983) was that the available evidence does not support the use of polygraph examinations in noncriminal investigations conducted in employment settings. One reason for this conclusion is that the only questioning technique with demonstrated validity, the guilty knowledge technique, cannot be applied in preemployment inquiries. The reliability and validity of the polygraph investigation declines so dramatically when one moves from investigations of specific events to a general evaluation of a job applicant's character that the polygraph examination is unlikely to provide a basis for valid decisions (Ben-Shakhar & Furedy, 1990).

There is little evidence that the polygraph examination does better than chance in correctly detecting deception when it is used in screening or other event-free investigations (Ben-Shakhar & Furedy, 1990; Office of Technology Assessment, 1983). The available research suggests that assessments based on the polygraph may have some validity when used in the investigation of a specific incident, but this technique has little if any validity or utility in contexts such as preemployment testing, where the character or propensity of individuals to engage in future dishonest acts is under investigation.

Another reason to be concerned with the application of the polygraph in employment settings is the potentially large number of false positive errors, where nondeceptive examinees fail the examination (see Ben-Shakhar & Furedy, 1990, and Office of Technology Assessment, 1983, for detailed discussions of false positive rates). Polygraph examinations can produce relatively large numbers of false positive errors for several reasons. First, the validity of the polygraph examination in employment settings is relatively low. More valid methods would lead to fewer decision errors. However, even if the polygraph examination were highly valid, there might still be a potentially large number of false positives.

The second major cause of false positive errors in polygraph testing is the potential discrepancy between the failure rate for these tests and the base rate for nontrivial deception. Consider the scenario illustrated in Table 4-2. Out of 100 job applicants, 20 stole nontrivial amounts (for example, more than $5 worth of merchandise and supplies a year) from their past employers. But 35 of them failed the polygraph examination. Given the discrepancy between the percentage who stole and the percentage who failed the examination, you must make some false positive errors. In the best case, you will falsely label 15 individuals as thieves. In the worst case, you will falsely label 35 individuals. In general, whenever the proportion failing the test exceeds the base rate for deception, the test must make false positive errors.

Murphy (1987) showed that, regardless of the failure rate, it is extremely difficult to avoid false positive errors when the base rate for deception is low (for criticisms of this study, see Manhardt, 1989, and Martin & Terris, 1991). Both the example presented in Table 4-2 and Murphy's analysis suggest that it is critical to estimate the base rate and to try to match the failure rate of the test to that base rate. In Chapter 1, I noted that base rates are often difficult to estimate, which implies that a precise match between the base rate and the selection ratio (that is, the number who fail the test) cannot be achieved. However, if you have good reason to believe that the base rate is low, it might be possible to minimize false positive errors by making the examination less stressful (for instance, by putting less emphasis on obtaining confessions) and to make the scoring of polygraph examinees conservative (that is, biased against concluding that a person has lied in the absence of strong evidence to the contrary). Failure to at least roughly match the base rate guarantees a number of predictable decision errors. When the base rate is low and the failure rate is high, as is sometimes the case when the polygraph is used for screening rather than for investigation of specific events, it may be impossible to reach sensible decisions on the basis of polygraph examination results.

Influence of polygraph recordings on the validity of polygraph examinations.   The polygraph apparatus is designed to record a number of physiological signs, such as pulse and breathing, that are

Table 4-2   *Best Case and Worst Case Scenarios When 35% Failed Test and 20% Stole*

	Best case [a]		Worst case [b]	
	TEST OUTCOME		TEST OUTCOME	
	Fail	Pass	Fail	Pass
Stole	20%	0%	0%	20%
Did not steal	15%	65%	35%	45%

[a] Decisions made on the basis of the best available test.

[b] Decisions made on the basis of a completely invalid test.

supposedly useful in the process of detecting deception. However, the outcome of a polygraph examination is not determined solely by these recordings; the polygraph interview is a contaminated procedure, in the sense that the polygrapher's judgments are affected by a great deal of nonphysiological information that is obtained in the preinterview phase, through observations of the subject and the like (Ben-Shakhar & Furedy, 1990). The process is further contaminated by the fact that a polygraph interview often elicits a confession rather than simply the examiner's judgment of the subject's deceptiveness.

It is interesting to speculate about the extent to which the physiological data recorded by the polygraph itself contribute to the validity of polygraph examinations. The machine might contribute in two very distinct ways. First, it is possible that the polygraph works in pretty much the way that its proponents claim—that is, the readings that are obtained from the polygraph itself might provide valid physiological indicators of deception (Reid & Inbau, 1977). Second, it is possible that the polygraph functions as a sort of "stage prop," in the sense that the machine is part of an elaborate process designed to convince the subject that his or her deceptions will indeed be detected (Lykken, 1981). Recall, for example, that a standard part of many polygraph examinations is the so-called stim test, which is used to demonstrate to subjects that the machine can indeed detect deception. The demonstration is itself often deceptive—the examiner may use a stacked deck of cards and then pretend to use the machine to guess what card the subject is looking at (Ben-Shakhar & Furedy, 1990; Lykken, 1981). However, as long as the subject believes that the machine in fact works, this sort of demonstration can be a highly valuable part of the whole process.

One piece of evidence for the stage prop hypothesis is the fact that many of the successes achieved in polygraph examinations are the result of the subject's admissions or confessions. Lykken (1981) claimed that 90 to 95% of all adverse reports in preemployment polygraph testing were based in part on admissions made by the subjects in the course of the examination. It is reasonable to believe that many of these admissions occurred because the subjects thought that attempts to cover up the damaging truth would be detected by the polygraph examiner. It also seems reasonable that the complex procedure and apparatus involved in polygraph examinations contribute substantially to the subject's belief that there is no use in lying. In fact, if you tried to invent a procedure meant to convince subjects that you had some foolproof method of detecting deception, you would probably end up with something very much like the polygraph examination. The mere presence of all the somewhat menacing machinery used in a polygraph examination may play a critical role in convincing many subjects to make admissions.

Another piece of evidence to support the hypothesis that the polygraph itself is little more than a stage prop comes from studies of polygrapher's judgments before and after they have had a chance to examine the physiological data recorded by the polygraph. In one study (Barland, 1988; cited in Ben-Shakhar & Furedy, 1990), fewer than 25% of the polygraphers studied reached different judgments after reviewing the physiological data from the ones they had reached before reviewing that data. This finding suggests that it is the behavior of the subject, answers to questions, and the like, and not the physiological data recorded by the polygraph, that most strongly influence polygraphers' decisions.

If you accept the premise that the mere presence of the polygraph machine and examiner heightens the anxiety of deceptive subjects (thus making it easier for a skilled examiner to detect attempts at deception) and makes them more liable to admit to wrongdoing, the next logical question might be whether the physiological recordings from the various sensors that make up a polygraph contribute in *any* way to the detection of deception. This question is harder to answer than you might think, in part because of the complexity of the whole examination process. For example, a study that simply gave trained examiners polygraph charts to read would not really be a fair test; a true polygraph examination always involves much more than reading a chart. A fairer test might involve the introduction of some sort of distortion to the polygraph readings that come out of actual examinations. For example, suppose you designed an apparatus that introduced random variation into the output of a polygraph. If the output recorded by the polygraph really is an important determinant of the validity of the polygraph, two things should happen. First, the polygraph examiner's judgments should be more valid when you turn off this apparatus (that is, when the polygraph gives true readings with no random noise inserted) than when you turn it on. Second, the more random noise you insert into the system, the worse the polygraph examiner's judgments should be. The alternative hypothesis is that the output of the polygraph is essentially meaningless, and the validity of the polygraph technique will not be affected whether the machine is functioning normally or abnormally or even if it ceased to function altogether. To my knowledge, studies of the sort described above have not yet been conducted.

Employee Polygraph Protection Act.   Prior to 1988, the polygraph was widely used in preemployment screening; more than three-quarters of all polygraphs given at that time, by more than 3500 polygraph examiners, were employment-related (Kleinmuntz, 1985; Libbin, Mendelsohn, & Duffy, 1988). In addition to the polygraph, other mechanical or electrical means of detecting physiological reactions presumably associated with lying, such as voice stress analysis, were widely used. As a result of long-standing concerns over the reliability, validity, and fairness of decisions rendered with the assistance of a polygraph or similar instrument, Congress passed the Employee Polygraph Protection Act of 1988. This act prohibits the use of polygraphs, voice stress analyzers, and similar techniques for preemployment screening by most private-sector employers. The act does permit testing of employees as part of a workplace investigation, but the circumstances under which this testing can be done are severely limited, as is shown in Table 4-3. In addition to the restrictions shown in this table, the act forbids employers from conducting either random or periodic screenings of their employees. In fact, employees cannot be tested, even at their own insistence, unless the employer meets the first seven conditions listed in Table 4-3.

Limited exemptions to this law exist for private security firms and drug companies licensed to handle or produce controlled substances, but even in these cases, testing is limited to employees in truly sensitive positions, such as employees who have direct access to drugs.[3]

Table 4-3 *Circumstances under Which Polygraph Examinations Are Allowed by the Employee Polygraph Protection Act of 1988*

An employer cannot suggest or require a polygraph test unless all of the following conditions are met:

1. The test is part of an investigation of a specific incident involving economic loss or injury to the business.
2. The employee to be tested had access to the property that is the subject of the investigation.
3. The employer has ground for reasonable suspicion of the worker's involvement in the incident.
4. The employee is given advance notice of the test, the employee's legal rights, the basis for suspicion, and all questions to be asked during the test.
5. The test meets a variety of procedural requirements, such as the guarantee of a right to counsel and the right to terminate or refuse the test without being demoted or fired for doing so.
6. Before taking action against the employee on the basis of test results, the employee must be given written copies of the questions, answers, and the examiner's opinion.
7. Examiners' qualifications must meet all relevant requirements, which may include licensing, bonding, or professional liability coverage.
8. No state or local law or collective bargaining agreement applies that is more restrictive than the act.
9. Records of polygraph exams are maintained for at least three years.

---

[3] There is some irony, or at least inconsistency, in the exemptions noted above. If the polygraph shows so little validity that it should be banned in most jobs, the rationale for retaining the polygraph in these highly sensitive jobs is not clear or convincing.

In general, the requirements of the Employee Polygraph Protection Act of 1988 are so restrictive as to practically outlaw the use of the polygraph, the voice stress analyzer, or any other similar device in most employment settings. The act does, however, leave employers a number of options. In particular, the act does not forbid or restrict the use of paper-and-pencil tests of honesty or integrity. These tests are examined in the following chapter.

Voice Stress Analysis

In addition to the polygraph, other mechanical methods have been applied in the detection of deception. In particular, voice stress analysis has been suggested as a method of detecting deception (Sackett & Decker, 1979). Although the exact methods used by different voice stress analysts vary, the conceptual underpinnings of this method are relatively consistent. Voice stress analysts believe that discernible patterns of voice production, sometimes referred to as microtremors in the voice, are indicative of deception. A number of electronic devices have been developed to measure these voice characteristics (for example, Hovarth, 1978, examined the accuracy of a device called the Psychological Stress Evaluator), and voice stress analysts have used the charts produced by these devices to assess deception in a variety of criminal and organizational settings.[4]

Proponents of voice stress analysis point to many potential advantages of this method, especially as compared to the polygraph. First, voice stress analysis appears to be less subjective than the polygraph. Polygraph examinations include extensive interviews, behavioral examinations, and the like in addition to the data that are obtained from the machine itself, and it is highly likely that polygraph examiners are affected by this information. Voice stress analyses do not involve these complex procedures; this method is often completely unobtrusive, so that the person being assessed might not be aware of it. As a result, voice stress analysts appear to rely more on the output of their machines and less on other verbal or behavioral information obtained during the analysis. Second, voice stress analysis is substantially less intrusive and intimidating than a polygraph examination, because voice stress analysis does not entail physically connecting an individual to a machine; voice stress analysis can even be carried out over the phone (Waln & Downey, 1987).

The unobtrusive nature of voice stress analysis creates its unique potential for invasion of privacy. One of the defining principles in deciding privacy rights in organizations is that individuals have the right to privacy in situations where they would reasonably expect that

---

[4] Lykken (1981) notes that voice stress analysis was used to "prove" that Lee Harvey Oswald was innocent of the assassination of President Kennedy.

their behavior or communications are not being monitored (Stone & Stone, 1990). The application of voice stress analysis to telephone conversations that are unobtrusively recorded raises many of the issues sometimes raised in debates over wiretapping—especially the question of at what point the employer's right to make managerial decisions overrides employees' privacy rights.

Reliability and validity evidence.   Although proponents of voice stress analysis claim high levels of accuracy, empirical research on the accuracy and validity of this method has been far from encouraging. First, the reliability of this method is highly suspect (Hovarth, 1979; Waln & Downey, 1987). The agreement between independent analysts' readings of the same voice stress charts is generally low, and correlations are also low between readings of the same interviews in their original form and as recordings that had been transmitted over the telephone (Waln & Downey, 1987). Second, the validity of judgments made on the basis of voice stress analysis appear to be questionable (Lykken, 1981). For example, studies by Hovarth (1978, 1979) showed a level of success approximating that of chance in identifying deception in mock crime situations. Similarly, a study by O'Hair and Cody (1987) showed that voice stress analyses were unsuccessful in detecting spontaneous lies in a simulated job interview. Voice stress analysis may be more successful in detecting real crimes or other nontrivial deceptions, where the level of stress is presumably higher, but even in this area, the evidence of validity is rather thin.

In the final analysis, the evaluation of voice stress analysis boils down to the same set of issues that underlie the evaluation of the polygraph—the presence or absence of some unique physiological reaction to deception. It seems clear that stress has identifiable physiological markers (although individuals differ substantially in reactions to stress), but this does not mean that there are reliable physiological indicators for deception. Most researchers accept Kleinmuntz and Szucko's (1984) assertion that lying has no unique physiological correlates. Mechanical methods that measure stress reactions will not provide adequate measures of deception; some individuals find deception stressful, but others do not.

Graphology

Another technique that is sometimes used to assess honesty is handwriting analysis, or graphology. The underlying theory is that various characteristics of a person's handwriting provide information about his or her personality, including traits such as honesty or loyalty. Although there are serious questions regarding the validity of assessments provided by this technique (Bar-Hillel & Ben-Shakhar, 1986;

Ben-Shakhar et al., 1989), it is widely used, especially in Israel (Ben-Shakhar, et al., 1986) and Europe (Ben-Shakhar & Furedy, 1990). In the United States, more than 2000 employers are thought to use graphology in preemployment screening (Sinai, 1988).

The graphologists' method. Graphology involves an examination of a number of specific structural characteristics of a handwriting sample, such as letter shapes and sizes, which are used to make inferences about the writer. Computerized systems for handwriting analysis exist (Berman, 1989), but most graphological analyses are still done by individual graphologists. Although this technique was originally used for forensic purposes (for instance, in determining whether a document is a forgery), it is now widely used as a method of personality assessment. Graphologists typically insist that the sample must be spontaneous and that handwriting samples that involve copying text from a book or writing a passage from memory will not yield a valid reading. The writing sample requested by a graphologist is often a brief autobiographical sketch or some other sort of self-description (Ben-Shakhar, 1989; Ben-Shakhar et al., 1986).

Graphologists claim that neither the content nor the quality of the writing sample (for example, qualities like fluency or clarity of expression) influence their assessments; they assert that their evaluations are the result of close examination of the features of letters, words, and lines in the sample. There are several reasons to believe that this claim is false and that even if graphologists try to ignore the content of the writing sample, their assessments are nevertheless strongly influenced by that content. First, several studies have shown that when the same biographical passages are examined by graphologists and nongraphologists, their assessments of individual examinees tend to agree, and graphologists' assessments are no more valid than those of nongraphologists (Ben-Shakhar, 1989; Ben-Shakhar et al., 1986). Because nongraphologists presumably do not attend in a systematic way to the graphological features of the writing but rather pay attention to the content of the stories, their ability to make assessments that are similar to and every bit as good as those made by professional graphologists strongly suggests that both groups are attending to the same material—the content of the writing samples. Indeed, in a study using a simple unweighted linear model to combine information from the various passages in each description into a prediction, Ben-Shakhar et al. (1986) showed that predictions based solely on the content of the writing sample were *more* valid than those obtained from professional graphologists. Second, when the content of the passages is not biographical in nature (for example, meaningless text, or text copied from some standard source), graphologists seldom make valid predictions. In their defense, graphologists claim that the production of such text does not reveal the same things about personality as is revealed in spontaneous biographical writing samples; however, it is not exactly clear why this might be true, and it is strange that graphological techniques work only when the content of the writing sample tells the graphologist something important about the examinee. Finally, it is not clear that people are able to ignore the content of what they read. If I tell you to not think about the pink elephant, you will find this very difficult to do. Similarly, if you attempt to look over the next paragraph without paying any attention to what it says (paying attention only to the shapes of the letters), you will find that very difficult to do.

One interesting trend in the use of graphology is that this technique, unlike polygraphs or integrity tests, is quite often used in assessing candidates for middle- and upper-management positions (Mowbray, 1988). There are a variety of potential explanations for this trend. First, graphologists claim that their method measures a broad spectrum of personality traits (Bar-Hillel & Ben-Shakhar, 1986). Whereas polygraphs and integrity tests focus mainly on honesty, graphology supposedly measures a number of personality traits thought to be critical to success, of which honesty is only one. Second, graphology is less invasive than the polygraph or some integrity tests. The candidate being assessed may not even know that his or her handwriting sample will be evaluated by a graphologist (thus raising some of the same privacy-related issues raised by the administration of voice stress analysis over the phone), although applicants are often informed of this fact. In any case, graphology supposedly has a broad range of application, and the assessment of honesty is only a small part of what graphologists claim to do.

Validity of graphological analysis.   In evaluating graphology, two separate questions might be asked. First, how good are the general predictions produced by a graphological analysis? For example, if graphology is used in personnel selection, we might ask the graphologist to predict who is more or less likely to perform well on the job. Second, how good are the specific assessments of particular personality traits? If graphology is used to measure specific traits, such as integrity, we might ask whether this method provides valid measures of that trait.

There is evidence that graphologists can make somewhat valid predictions of a job applicant's overall performance, but it is also clear that nongraphologists who examine the same material make equally valid predictions (see Ben-Shakhar, 1989, for a review of the relevant research). This research suggests that little is to be gained from attending to the purely graphological aspects of the writing sample. Interestingly, the development of computerized systems for graphological analysis may finally provide a fair test of graphologists' claims.

Unlike the human graphologist, a computer can ignore the content of the writing sample and attend solely to the structural characteristics of the writing. Perhaps if these systems prove successful, it will be necessary to reevaluate graphology.

The available evidence casts doubt on graphologists' ability to make even the most general assessments of individuals or at least to do a better job than nongraphologists given the same materials, suggesting that graphological assessments of specific characteristics such as

Box 4-2   *Graphological Analysis*

The use of handwriting analysis to make inferences about personality has a long history (Battan, 1984; Crepieux-Jamin, 1909; Downey, 1919; Lumley, 1875). Although there is some variability in the methods applied by different graphologists, it is possible to give you a sense of the method by describing the various features of letters, words, and writing style that are assessed in a graphological analysis and the meanings attached to those features.

Battan (1984) provides a fascinating account of graphological analysis; some aspects of handwriting considered in his system are listed below.

Movement
>   *Slant*—A right slant represents future and outwardness; a left slant represents past and inwardness.
>   *Pressure*—The depth of force and pressure used in writing is related to physical strength, conscious and unconscious drive, and sexual energy.

Structure
>   *Zones*—An emphasis on the upper, middle, or lower portion of a letter represents unconscious behavior and motivation, ego or self, and superego or conscience, respectively.

Type of Script
>   *Form*—The use of angular script (formed by straight lines, changing direction) shows a serious approach to problems and goals.

General Characteristics
>   *T-bars*—The normal T-bar crossing indicates conformity and a practical nature.

I should emphasize several things about this list. First, it is only a partial account of the various graphological features considered in an analysis. Second, the meanings of the features are more complex than the summaries presented here. Third, these features are not supposed to be considered in isolation; rather, the presence of another feature may change or modify the interpretation of any particular feature. However, this list does give you a more concrete idea of how graphological analyses work.

honesty and integrity will not be successful. Little, if any, empirical research adequately evaluates the accuracy of specific assessments made by graphologists, such as assessments of a job applicant's honesty, but given the generally dismal track record of graphologists in making global predictions, there is very little reason to believe that their more specific predictions will be any more accurate.

Behavioral Cues to Deception and Dishonesty

As I noted at the beginning of this chapter, it has long been believed that there are a number of behaviors that indicate deception, ranging from sweating or halting speech to an unwillingness to look another person in the eye. Interviewers are sometimes trained to recognize these behaviors and to use them to infer deception. For example, in describing the "integrity interview," Buckley (1989) suggested that repeated observations of the following behaviors might indicate attempts to deceive: (1) hesitancy in answering, (2) sudden movement of the upper or lower body away from the examiner, (3) grooming or cosmetic gestures, such as arranging clothing or jewelry, or adjusting and cleaning glasses, (4) hiding hands or crossing arms or legs. Johnson (1987) described a more subtle system, which involves observing the subject's eye movements. This system is based on the belief of researchers in neurolinguistic programming that the direction of eye movements indicates the type of mental activity the subject is engaging in. For right-handed subjects, looking to the left is considered to show that the subject is searching his or her memory, whereas looking to the right is believed to indicate thoughts about the future. Therefore, if you ask a person about incidents in the past, such as theft from previous employers, and he or she looks to the right (that is, thinks about the future rather than the past), this might indicate deception. I should note that this specific claim about the relationship between direction of gaze and deception is not widely accepted; for a review of research on neurolinguistic programming and its interpretation, see Druckman and Swets (1988).

Unfortunately, the literature and lore concerning the behavioral cues to deception represents a jumble of intuition, folk tales, and well-established facts. Researchers have attempted to identify behavioral correlates of deception, with only partial success. Table 4-4 presents examples of behavioral correlates of deception that have been identified in the research literature (for example, DePaulo, Stone, & Lassiter, 1985; Ekman, 1973, 1975; Ekman & O'Sullivan, 1991). Although all these behaviors are correlated with deception, the correlations appear weak. These behavioral indicators may allow a skilled observer to do better than chance in detecting deception, but they do not make for a high degree of accuracy.

Table 4-4   *Some Behavioral Cues Associated with Deception*

Verbal
   Hesitation in speaking
   Higher pitch
   Speech errors
Nonverbal
   Increased blinking
   Frequent swallowing
   Fast or shallow breathing
   Self-manipulative behaviors—for example, rubbing or scratching
   More masking smiles; fewer enjoyment smiles

Studies on the detection of deception through the observation of behavioral cues such as those listed in Table 4-4 have consistently shown the exact pattern of results described above—an ability to detect deception that is only slightly better than chance (DePaulo, 1988; DePaulo & DePaulo, 1989; DePaulo et al., 1989). For example, in a recent study Ekman and O'Sullivan (1991) asked police, judges, FBI and CIA polygraph examiners, and U.S. Secret Service agents to attempt to detect deception in a realistic laboratory task. Only Secret Service agents performed better than chance. Ekman's (1973) research suggests why this is the case. He proposes that few behaviors, if any, are universal indicators of deception, noting that "no clue to deceit is reliable for all human beings" (p. 97). His extensive program of research indicates that many individuals show consistent behavioral cues when they lie, but that the specific behaviors that indicate deception vary from person to person. One person might usually sweat and hesitate in speaking, while another might change his or her pitch. If the behaviors that indicate deception are indeed idiosyncratic, it may be pointless to train interviewers, supervisors, or others to look for the signs of deception: these signs might be completely different for each potentially deceptive person.

One reason that behavioral cues provide only weak evidence of deception is that most behaviors are multiply determined (that is, several causes contribute to the behavior) and contextually dependent (that is, the same behavior may mean different things in different contexts). These qualities mean that deception might prompt different behaviors in the same person at different times and that the same behavior that is prompted by deception in one context might indicate something else, such as stresses that have nothing to do with deception, in another. Although behavioral cues provide some weak evidence of truthfulness, age-old beliefs that a weak handshake, an unsteady gaze, a dry mouth, and so on indicate deception are such oversimplifications that they will result in wrong judgments more often than in right ones.

Employee Drug Testing

As part of a nationwide campaign against drug abuse that began in the 1980s, employee drug testing grew from a relative rarity to a common practice. Although this method is not used to infer overall integrity, it is used to deter and detect one type of counterproductive behavior that is thought to be extremely costly in the workplace—drug abuse. Some paper-and-pencil tests are used to measure or infer drug abuse (Crown & Rosse, 1988), but the most common methods involve biochemical tests for the presence of drugs in the system. Like the polygraph and the voice stress analyzer, drug tests use test results to make an inference about the likelihood of deceptive behaviors. In the case of drug tests, a positive result (that is, a confirmed finding of drug by-products in an individual's system) usually leads to an inference that the individual might use drugs in a work setting or that drug impairment might compromise safety, productivity, or both.

Before describing research on employee drug testing, it is useful to comment briefly on why the topic is included in this book at all. Drug tests are not designed to provide assessments of overall honesty or integrity, which makes them different (in theory) from polygraph examinations, integrity tests, and the like. My rationale for including drug tests in this chapter is that they represent an indirect method for detecting and discouraging a specific type of behavior, drug use in work settings, that is thought to be a major component of production deviance and that is, on the face of it, deception and dishonesty. Thus, this method is conceptually similar to although more narrowly focused than other indirect methods of detecting deception.

Drug testing policies and practices. Employee drug testing programs are now common (Anglin, 1988; Gust & Walsh, 1989; Walsh & Hawks, 1988). O'Boyle (1985) reported that in 1985 25% of Fortune 500 companies screened applicants, employees, or both for illegal drug use. A more recent survey by Guthrie and Olian (1989) of 378 private-sector firms showed that 49% tested for drugs and that another 5 to 11% were considering testing in the near future. Surveys by the Department of Labor's Bureau of Labor Statistics show lower figures for some industries, particularly for small companies, but still suggest that large numbers of individuals will be subject to drug testing. The most common method of drug testing involves some type of bioassay, usually through urine testing, although both blood tests and hair sample analyses are sometimes used (Murphy & Thornton, 1992; Reid, Murphy, & Reynolds, 1990). All these methods test for the presence of drug metabolites in the system, which would indicate somewhat recent drug usage; metabolites of some drugs, such as marijuana, may stay in the system for up to three weeks, but for many drugs, the presence of metabolites indicates drug use within the last few days. Significantly, none of the widely used methods tests for drug use at work or drug impairment at work. Thus most drug testing programs might indicate who uses drugs, but few programs pinpoint the use or the effects of drugs in a work setting.

The drug testing policies, practices, and strategies of different organizations are far from uniform (Stevens, 1988). Rather, there appears to be wide variability in the drug testing practices of different organizations. In general, employee drug testing programs can be characterized in terms of four variables: (1) who is subject to testing, (2) the circumstances that lead to testing, (3) the administrative procedures used in testing, and (4) the consequences of failing a drug test (Lorber & Kirk, 1987). Drug testing is more common in labor and lower management positions than in executive ones (O'Boyle, 1985) and appears more likely for people whose jobs involve high levels of perceived risk to the public, such as airline pilots, than for those in which the hazards associated with drug-impaired performance are minimal, such as typists (see Murphy, Thornton, & Prue, 1991). Drug testing is more common when there is "just cause" or a reasonable suspicion of drug use, but some organizations test all applicants or a random sample of job incumbents (Guthrie & Olian, 1989; Murphy & Thornton, 1992). Some organizations (for example, the military and federal agencies) take elaborate precautions to prevent cheating and screen for a wide variety of drugs, while others employ less invasive or more tightly focused procedures. Finally, the consequences of failing a drug test vary considerably from organization to organization. A single confirmed positive test will lead almost all of the organizations that test to reject a job applicant, whereas a minority of the companies that test will dismiss an employee who fails a test (Guthrie & Olian, 1989; Murphy & Thornton, 1992).

Despite the extensive variability of employee drug testing practices in different organizations, some common threads appear. Murphy and Thornton (1992) surveyed more than 300 organizations concerning their drug testing practices. Characteristics that were present in the majority of the organizations engaged in drug testing included (1) testing all applicants and refusing to hire those who fail the test, (2) testing for cause (that is, on reasonable suspicion of drug use), (3) using drug tests to discourage drug use on the job, screen out abusers (but not necessarily casual users), and protect the health and safety of workers, (4) circulating written descriptions of the program to employees and designating some person or department responsible for the program, (5) training supervisors to recognize impairment, (6) taking steps to minimize false positives (for instance, administering follow-up tests or notifying employees of legal substances that could cause false positives), and (7) some form of ongoing evaluation of the testing program.

Validity evidence. Public discussions of employee drug testing often focus on the possibility that drug tests will make false positive errors—that they will indicate that a nonuser has drugs in his or her system. Personnel specialists often focus on a different set of questions—that is, whether the results of drug tests have any relevance for safety, absenteeism, productivity, and other behaviors at work. In discussing research on employee drug tests, it is useful to separate these two distinct meanings of the term *validity*. The question whether employee drug tests provide valid information about the presence or absence of drugs in an individual's system is quite distinct from the question of whether people who fail drug tests are likely to be less safe, less productive, and so on than those who pass. In other words, we need to distinguish between the ability of drug tests to detect drug by-products in one's system on the one hand and the validity of inferences about job performance, safety, and behavior in the workplace that are made on the basis of those tests on the other.

The National Institute on Drug Abuse has issued a number of guidelines for drug testing programs, covering issues such as testing methods; chain of custody procedures (procedures for preventing accidental or purposeful mislabeling or switching of samples); procedures for confirming the results of screening tests and for ruling out foods, prescription drugs, and the like as causes for positive results; lists of recommended labs for processing samples; and so on. There is clear evidence that when all these procedures are followed, drug tests are highly accurate, and the likelihood of false positives is minimal (Normand, Salyards, & Mahoney, 1990; Walsh & Hawks, 1988). However, there is also evidence that many organizations fail to follow the procedures needed to achieve high levels of accuracy in testing (Murphy & Thornton, 1992). Therefore, although it is well known that drug tests can be highly accurate, that does not necessarily mean that they will be accurate in the field.

Even when the test gives an accurate reading, it is important to reiterate that these tests do not measure either drug use or drug impairment at work. Bioassay methods (for example, blood or urine testing) test for specific by-products or metabolites of one or more illicit drugs. Depending on the drug involved, the presence of metabolites could indicate that a person had taken an unknown amount of the drug anytime within the last few days or even weeks (Reid, Murphy, & Reynolds, 1990). Recent drug use might very well indicate a higher probability of future drug use, but it is a substantial leap of inference to conclude that drug tests will predict drug use on the job. It is an even greater leap to conclude that drug tests will predict drug impairment on the job. Individual differences in patterns of both drug use and drug impairment are substantial, and the implications of preemployment tests (or periodic tests given to current employees) for drug use and impairment on the job are not necessarily clear.

Although many studies of the criterion-related validity of employee drug tests have a number of shortcomings, evidence is growing that the results of employee drug tests are related to a number of job-relevant criteria, including absenteeism, involuntary turnover, and perhaps overall job performance (McDaniel, 1988; Normand, Salyards, & Mahoney, 1990; Walsh & Hawks, 1988). However, the relationships between the results of drug tests and these criteria appear to be both weak and inconsistent. In part, this weakness is probably due to simple statistical artifacts, such as sampling error (Hunter & Schmidt, 1990). However, it also appears to reflect the substantial variability in the testing policies, practices, and methods of different organizations (Murphy & Thornton, 1992).

If you accept the conclusion that, when the testing is done carefully, employee drug tests appear to have some validity as predictors of work-related criteria, the next question is why these tests are valid (Murphy, 1991). One possibility is that they deter drug use or screen out drug users and therefore decrease drug use and drug impairment at work. Although drug tests may well do these things, there is surprisingly little solid evidence that drug use or drug impairment at work is in fact a widespread phenomenon. Another possibility is one I have heard referred to as the "low-life" hypothesis. Many individuals are basically irresponsible, resist authority, engage in a number of illegal activities, and so on; for want of a better label, call these people low-lifes. It is probable that many of the people who fail employee drug tests would fit into this category. Because low-lifes are unlikely to be good employees, any test that screens out a number of these individuals is likely to lead to an overall improvement in the workforce. If this hypothesis is true, drug tests are an expensive, cumbersome, and very roundabout way of identifying and screening out the low-lifes; we have personality tests, interview protocols, and other methods that could probably do this better at a much lower cost.

Reactions to drug testing. Despite its increasing frequency, employee drug testing is still controversial. Several authors (for example, Crant and Bateman, 1989; Murphy, Thornton, & Reynolds, 1990) have suggested that workers and job applicants might react negatively to drug testing, especially where the justification for the testing program was not apparent. There is also evidence that these negative reactions can have real consequences for the organization. In particular, Murphy and Thornton (in press, a) present evidence that individuals with negative attitudes toward employee drug testing are less likely to apply to and may be less likely to accept jobs in organizations that test for drugs.

Recent research has confirmed the frequent presence of negative reactions to drug testing (Murphy, Thornton, & Prue, 1991; Stone & Kotch, 1989), but also suggests that this reaction is not inevitable. Testing programs that are run in a sensible fashion, with due concern for the accuracy of test results, for the rights of employees, and for the welfare of the workers (both those who pass and those who fail drug tests) may not provoke negative reactions. Murphy and Thornton's (1992) study suggested that many organizations do make efforts to explain their programs to employees and to involve them in the process of designing a drug testing program. However, some organizations still seem to impose testing programs with little consultation or apparent justification. The research cited here suggests that they are looking for trouble.

Reactions to employee drug testing vary considerably, depending on the job or jobs in question. Drug testing for airline pilots is widely accepted, whereas testing priests or professors is accepted by some individuals and viewed negatively by others (Murphy & Thornton, in press, b). In general, drug testing is most acceptable in jobs where impairment might endanger the public or co-workers and in jobs where specific abilities that seem to be impaired by drugs, such as psychomotor abilities, are critically important.

As with many other methods of inferring honesty, integrity, dependability, and the like, employee drug testing may be regarded as an invasion of privacy (Stone & Stone, 1990). Urine testing may be an especially sensitive area; being required to provide urine samples strikes some people as offensive, and being required to do so in front of witnesses, or under tightly monitored conditions, might seem especially so. Both employees and applicants have legitimate concerns about their privacy, especially in the case where activities that are carried out away from work might affect this job-related test. Drug testing policies and practices that respect the dignity and privacy of workers are less likely to be a source of dissatisfaction than are those that are unduly invasive or threatening.

SUMMARY

Polygraph examinations, voice stress analyses, graphological analyses, observations of behavioral indicators of deception, and drug tests all represent indirect strategies for inferring deception. Some methods, such as the polygraph, attempt to detect deception as it occurs. Others, such as graphology or drug testing, attempt to identify people who are more or less likely to be either generally dishonest or to engage in a specific form of counterproductive behavior, such as drug abuse, that is of considerable concern to many organizations.

On the whole, the evidence for the validity of these procedures is weak. Some procedures, such as graphology or voice stress analysis, have received little empirical support from independent investigators. Although the proponents of these methods claim to have conducted large numbers of studies demonstrating the validity of their methods, these studies often do not exist in written form, cannot be located, or cannot be replicated by independent researchers. Some evidence exists for the validity of assessments based on the polygraph in certain criminal investigations, but there are a number of reasons to believe that this research does not translate into the work setting, particularly when these tests are used for preemployment screening. As a result, the use of polygraphs and similar techniques in employment settings is now severely restricted by law. Drug tests have shown some evidence of validity, but a number of questions still exist about the value of these tests in personnel selection and assessment (Murphy, 1991).

There are several probable reasons for the general failure of these indirect methods for detecting or inferring deception and dishonesty. The most important explanation is that there is no unique physiological or behavioral response to deception, nor are there universal behavioral indicators of honesty (Kleinmuntz & Szucko, 1984). It is easy to measure tremors in the voice, changes in pulse and respiration rates, the shapes and orientations of letters in a writing sample, increased blinking or swallowing, or the presence of drug metabolites in the bloodstream. The problem is that it is hard to know what to do with that data. Any of these factors might indicate deception, and for some people in some situations, all of them might. The problem is that none of the potential indicators of deception or dishonesty mentioned in this chapter are sufficiently general for them to be used as reliable and valid indicators of honesty in the workplace.

The next chapter considers a variety of more direct indicators of deception, all of which use information obtained from the individual to infer his or her honesty. Evidence for the validity of these techniques is somewhat more encouraging, but as with the methods reviewed in this chapter, a number of controversial questions remain unresolved regarding these procedures for detecting deception or inferring honesty in the workplace.

CHAPTER FIVE

Using Self-Reports to Detect Deception and Dishonesty

The previous chapter discussed a number of indirect methods that might be used to infer deception on the basis of behavioral, physiological, or biochemical measures. This chapter examines a more direct strategy, which involves inferring honesty on the basis of information provided by the examinee. In psychological testing, the term *self-report* refers to a class of measurement instruments in which the individual is asked to report his or her feelings, attitudes, preferences, beliefs, and the like (Murphy & Davidshofer, 1991). In this chapter, I will use the term to refer to a group of techniques that all depend on information provided directly by the individual to make inferences about integrity. This group of techniques includes paper-and-pencil integrity tests, interviews designed to assess integrity, the use of biographical and demographic information to infer honesty, and applications of general personality tests (as well as inventories used to assess psychopathology) in assessing integrity.

Physiological methods such as the polygraph or the voice stress analyzer attempt to detect deception as it occurs. These methods involve an interrogation of the subject, together with some attempt to sort honest from dishonest answers. Integrity tests and other similar techniques are usually used to identify general propensities toward honest or dishonest behavior, although they may also be used in investigating specific incidents of workplace dishonesty. Many tests focus on constructs such as "theft proneness" (Ash, 1991), while others attempt to identify people who are likely to engage in a wide range of dishonest behaviors.

Integrity Tests

Although paper-and-pencil integrity tests have been in existence since at least the 1950s (Ash, 1976), their widespread use is relatively recent. In particular, the use of these tests grew considerably following the 1988 Employee Polygraph Protection Act. O'Bannon, Goldinger, and Appleby (1989) report that these tests are used by 10 to 15% of all employers, concentrated in the retail sales, banking, and food service industries, and that in excess of 2.5 million tests are given by more than 5000 employers each year. There are several reasons to believe that the current figures for integrity test use are even higher; these include growing awareness of the extent of employee theft and increasing evidence of the validity of several widely distributed tests.

Despite its increasing frequency, integrity testing remains a controversial topic. In part, this controversy results from the content of the tests; many tests ask questions that could be regarded as invasive or insulting. More fundamentally, integrity testing has been controversial because of the intensely personal nature of what is being tested. Many people can fairly readily accept, for example, being denied a job because they appear to lack the skills or abilities necessary to perform the job, but the idea of being denied a job because a test implies that the applicant is dishonest strikes many people as grossly unfair. The notion that any test can adequately measure characteristics such as integrity and honesty is itself a controversial idea.

To understand the controversy over integrity testing, it is important to first describe the tests themselves, then examine the research on their use, the validity of inferences based on the tests, and concerns that have been raised by critics of integrity testing.

What Do Integrity Tests Measure?

O'Bannon, Goldinger, and Appleby (1989) reviewed most available integrity tests. Although the individual tests differed in a number of specifics, a number of features were common to virtually all the tests. In particular, integrity tests usually include items that refer to one or more of the following areas: (1) direct admissions of illegal or questionable activities, (2) opinions regarding illegal or questionable behavior, (3) general personality traits and thought patterns believed to be related to dishonesty (for instance, the tendency to constantly think about illegal activities), and (4) reactions to hypothetical situations that may or may not feature dishonest behavior.

A distinction is usually drawn between tests that inquire directly about integrity—for example, asking for admissions of past theft or asking about the degree to which the examinee approves of dishonest behaviors—and tests that indirectly infer integrity on the basis of responses to questions that are not obviously related to integrity. Several authors (for instance, Sackett, Burris, & Callahan, 1989) refer to the former as "overt" tests, and to the latter as "personality-based" tests. I prefer to call them "clear-purpose" and "veiled-purpose" integrity tests, in part because the major distinction between them is how obvious it is that the test measures integrity. However, the label *overt* is both reasonably descriptive of the tests themselves and widely accepted, and I will use this label to refer to clear-purpose tests where appropriate.

Examples of tests usually classified as either clear-purpose or veiled-purpose integrity tests, together with descriptions of dimensions measured by the tests (in some cases, these refer merely to the labels attached to scale scores reported) are presented in Table 5-1; detailed descriptions of the dimensions measured by 43 integrity tests are presented in O'Bannon, Goldinger, & Appleby (1989). As the table suggests, the distinction between clear-purpose and veiled-purpose tests is not always a simple one (O'Bannon, Goldinger, & Appleby, 1989; Office of Technology Assessment, 1990). Many clear-purpose tests include items, scales, and the like that are not obviously related to integrity, while many veiled-purpose tests include items and scales that seem very similar to those characteristics of clear-purpose tests.

Many integrity tests seem similar in terms of the dimensions actually measured. Examples of the dimensions that appear to underly the items included on most integrity tests are presented in Table 5-2. (See Cunningham and Ash, 1988, Harris and Sackett, 1987, and O'Bannon, Goldinger, and Appleby, 1989, for research examining the factors underlying integrity tests.) Although many distinct factors are tested, some evidence shows that a general honesty factor may pervade at least some tests (Harris & Sackett, 1987), so that tests of this type measure general integrity, as well as more specific dimensions. As I noted in Chapter 1, there is some disagreement whether any such thing as "general integrity" or "honesty" actually exists; it is clear that honest behavior is affected by characteristics of both the person and the situation. Nevertheless, research seems to show that many integrity tests provide information about the overall likelihood of dishonest behavior, and that a person with poor scores is more likely to behave in

Table 5-1 *Examples of Clear-Purpose and Veiled-Purpose Integrity Tests*

Clear-purpose	Dimensions measured or scores reported
Reid Report	Honesty attitude, social behavior, substance abuse, personal achievements, service orientation, clerical/math skills
Stanton Survey	Honesty attitude, admissions of previous dishonesty
Personnel Selection Inventory (Version 7)	Honesty, drug avoidance, customer relations, work values, supervision, employability index, validity scales
VEILED-PURPOSE	
Personnel Reaction Blank	Dependability/conscientiousness
Hogan Reliability Scale	Hostility to rules, thrill-seeking impulsiveness, social insensitivity, alienation
PDI Employment Inventory	Productive behavior, tenure

Table 5-2 *Dimensions Often Reported in Factor Analyses of Integrity Tests*

1. Perceived incidence of dishonesty: Less honest individuals are likely to report a higher incidence of dishonest behavior.
2. Leniency toward dishonest behavior: Less honest individuals are more likely to forgive or excuse dishonest behavior.
3. Theft rationalization: Less honest individuals are likely to come up with more excuses or reasons for theft.
4. Theft temptation or rumination: Less honest individuals are likely to think about theft.
5. Norms regarding dishonest behavior: Less honest individuals are likely to view dishonest behavior as acceptable.
6. Impulse control: Less honest individuals are likely to act on their impulses.
7. Punitiveness toward self or others: Less honest individuals are likely to have more punitive attitudes.

a dishonest fashion across a wide range of situations than a person with higher scores.

Faking and admissions.   Many integrity tests, as well as more general personality tests, require some sort of self-description. A clear-purpose integrity test might require the respondent to describe his or her attitudes toward theft, or beliefs about the frequency of theft, as well as describing his or her own history of theft and misdeeds. Veiled-purpose tests may not require such direct self-description, but even these tests often include many items that inquire into the individual's opinions, beliefs, and self-perceptions (O'Bannon, Goldinger, & Appleby, 1989). The possibility that individuals will distort their responses to scales of this type has long troubled measurement specialists, who have employed a variety of strategies either to control distortion or to detect and attempt to correct for it in responses to these tests (Cronbach, 1990).

The most common strategy for detecting distortion is to include supplementary scales or indices that are used to identify unusual or potentially invalid response patterns.[1] For example, score reports from the Strong-Campbell Interest Inventory (an inventory designed to measure general vocational interests) typically include counts of the total number of responses, the number of infrequent responses, and the frequency of specific responses. Test blanks that include few responses or unusual response patterns may not represent valid measures of the individual's interests. Other tests, such as the Minnesota Multiphasic Personality Inventory (an inventory used in psychiatric diagnoses and personality research) include more elaborate validity

[1] Drasgow and Hulin (1991) describe a number of appropriateness indices that might be used to identify specific types of distorted or aberrant responses.

scales (Murphy & Davidshofer, 1991). Although these scales can detect some specific types of distortion, efforts to correct for distortion have been far from successful (Cronbach, 1990). These scales may help identify specific types of distortion, but it is virtually impossible to use these indices to infer what the respondent's responses would have been in the absence of distortion. When distortion indices indicate that test scores are unlikely to be accurate (whether because of, for example, careless, inconsistent responding or because of conscious distortion), it is probably better to disregard the score than to attempt to create a "corrected" score.

Effects of faking on test validity. In several studies, Hough et al. (1990) tested the hypothesis that intentional distortion of responses to personality scales—in other words, faking—would affect the validity of these scales as predictors of job performance. Their research suggests that faking is not, in fact, a major problem. First, the evidence suggests that faking is not widespread. Second, when it does occur, faking has relatively little effect on the validity of the tests. That is, although people can distort their responses to personality tests and other similar instruments (for example, they can distort responses to an integrity test to make themselves seem more honest), doing so does not necessarily affect the relationship between test scores and performance. Faking may affect the overall mean test score, but it does not seem to substantially affect the rank-ordering of individuals. Nevertheless, Hough et al. (1990) suggest that tests that are potentially susceptible to faking should contain response validity scales, which would help to identify inaccurate self-descriptions, and that respondents should be warned that efforts will be made to identify inaccurate self-descriptions.

Overt integrity tests, which inquire directly about attitudes toward and past history of theft and other questionable behaviors, are probably more susceptible to distortion than veiled-purpose tests; research has shown that it is relatively easy for individuals to "fake good" on clear-purpose tests (Ryan & Sackett, 1987). You might therefore think that few individuals would be willing to admit to past thefts, or to exhibit favorable attitudes toward theft and other illegal behaviors. In fact, research on overt integrity tests suggests that people are surprisingly willing to admit to a variety of misdeeds, especially when they believe that their responses might be checked, and to indicate favorable attitudes toward the same misdeeds (Cunningham, 1989; McDaniel & Jones, 1988; O'Bannon, Goldinger, & Appleby, 1989). For example, McDaniel and Jones (1988) reviewed a number of studies of the Personnel Selection Inventory, an overt integrity test designed to measure honesty, emotional instability, and propensity toward drug use. The test showed fairly high levels of validity in all studies, which implies that the self-reports were reasonably accurate, at least in a relative sense (that is, individuals with more favorable attitudes toward and more incidents of questionable acts were probably more likely to report them). The validity of predictions made on the basis of this test was highest when subjects were aware that the investigators had other sources of information about their honesty, but the effects of this independent confirmation on the validity of the test were relatively slight.

Although the research discussed above suggests that people are somewhat willing to admit to wrongdoing and to reveal their attitudes toward wrongdoing, it does not completely rule out distortion in overt integrity tests. One possibility is that only some individuals distort their responses. In particular, it is possible that the more intelligent respondents realize that honest responses may have negative consequences (for example, if the test is used in preemployment screening, they might not get the job) and are therefore more likely to distort their answers. Werner, Jones, and Steffy (1989) examined this hypothesis. Their studies showed that integrity test scores were not highly correlated with measures of educational level or intelligence and that theft admissions were not highly correlated with intelligence. Their studies cannot be regarded as definitive, because of relatively small samples and less than optimal measures of intelligence. Nevertheless, their results, together with the results of other similar studies reviewed by Sackett, Burris, and Callahan (1989), suggest that intelligent individuals may not be especially likely to distort their responses to overt integrity tests.

Cunningham (1989) suggests that faking in response to items on an integrity test might itself be an indication of dishonesty. He demonstrated that a number of test-taking attitudes that are related to faking are also related to admissions of past misdeeds. While the use of test faking as an indicator of general honesty is an interesting idea, it is important to keep in mind that there is relatively little evidence that individuals who engage in faking when answering a test will later engage in other dishonest behaviors.

Uses of Integrity Testing

As with employee drug testing (see Chapter 4), it is useful to distinguish between preemployment testing and testing of incumbents. Preemployment testing is most common, and in most cases a score below the cutoff used by any particular test will result in the applicant being withdrawn from consideration. Integrity tests may also be used with incumbents; O'Bannon, Goldinger, and Appleby (1989) review several tests constructed for this purpose.

When testing job applicants, integrity tests function as a broad screening tool. Tests administered to job incumbents are often, though not always, part of a more focused investigation. For example, if a department is experiencing an unusually high shrinkage rate (that is, unexplained loss of materials, parts, and the like), integrity tests might be given to employees in that department as part of an investigation. It is unusual to use an integrity test score as the sole basis for actions taken against an employee, such as dismissal, whereas in preemployment screening a low test score might be a sufficient reason for dropping the candidate.

The contribution of integrity tests to the quality of decisions made about job applicants and incumbents is affected by a number of characteristics of the tests, the examinees, and the situation. The most obvious characteristic to consider is the validity of these tests; in later sections of this chapter, I will examine research on integrity test validity. As has been noted in earlier chapters, the base rate for deception and the failure rate for the test are also important.

Base rates and failure rates for integrity tests.   It is common for 30 to 60% of the individuals who take integrity tests to fail them (that is, to receive scores below the cutoff for "not recommended" or some similar classification) (see Office of Technology Assessment, 1990; Sackett, Burris, and Callahan, 1989). As I noted in Chapters 3 and 4, the match between this failure rate and the base rate for workplace dishonesty is a potentially important determinant of the value of *any* test. For example, if 10% of all workers are likely to engage in nontrivial theft (such as theft of more than $10 worth of goods and materials) but 60% of them fail the test, it follows that at least 50% of the individuals who take the test will be improperly classified. Martin and Terris (1991) and others (APA Task Force, 1991) note that false positive errors (for example, when a nondeceptive individual fails an integrity test) are not solely a product of the test itself, and that if integrity tests were replaced by less valid methods of inferring integrity (such as the polygraph), the false positive rate would be even higher. This argument is based, however, on the assumption that the replacement test has a failure rate equivalent to the old one. If integrity tests were replaced by *less* valid tests that had a failure rate closer to the base rate of nontrivial deception, the false positive rate could be reduced dramatically.

An example is presented in Table 5-3. Assume that there are two tests, both of which are designed to measure integrity. The two tests have validities (that is, correlations with some valid indicator of integrity or theft) of .50 and .20, respectively, and failure rates of 50% and 20%, respectively. If 100 workers are tested, of whom 20 routinely steal (so that the base rate is .20), use of the more valid test (which also has

Table 5-3 *Approximate Number of False Positives and Total Decision Errors per 100 Examinees for Tests That Differ in Terms of Validity and Failure Rates*

Base rate	Test #1 (validity = .50; failure rate = .50)		Test #2 (validity = .20; failure rate = .20)	
	FALSE POSITIVES	TOTAL ERRORS[a]	FALSE POSITIVES	TOTAL ERRORS
.20	39	48	13	26
.30	24	28	11	22
.40	18	26	8	26

[a] Total errors = number of false positives + number of false negatives

the higher failure rate) will lead to 30 false positive errors, whereas use of the less valid test will lead to 13 false positive errors. Furthermore, use of the less valid test will lead to fewer total decision errors (26 versus 48) than use of the more valid one. If the base rate is .30, the more valid test will make more false positive errors and more total errors than the less valid test (24 versus 11 for false positives, 28 versus 22 for total errors). Finally, if the base rate is .40, the more valid test will make more false positive errors (18 versus 8), although in this case the total number of decision errors will be the same (26 for each test).

The preceding paragraph seems to contradict a basic assumption of test theory, that more valid tests are usually preferable to less valid ones. However, the situation is not so simple when (1) the test and the criterion are both dichotomous (that is, pass/fail, or honest/dishonest), and (2) the failure rate for the less valid test is closer to the base rate. Whenever tests yield dichotomous scores, the match between the failure rate and the base rate of the criterion they are designed to predict is an important factor in the overall evaluation of the test.

The simplest way to reduce the number of false positives arising from the use of an integrity test would be to adjust the passing score so that the failure rate approximated the base rate for nontrivial dishonesty. Unfortunately, as I have noted earlier, this base rate is often unknown. Even when it is known, it is not clear whether test publishers have the means or would be willing to incorporate this information into their test-scoring formulas. Martin (1988) suggests a number of other, perhaps simpler, methods of reducing false positives, including the use of multiple tests.

Validity of Integrity Tests

Questions about the validity of integrity tests are framed in two ways. The first approach focuses on the validity of measurement and leads to the question whether these tests really measure integrity, honesty, and so on. The second approach focuses on the use of test scores, and leads to the question whether scores on integrity tests are related to other phenomena of interest (such as absenteeism and job performance) and whether use of these tests will lead to better decisions (Murphy & Davidshofer, 1991). In Chapter 3, I noted that both aspects of validity could be considered as components of the overall construct validity of the test. Nevertheless, for interpretative purposes it is useful to distinguish between what these tests purport to measure and what they predict.

Although some studies do examine the validity of measurement for integrity tests (Ash, 1991), most studies of integrity test validity have followed a criterion-related approach, in which scores on these tests are related to a variety of external criteria. Within this broad approach are a number of possible research strategies; several have been used in an attempt to determine the criterion-related validity of integrity tests.

Validation strategies.   Research on the validity of integrity tests is difficult to carry out, in part because of the lack of good criteria (APA Task Force, 1991; O'Bannon, Goldinger, & Appleby, 1989; see also reviews by Sackett, Burris, & Callahan, 1989; Sackett & Decker, 1979; and Sackett & Harris, 1984). A variety of research strategies has been used in empirical assessments of integrity tests; characteristics of some of the more common strategies are presented in Table 5-4.

As O'Bannon, Goldinger, and Appleby (1989) note, potential problems exist with all these strategies. The contrasted groups strategy often seems to show large differences between groups, but the use of

Table 5-4   *Strategies for Investigating Integrity Test Validity*

Strategy	Characteristics
Contrasted groups method	Test scores of people known to be dishonest (such as convicted thieves) are compared to scores of individuals who show no signs of dishonesty.
Background check method	Outcomes of background checks (such as the number of criminal convictions) are correlated with test scores.
Admissions method	Admissions of dishonest acts are used as a criterion for validating tests.
Predictive method	Future behavior is used as a criterion, and test scores are kept confidential until after criterion data are collected.
Time series method	Indicators of group performance, losses, shrinkage, and so on are collected both before and after the use of tests, and trends in these indicators are compared before and after testing.

criminals may stack the deck in favor of such a test. It is probably much easier to discriminate between convicted felons and people in general than it is to discriminate among job applicants who may or may not engage in small-scale employee theft.

Strategies that rely on background checks are probably limited in their usefulness, because many of the most frequent and, in the long run, most costly forms of property and production deviance will not show up on a standard background check. For example, instances of production deviance such as goldbricking, doing personal business on company time, or taking extra-long breaks will rarely if ever show up on a background check, yet these behaviors are both frequent and costly.

Validating tests against admissions of wrongdoing is a risky undertaking, because you never know whether all admissions are truthful or whether admissions of all instances of theft or other undesirable behavior can be obtained. Validation against admissions is especially problematic for clear-purpose integrity tests, because the tests themselves contain items that require admissions. A recent review of integrity test validities (Ones, Viswesvaran, & Schmidt, 1992) did indeed report extremely high validity coefficients for one overt integrity test; it is possible that this level of validity was obtained by correlating the test against a criterion that is essentially identical to some of the items on the test itself. Even when the test itself does not call for admissions, the potential for criterion contamination is introduced by the fact that test results are sometimes used to prompt confessions of past misdeeds (O'Bannon, Goldinger, & Appleby, 1989).

True predictive validity studies are rare, and the ones that are carried out often are plagued by small samples or a variety of design flaws. In fairness, the same can be said of validation research for other types of tests (for example, cognitive ability tests). A true predictive study is very hard to carry out, and even when it is technically possible, a number of practical and ethical difficulties discourage researchers and organizations from attempting it (Murphy & Davidshofer, 1991). In order to carry out a true predictive validity study, you must give an integrity test, hire individuals without consulting their scores on the test, and then wait to see what happens. To many people, it seems both unethical and stupid to hire people who you have reason to believe will steal (that is, individuals with very low scores on the integrity test), then stand by and wait for them to actually steal. Thus, it is unlikely that we will ever see the number of predictive validity studies that would, from a strictly scientific viewpoint, be desirable.

There have been a number of time series studies, which have generally produced encouraging results. In particular, many studies have suggested that theft, shrinkage, counterproductive behavior, and the like decline after the introduction of integrity tests and that this decline persists over time. Unfortunately, there are often a number of competing explanations for this change, which may have nothing at all to do with the validity of the tests. The simplest explanation is that the introduction of an integrity test heightens everyone's awareness of employee theft, which will itself reduce theft opportunities. For example, if I introduced into an organization a test labeled (in large letters) the "Murphy Integrity Inventory," I would probably get people thinking about employee theft, which would increase the vigilance of the honest employees and increase the caution of the thieves. Even if the test had no value in discriminating honest from dishonest subjects, the mere fact that the organization was visibly paying attention to integrity should help reduce the incidence and seriousness of employee theft.

In addition to validity studies, a number of test publishers and users have conducted adverse impact studies, designed to determine whether integrity tests are likely to screen out members of some particular group (such as younger workers or minorities) in disproportionate numbers. In general, these studies suggest that different groups in the population receive roughly comparable scores, although males are somewhat more likely to fail such tests than females and younger workers are more likely to fail than older workers (O'Bannon, Goldinger, & Appleby, 1989). These results are important because they suggest that integrity tests do not systematically discriminate against minorities or other groups that have historically fared less well with other types of testing. One of the principal reasons for ongoing controversy over the use of cognitive ability tests in education and industry is the fact that average test scores differ as a function of race, leading to an adverse impact; in other words, these tests have different impacts on white and minority populations. The fact that integrity tests seem to show little adverse impact may have important practical and societal implications.

Validity evidence.   Sackett and his colleagues have conducted several reviews of research on the reliability, validity, and usefulness of integrity tests (Sackett, Burris, & Callahan, 1989; Sackett & Decker, 1979; Sackett & Harris, 1984, 1985); Ones, Viswesvaran, and Schmidt (1992) and McDaniel and Jones (1988) have subjected some of the same studies to meta-analyses designed to quantitatively summarize the outcomes of multiple validity studies. O'Bannon, Goldinger, and Appleby (1989) have reviewed this research as well, and they have also given attention to a variety of practical issues surrounding the administration and use of integrity tests. Although each review raises different concerns, and most reviews lament the shortcomings of research on the validity of integrity tests, the general conclusion of the more recent reviews is positive. Earlier reviews of research on integrity tests were sharply critical, but it appears that both the research and the tests themselves have improved, partly as a result of the earlier criticism. There is now a reasonable body of evidence showing that integrity tests have some validity for predicting a variety of criteria that are relevant to organizations. This research does not say that tests of this sort will eliminate theft or dishonesty at work, but it does suggest that individuals who receive poor scores on these tests tend to be less desirable employees.

In discussing validity evidence, it is important to identify the specific criteria used in different studies. Some studies have validated integrity tests against measures of counterproductive behavior, whereas others have validated these tests against measures of general job performance. These two criteria are clearly not independent; employees who engage in a wide variety of counterproductive behavior are unlikely to be good performers. Nevertheless, there are important differences between the two criteria and, more important, differences in the validity of integrity tests for predicting the two; Ones, Viswesvaran, and Schmidt (1992) suggested substantially higher levels of validity for predicting counterproductive behaviors than for predicting job performance.

Reviewers have examined several different facets of integrity test validity and have reached somewhat different conclusions regarding many of the fine points. For example, Sackett, Burris, and Callahan (1989) suggested that the validity of overt and veiled-purpose tests was roughly equivalent, although each test may be aimed at somewhat different criteria. A more detailed analysis by Ones, Viswesvaran, and Schmidt (1991) suggests that, depending on the criterion, overt tests may show higher validities. However, some of the studies examining the validity of overt tests correlated scores on these tests with admissions of past misdeeds. Because the tests themselves often call for similar admissions, it is not surprising that the validity coefficients are sometimes quite high.

Although the results of recent validity studies are generally positive, these results have not quieted the controversy over integrity testing. In response to the continuing debate over the use of tests to infer honesty, dependability, and trustworthiness, two major recent assessments of integrity testing have been made, one conducted by a special task force of the American Psychological Association (APA Task Force, 1991) and the other by the U.S. Congress's Office of Technology Assessment (Office of Technology Assessment, 1990). These two reviews covered somewhat different sets of studies (the OTA review concentrated on the most methodically sophisticated studies, while the APA review looked at a wider range of studies) and were conducted with somewhat different purposes in mind. As a result, they did not always reach identical conclusions. However, they did agree in several areas; I will review these areas of agreement before discussing differences between the conclusions reached in the two reviews.

OTA versus APA: areas of agreement.   Both reviews reached similar conclusions in at least four important areas. First, it is exceedingly difficult to define honesty, integrity, or whatever attribute these tests are designed to measure. Different tests seem to focus on very different attitudes, beliefs, or behaviors. For example, employee theft can be defined in a number of ways. Researchers often distinguish between trivial and nontrivial theft; conclusions about the extent of theft depend largely on whether taking articles of little value, such as pencils and paper, is included in one's definition of theft. Goldbricking, taking long lunch breaks, using company time to carry out personal business, and similar activities are sometimes labeled "time theft." As I have noted earlier, a wide variety of dishonest behaviors occur in organizations, and lumping them all into a single category (that is, dishonest as opposed to honest behavior) is unlikely to advance our understanding of these behaviors.

Both reviews raise a related issue that has been a source of controversy since the time of Hartshorne and May (1928): the question whether honesty is a distinct trait. Most researchers believe that situational factors have a very strong impact on the tendency to engage in honest or dishonest behaviors (Saxe, 1990) and that labeling a person as "honest" or "dishonest" is a serious oversimplification. Both reviews lead to the conclusion that we do not really know what integrity tests measure, but whatever it is, it is not quite the same thing as "honesty."

Second, it is hard to distinguish integrity tests, particularly veiled-purpose tests, from other personality inventories. It is clear that our understanding of integrity tests would be advanced considerably if the constructs measured by these tests could be compared to those assessed by existing, well-validated measures of general personality. Several authors (for example, O'Bannon, Goldinger, & Appleby, 1989; Ones, Viswesvaran, & Schmidt, 1992) have suggested that integrity tests are highly similar to tests designed to measure conscientiousness, but to date, little direct research has been conducted on this hypothesis. Assuming that the hypothesis turns out to be correct, the next logical question may be whether any need exists for a special category of tests labeled "integrity tests." Integrity test publishers are likely to answer affirmatively, but to date, the evidence has been insufficient to demonstrate that these tests accomplish much that could not be accomplished with existing personality inventories.

Third, informed consent is a potentially serious issue in integrity testing. The OTA review notes that integrity test publishers advise *against* informing examinees of their test scores—so that if an individual is denied employment on the basis of a score on an integrity test, he or she would not be so informed. The *Standards for Educational and Psychological Testing* (1985) and the *Ethical Principles of Psychologists* (1989) make it clear that psychologists involved in integrity testing are obliged to inform examinees about the risks and consequences of taking the test and those of refusing to take the test, about the purpose and nature of the test, and about the way in which test scores will be used (Lowman, 1989). The ethical standards described in these documents do not imply that examinees need to know their final test scores, but they do seem to imply that examinees receive a good deal more information about the tests and their use than is typical in actual testing situations.

Fourth, there are serious concerns over the way in which integrity tests are scored and in which scores are reported. Despite the claims of some test publishers, it is common to use some sort of dichotomous scoring, such as pass/fail, in integrity testing. More sophisticated tests sometimes report test scores in terms of a small number of "zones"— that is, high danger, moderate danger, average danger, or low danger of theft, substance abuse, and so on. There is an extensive literature dealing with the highly complex psychometric and legal issues involved in setting cutoff scores (see Cascio, Alexander, & Barrett, 1988, for a review), but it is not clear whether any of this literature is taken into account by some test publishers. Test scores that are reported on a pass/fail basis are inherently suspect, because they blur potentially meaningful differences between individuals in each of the two categories; it is unlikely, for example, that all individuals who fail present the same risks.

OTA versus APA: areas of disagreement.   The OTA and APA reviews were prepared for somewhat different purposes (legislation versus scientific research), for different audiences (Congress versus psychologists), and using different methods (selective versus broad coverage of the literature), and it would be unreasonable to expect complete agreement. Comparison of the two reports shows that they disagree in two ways. First, the bottom line of these reviews differs. The OTA review concludes that "the research on integrity tests has not yet produced data that clearly supports or dismisses the assertion that these tests can predict dishonest behavior" (Office of Technology Assessment, 1990, p. 8). The APA review concludes that "to the extent that evidence is available, it is consistent with the idea that these tests reflect aspects of personal integrity, dependability, or trustworthiness" (APA Task Force, 1991, p. 26). One reason that the APA report reviews integrity tests somewhat more favorably is that it compared these tests to other procedures that might reasonably be used in their place, such as polygraphs, whereas the OTA review considered integrity tests in isolation. The APA position is that if integrity tests are banned, something else will be used in their place, and the replacement will almost certainly be worse. While the APA's endorsement of these tests is far from ringing, its review suggests that if integrity tests are evaluated by the standards used to evaluate other psychological tests, a reasonable amount of evidence points to their validity and utility. Furthermore, attempts to hold these tests to a higher standard or level of scrutiny than that given to other selection tests may in the end be counterproductive. Organizations have legitimate concerns regarding the integrity of current or prospective employees, and a well-designed paper-and-pencil test is more likely to prove valid, useful, and fair than any other method currently available for assessing integrity.

A second difference between the two reviews is the attention given to the actual use of integrity tests in the field. The APA review has a good deal more to say about the integrity test industry, and much of it is strongly critical. Although the APA review notes that some integrity test publishers are highly responsible in their approach, it also notes that many test publishers fail to live up to the technical and ethical requirements in the *Standards for Educational and Psychological Testing* (1985). Some test publishers fail to carry out or adequately report research on the validity of their tests, whereas others resist any independent scrutiny of their instruments. The psychometric quality of some tests is either unknown or so poor that the test publishers are acting irresponsibly in distributing them.

The marketing of integrity tests is, in many cases, a disgrace. The APA report notes that the claims made for some of these tests are so excessive and overblown as to be fraudulent. Indeed, if you want to see examples of dishonesty in the workplace, you need not look much further than the marketing brochures for some integrity tests. Experts in consumer fraud warn us that claims that look too good to be true often *are* too good to be true. A marketing brochure that claims that a simple test will eliminate most or all of an organization's theft and shrinkage problems should not be taken seriously.

At least two groups suffer from the failure of some test publishers to live up to the standards that govern other types of testing: test consumers and the many integrity test publishers who do live up to these standards. Both organizations and individuals suffer when tests with limited validity or relevance are used to make important decisions. The entire integrity testing industry suffers because of the actions of those publishers who fail to conform to appropriate technical and ethical guidelines.

Why integrity tests predict performance.   The available evidence suggests that individuals who score poorly on integrity tests turn out to be worse employees. They may not necessarily be involved in theft or other types of serious wrongdoing, but they are probably more likely to be undependable, irresponsible, absent, late, and so on than individuals with higher scores are (Ones, Viswesvaran, & Schmidt, 1991). Although encouraging from a practical point of view, since these results suggest that integrity testing can help improve the quality of personnel selection decisions, this finding is potentially puzzling. In particular, it is not at first obvious why integrity test scores should be related to job performance. Their potential relevance to more narrow criteria such as theft or other forms of property deviance is clear, but their broad relevance to global measures of job performance is not.

One potential explanation for the validity of integrity tests as predictors of job performance is that many of the forms of workplace dishonesty that these tests are designed to predict themselves constitute poor performance. In particular, many counterproductive behaviors, such as goldbricking and irresponsibility, are themselves components of poor performance, and a test designed to predict these behaviors should naturally tell us something about performance.

Another potential explanation for the relationship between integrity test scores and job performance was suggested by Murphy and Lee (1991). They noted that most integrity tests either directly or indirectly measure the personality trait conscientiousness. Conscientiousness is in turn positively related to performance in a wide range of jobs (Barrick & Mount, 1991). It is possible that the relationship between conscientiousness and both job performance and integrity test scores is partly or fully responsible for the relationship between integrity and job performance. This hypothesis is illustrated in Figure 5-1; the shaded portion of this figure represents the portion of the relationship be-

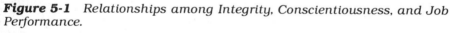

Figure 5-1   *Relationships among Integrity, Conscientiousness, and Job Performance.*

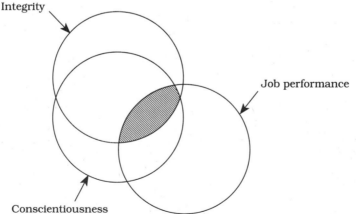

Note: The shaded portion of the figure represents the overlap between integrity and performance that may be explainable in terms of conscientiousness.

tween integrity and performance that might be explained in terms of conscientiousness.

The best way to understand this hypothesis is to think about people who exhibit low levels of conscientiousness (which results in poor scores on most integrity tests). These individuals are undependable, avoid extra work (and even their regular work, if they can get away with it), are sloppy, and require close and constant supervision. This is hardly the picture of a model employee. To test the hypothesis that the conscientiousness factor either fully or partly explains the relationship between integrity and job performance, Murphy and Lee (1991) collected data from two samples. On the basis of existing meta-analyses (Barrick & Mount, 1991; Ones, Viswesvaran, & Schmidt, 1992), they were able to estimate the correlations between integrity and performance and between conscientiousness and performance. Their study was designed to estimate the strength of the relationship between integrity and conscientiousness. Their results suggested that scores on both overt and veiled-purpose integrity tests are positively related with measures of conscientiousness, but that these correlations are not so strong as to explain the correlation between integrity and performance. This study suggests that conscientiousness represents a partial explanation for the correlation between integrity and performance, but that factors other than conscientiousness are also important for understanding this relationship. At present, however, it is difficult to determine precisely what those other factors might be.

Reactions to Integrity Testing

Integrity testing is still highly controversial (Office of Technology Assessment, 1990), and it is widely believed that individuals react very negatively to integrity tests. Two studies by White (1984) suggested that the use of the polygraph might lead to negative reactions. Similarly, Murphy, Thornton, and Reynolds (1990) suggested that many individuals might react negatively to drug tests. However, research on reactions to paper-and-pencil integrity tests suggests that negative reactions may be rare, even when clear-purpose tests are used (O'Bannon, Goldinger, & Appleby, 1989; Ryan & Sackett, 1987). A laboratory study by Stone and Herringshaw (1991) suggests that the use of integrity tests to detect theft by job incumbents is more controversial than the use of these tests in preemployment screening; similar results have been found in research on employee drug testing. On the whole, however, little evidence supports the idea that job applicants or incumbents find integrity tests objectionable.

Research on attitudes toward employee drug testing (for example, Murphy, Thornton, & Prue, 1991; Murphy, Thornton, & Reynolds, 1990) suggests that reactions to this form of testing depend on both the perceived relevance of the test (testing is regarded most favorably in jobs in which impaired performance could threaten the safety of co-workers or the public) and on the perceived accuracy of the test (testing programs that employ highly sensitive tests and independent confirmation of initial test results are viewed most favorably). Stone and Herringshaw (1991) suggest that the same factors might affect reactions to integrity tests. Organizations can probably minimize negative reactions by clearly explaining their rationale for integrity testing and by including safeguards, such as the use of multiple tests or testing methods, to help minimize the possibility that an individual is adversely affected by his or her score on a particular test of integrity.

White (1984) notes that integrity testing (in this case, polygraph testing) may have an unanticipated and unwanted effect. By heightening applicants' awareness of the organization's concern over integrity, integrity testing may lead to the impression that dishonesty is a substantial problem in this organization and that dishonest behavior is somewhat common. There is clear evidence that beliefs about the occurrence of theft are related to theft (individuals who think that theft is common are more likely to steal), and it is possible that testing procedures that lead individuals to believe that theft is common may also lead to more theft.

Privacy and integrity testing.   Paper-and-pencil tests of honesty and integrity have been criticized as unwarranted invasions of privacy (Libbin, Mendelsohn, & Duffy, 1988), in part because such tests may include questions about the respondents' attitudes toward religion or sex, family relations, personal habits, and private interests. Even though responses are used to make inferences about integrity or related behaviors and attitudes that may indeed be job-related, the fact that a test inquires about attitudes, beliefs, behaviors, and the like that are not themselves the legitimate concern of the employer is potentially problematic.

Stone and Stone (1990) reviewed research and theory relevant to privacy in organizations. Their review suggests that organizations and individuals differ considerably in what they deem private as opposed to public and that any inquiry into topic areas as sensitive as past misdeeds is likely to be regarded by some as an unwanted invasion of privacy. The potential gain to an organization resulting from the use of a well-designed integrity test might outweigh concerns over invasions of privacy. Nevertheless, it is important to keep in mind that this class of tests is likely to stir up opposition on the basis of potential invasions of privacy and that organizations must be sensitive to privacy-related concerns if they use integrity tests.

Trends in Integrity Testing

O'Bannon, Goldinger, and Appleby (1989) cite a number of trends in integrity testing. First, these tests are becoming increasingly broad. Many integrity tests now include subscales designed to make inferences about turnover, drug use, emotional instability, and potential for violence. While the development of broader tests is probably a good thing, caution must be observed in interpreting these subscale scores literally. To date, evidence of the criterion-related validity of integrity tests has focused largely on the integrity scales themselves; there is no clear evidence yet that a high score on a scale labeled, for example, "drug use" will in fact indicate a high probability of actual drug use.

A second trend in integrity testing is increased attention to privacy rights and to potential violations of civil rights. In general, the evidence suggests that different subgroups in the population (for example,

Box 5-1 *Legal Issues in Integrity Testing*

Attempts to evaluate the integrity of job applicants and incumbents have long been the source of legal controversy. Since the passage of the Employee Polygraph Protection Act, legal scrutiny has shifted from polygraphs and similar devices to paper-and-pencil testing. Several states have considered or passed laws banning or limiting the use of integrity tests in employment contexts.

In states where integrity testing is permitted, two legal issues have received considerable attention: adverse impact and invasion of privacy. Adverse impact exists when the use of a test has a substantially different impact on some group in the population (for instance, women or racial or ethnic minorities) than on others. For example, if most women fail a specific test and most men pass, the use of that test in employment screening will deny jobs to women. Equal opportunity laws forbid such discrimination, unless it can be shown to be job-related. However, O'Bannon, Goldinger, and Appleby's (1989) review suggests that integrity tests do not tend to show adverse impact and therefore do not appear to be discriminatory. The likelihood of failing such a test is essentially unrelated to race and only weakly related to gender (males are more likely to fail).

Jones, Ash, and Soto's (1990) review suggests that concerns about litigation over invasion of privacy may be somewhat exaggerated. They note that although 12 states have explicit guarantees in their constitutions for privacy, and although current interpretations of the U.S. Constitution imply federal protection of privacy rights, few serious attempts have been made to challenge integrity tests on privacy-related grounds. In fact, Jones, Ash, and Soto were unable to locate any cases involving integrity testing in which questions related to privacy were an important aspect of the case.

male, female, old, young, white, minority) receive roughly similar scores on many tests, which implies that the tests might not systematically discriminate against specific groups. Nevertheless, individuals' rights to privacy and to fair treatment might be compromised by some integrity tests, and both test publishers and test users are showing increasing concern for these issues.

A third trend noted in several other reviews (for instance, APA Task Force, 1991) is an increasing level of cooperation between many integrity test publishers and researchers interested in integrity testing.[2] The amount and the sophistication of the research on integrity testing has increased dramatically in recent years, and it is likely that this cooperation will ultimately benefit both test users and test publishers.

Other Self-Report Methods

Integrity tests represent the most widely used and most controversial method of using self-reports to assess or infer honesty or integrity. A variety of other methods exist, ranging from those that use information from the application blank to infer integrity to those that involve intensive face-to-face interviews. As with integrity tests, the rationale behind all of these methods is that information provided by the indi-

Box 5-2 *Model Guidelines for Preemployment Integrity Testing Programs*

The Association of Personnel Test Publishers has issued a set of guidelines for integrity testing programs, which if followed might substantially reduce the negative reactions often associated with this type of test. For example, these guidelines suggest that all test users:

1. select testing programs that are professionally developed and validated;
2. use testing programs only for the purpose for which they are designed;
3. administer tests in a proper testing environment;
4. train qualified testing personnel to administer the program and to handle and protect all forms of relevant employment data;
5. select testing programs that are fair to protected subgroups in the population; and
6. provide and enforce written guidelines on all matters related to test security and confidentiality.

---

[2] As an example of this cooperation, in a recent research project (Murphy & Lee, 1991), I contacted three integrity test publishers for permission to use their tests in my research. Not only was I given permission to use the tests, but I was also given a number of tests, as well as test-scoring services, free of charge for use in the project.

vidual may help to indicate an overall likelihood to either engage in or avoid various types of dishonest behavior.

Using Biographical Data

Self-report methods are usually used to assess a person's attitudes, beliefs, values, and the like. Although not technically a self-report, the application blank that virtually all applicants fill out represents a method of obtaining information from the respondent that might be useful in inferring his or her integrity. Several authors (for example, McDaniel, 1989) have suggested that a weighted application blank might be used to infer honesty. The basic idea here is to identify items on job applications that consistently discriminate those who steal or commit dishonest acts from those who don't. For example, if you found out that individuals who give a post office box address rather than their home address often steal, but those who give their home address rarely steal, this question on the application blank could be used to predict future theft. Items that more clearly discriminate honest from dishonest individuals are then given more weight, and a composite score based on responses to several questions on the application blank is used to predict future honesty.

Rosenbaum (1976) applied this technique to predict theft in the retail industry. Some items reported to be related to theft are (1) number of previous jobs, (2) local versus out-of-town address, (3) length of time at present address, (4) number of dependents, (5) ownership of an automobile, and (6) whether the applicant wants a relative contacted in case of emergency. It is well known that individuals with loose ties to the organization or the community are more likely to steal than individuals with long-standing connections (Hollinger & Clark, 1983); several of the items identified by Rosenbaum seem to relate to this theme.

McDaniel (1989) studied the validity of biographical measures obtained from background investigations. Although conceptually similar in many ways to the biographical data obtained from application blanks, background investigations often concentrate on negative information, such as drug use, criminal convictions, or bad credit history. He found that a number of background factors, including school suspension, drug use, quitting school, poor grades and failure to become involved in extracurricular activities, and previous contact with the legal system were all significantly correlated with unsuitable discharges from the military.

The use of biographical data to predict theft and infer integrity has many advantages. This type of data can often be verified, reducing the likelihood of faking, and this method is highly unobtrusive. Job applications are virtually universal, and it is quite possible that an individual will never find out that his or her application is used to infer integrity. However, a variety of problems are inherent to this approach. First, weighted application blanks can be openly discriminatory, particularly if factors such as race, gender, or income are directly entered into the equation. Second, the weights may be unstable, especially if they were originally estimated in small samples. Third, this approach lacks face validity. In other words, the relevance of many items on an application blank for predicting integrity is not always obvious, and even if this method leads to valid decisions, accepting decisions based on weighted application blanks may present substantial problems.

There are often legal restrictions on the use of background data. For example, in most states, it is illegal to inquire about previous arrests and, in some cases, about prior convictions that are not clearly job-related. Similarly, making decisions on the basis of demographic data (for example, race or gender) is often illegal, and even where it is permitted, the threat of lawsuits often looms.

Personality Tests and Integrity

Lewicki (1983) reviewed research on a variety of personality characteristics that may be related to lying. These involve the individual's stage of moral development (Kohlberg, 1969), level of Machiavellianism (Gies & Moon, 1981), and internal versus external locus of control (Hegarty & Sims, 1978). Trevino (1986) suggested that ego strength and field independence might both be related to ethical behavior in managers. Other studies have examined the relationships between a number of personality traits and scores on integrity tests (Hogan & Hogan, 1989; Korchkin, 1987; Logan, Koettel, & Moore, 1986). More recent personality theory has concentrated on a personality trait that may be critical for understanding both honesty at work and job performance: conscientiousness.

The most widely accepted theory of personality suggests that human personality can best be understood in terms of five factors or dimensions, often referred to as the "big five" (Barrick & Mount, 1991; Digman, 1990; McCrea & Costa, 1985, 1986, 1987, 1989). These five factors, described in Table 5-5, repeatedly emerge from analyses of personality data obtained using different tests and methods (for example, tests versus self and peer ratings) in different cultures and samples. All five appear to be relatively independent of cognitive ability.

Of the five factors listed in Table 5-5, conscientiousness seems most closely allied to honesty. Indeed, a number of paper-and-pencil tests of integrity and honesty include scales labeled "dependability," which is thought to be one aspect of conscientiousness. A recent analysis by

Table 5-5 *The Five-Factor Model of Personality*

Factor	Definition
Extroversion	People high on this dimension are sociable, gregarious, assertive, talkative, and active.
Emotional stability	People low on this dimension are anxious, depressed, angry, emotional, embarrassed, and insecure.
Agreeableness	People high on this dimension are courteous, flexible, trusting, good-natured, cooperative, and tolerant.
Conscientiousness	People high on this dimension are dependable, careful, thorough, responsible, hard-working, and persevering.
Openness to experience	People high on this dimension are imaginative, cultured, curious, original, and artistically sensitive.

Barrick and Mount (1991) suggests that conscientiousness is also related to a number of objective and subjective measures of job performance. They examined 117 studies that reported correlations between personality tests and measures of job performance, training proficiency, and such characteristics as absenteeism, turnover, tenure, and salary level in professional, managerial, police, sales, and skilled/semiskilled jobs. Their analyses suggest that conscientiousness is the only personality dimension that is consistently related to measures of job performance (although the validity coefficients are usually small). Furthermore, the validity of conscientiousness as a predictor of performance is essentially constant across different types of jobs and different types of performance measures. Other personality dimensions are important in some jobs or are related to specific performance measures (for example, Hough et al., 1990, review research on personality as a predictor of performance in the military), but the dimension of conscientiousness is potentially unique in its broad relevance.

Conscientiousness is a critical component of most paper-and-pencil tests of integrity. Most veiled-purpose tests directly measure conscientiousness or some closely related personality construct (Sackett, Burris, & Callahan, 1989). Overt integrity tests are not necessarily designed to measure this personality characteristic, but even these tests are probably influenced by the respondent's level of conscientiousness. Highly conscientious individuals are probably less likely to commit illegal or questionable acts, so that they simply have less to admit when responding to tests that call for admissions of past thefts, crimes, or other questionable behaviors.

As we noted earlier, Murphy and Lee (1991) presented evidence that conscientiousness was related to scores on several measures of integrity. Pooling across the two samples included in their study, they found that scores on a conscientiousness scale were moderately correlated (with correlations ranging from .28 to .36) with scores on both clear-purpose and veiled-purpose tests.

Measures used to assess psychopathology.   There is increasing interest in screening employees for various forms of psychopathology, using instruments such as the Minnesota Multiphasic Personality Inventory (and its recent revision, the MMPI-2; see Butcher, 1991; Lowman, 1989). In part, this kind of screening continues an earlier tradition in which inventories such as the MMPI and the California Personality Inventory, as well as projective devices such as the Rorschach Inkblot Test, were used in an attempt to detect delinquency and criminality (Hollinger & Clark, 1983).

Although assessments of psychopathology do not always deal directly with integrity, they are very likely to deal with related concepts, such as problems in dealing with authority, emotional stability, responsibility, and the like. The use of MMPI subscales in screening for integrity is increasingly common, especially in police departments and in the security and nuclear power industries (Lowman, 1989). To date, however, little evidence shows that this test can validly predict honesty in the workplace (Office of Technology Assessment, 1990). More generally, there is little compelling evidence that preemployment screening for psychopathology will have a noticeable impact on honesty, theft, and so on in the workplace (Lowman, 1989). Pre-employment screening for psychopathology is both useful and important, but it does not appear to provide a valid substitute for integrity tests or other reasonably valid methods of inferring honesty or dishonesty.

Lowman (1989) notes that when the MMPI is used in preemployment screening, individuals with clinically elevated scores on this test are usually subjected to additional methods of assessment and screening. The same is not true when the MMPI is used to screen for integrity. When the MMPI is used as a type of integrity test, individuals who receive poor scores on the scales being used to screen for integrity are likely to be rejected without any independent confirmation of the MMPI scores (Office of Technology Assessment, 1990).

Personality inventories and integrity tests.   Both the APA and OTA reviews raised the question whether veiled-purpose integrity tests are meaningfully different from more general personality tests. First of all, some integrity tests and scales are directly derived from existing personality inventories. For example, Hogan and Hogan (1989) discuss a measure of employee reliability derived from the Hogan Personality Inventory. Second, many of the items on veiled-purpose integrity tests seem similar to those on other personality inventories.

Third, there is evidence of positive correlations between integrity tests and measures of some more broadly defined personality traits.

It is probably best to think of veiled-purpose integrity tests as a type of narrowly focused personality inventory. Such tests do not tell you as much about an individual's personality as do more broadly defined inventories, such as the 16PF. They may, however, provide more valid predictions of specific criteria, such as counterproductive behaviors, than can be obtained using more general personality measures. Because of the lack of methodologically adequate studies, this hypothesis has not yet been fully tested by researchers.

However, research on trade-offs between bandwidth and fidelity suggest that this hypothesis is likely to be true. In psychological testing, there is an inevitable trade-off between attaining a high degree of precision in measurement of any one attribute or characteristic and obtaining information about a large number of attributes or characteristics. For example, if a test you are administering is to have 25 items, you may have to choose between measuring one thing well or five things poorly. This conflict is referred to as the "bandwidth–fidelity dilemma" (Cronbach & Gleser, 1965). Integrity tests probably have more fidelity: they probably tell you more about one specific characteristic, integrity, than you would learn from a more general personality inventory. Multifactor personality inventories probably have more bandwidth: they tell you more about the whole person than you will probably learn from the integrity test.

Integrity Interviews

A number of interview protocols have been developed that are designed to obtain information about an individual's integrity (Buckley, 1989). Although not as standardized as written tests, these interviews resemble overt or clear-purpose integrity tests in that they involve frank discussions of past misdeeds, thefts, and the like.

Like all interviews, the validity of this method probably depends as much on the interviewer as on the interview protocol itself (Landy, 1985). Some interviewers are probably better than others at putting the respondent at ease and building up an atmosphere in which he or she will be honest about past behavior. It is therefore difficult to make a meaningful statement about the reliability or validity of integrity interviews. In the hands of a well-trained, skilled interviewer, a carefully constructed interview protocol can probably yield valid information about integrity. On the other hand, the number of qualifications in the preceding sentence suggests a number of ways in which the process could go wrong. Poor training, lack of interpersonal skills, poorly chosen questions, or any combination of these factors could seriously compromise the validity of this technique.

The similarity of integrity interviews and overt integrity tests is both a blessing and a curse. If the questions used in such an interview are similar to those used in a well-validated test, this similarity might provide indirect evidence for the validity of the interview. On the other hand, if the interview is so similar to the test, you might wonder why you should bother giving the interview at all. Written tests are cheaper and simpler to administer, and they are not subject to the large number of biases thought to plague most interviews (Arvey & Faley, 1988).

—————————————*SUMMARY*—————————————

All the methods discussed in this chapter involve the assumption that honesty or integrity is a reasonably general characteristic of the person and can be measured or inferred on the basis of information supplied by that person. As we saw in Chapter 1, the assumption that honesty is a trait is only partly true: honest behavior is affected by characteristics of both the person and the situation. Nevertheless, it is clear that some people are more likely to be dishonest in a wider range of situations than others. It also seems clear that measuring relevant characteristics of the person can help in predicting honest and dishonest behavior.

Although integrity testing has recently caused a great deal of controversy, such tests do not appear fundamentally different from many other widely used psychological tests. Overt tests may strike some individuals as offensive and invasive (although research on reactions to integrity tests suggests that negative reactions to such tests are not common), but both overt and veiled-purpose integrity tests share a number of characteristics with more general measures of personality.

On the whole, the available evidence supports the use of integrity tests as one component of the complex process of personnel selection, as long as certain limitations of this class of tests are kept in mind. First, like all psychological tests, integrity tests are fallible measures. These tests do not provide a window into a person's soul, and neither do any other tests; rather, they provide some information that must be considered in the light of everything else that is known about an applicant and incumbent. Second, the tests are more valuable for ranking individuals than for screening out those who "fail." Whenever test scores are dichotomous (pass/fail), information is probably being lost, and decisions made about individuals near the cutoff score are especially risky. Third, these tests do not solve all problems involving the integrity of an organization's work force. An organization that relies exclusively on integrity tests for hiring and rejects all low scorers may still experience high rates of theft and counterproductive behavior if the relevant situational factors favor these types of behavior—for example, if there is little security and strong norms support theft or goldbricking. An organization that ignores integrity test scores might have very few problems with dishonesty if the situation is right.

The use of biographical data, scores on more standard personality inventories, or outcomes of interviews to infer integrity has not received the attention currently devoted to integrity tests. In general, all these methods show some promise, but in the final analysis none of them is likely to be more valid or economical than a well-validated integrity test.

CHAPTER SIX

Situational Causes, Correlates, and Methods of Control

In Chapter 1, I noted that honesty in the workplace is affected by characteristics of both people and situations. Chapters 4 and 5 examined person-oriented methods of assessing or deterring dishonesty and deception. The present chapter examines situational causes and correlates of honesty and dishonesty and discusses ways of modifying situations to increase honesty and decrease dishonesty.

This chapter opens by discussing what constitutes a situation and what situational factors are most likely to affect honesty in the workplace. This discussion is structured in terms of three potential processes by which situational factors might influence honesty and dishonesty: (1) by increasing the apparent necessity or attractiveness of dishonest behaviors, (2) by defining norms that either encourage or discourage dishonesty, and (3) by providing or restricting opportunities for dishonest behaviors. Given the importance of normative influences, the development and enforcement of norms is examined in detail, with special attention to situational factors linked to norms that encourage or tolerate various forms of workplace dishonesty. Finally, this chapter examines a variety of strategies for changing the situation in ways that might encourage honesty or discourage dishonesty in the workplace.

Defining Situations

Although security experts have devoted considerable attention to some features of work situations that might promote or deter specific forms of workplace dishonesty (usually theft), managers and behavioral scientists have not devoted sufficient attention to the situational factors that affect honesty in the workplace. For example, whereas integrity testing represents a multimillion dollar industry, it is hard to cite many large-scale attempts to change situational factors—other than those involving physical security and monitoring—thought to affect dishonest behavior in the workplace. One reason for this relative lack of attention to situational or contextual factors is the difficulty in defining exactly what constitutes a "situation."

The term *situation* refers here to a diverse mix of variables in the environment that are potentially relevant to the individual's decision to engage in or refrain from committing specific dishonest acts. The exact variables that define the relevant situation might vary across individuals, over time, across settings, or even as a function of the behavior in question. For example, the situational factors that affect decisions regarding employee theft might be quite different from those that affect decisions regarding mild forms of production deviance. The situational variables that affect workers in one part of an organization might be quite different from those that are relevant in other areas or divisions.

Although situational variables are features of the external environment, it is a mistake to think of the situation as a fixed, objective entity. Rather, situational variables are partly psychological in nature (Magnusson & Endler, 1977). First, the variables that become relevant in defining honest or dishonest behavior in the workplace depend in part on the individual. If general economic conditions motivate employee A to steal but have no effect on employee B's decision to steal or refrain from stealing, these conditions are part of the relevant situation as far as employee A is concerned, but not for employee B. Second, individuals act on their perceptions of environmental variables, not directly on the variables themselves. Two different individuals placed in the same objective environment may perceive substantial differences in their respective situations.

Cleveland and Murphy (1992) suggested that one key to defining situations is to think about the various levels of situational variables that may be affecting behavior at any given point in time (see also Murphy & Cleveland, 1991). In particular, proximal and distal influences are distinguished. Proximal influences are those features of the immediate work situation that directly affect honest or dishonest behavior. Examples include the norms, beliefs, and values of members of the immediate work group, the presence or absence of adequate security, and the availability of materials, goods, information, and the like that can readily be stolen, transferred, or misused. Distal influences are those features of the more general environment that indirectly affect honesty or dishonesty in the workplace. Examples include economic or competitive pressures, legal and procedural sanctions for dishonesty in the workplace (such as organizational policies regarding prosecution or punishment of various forms of dishonesty), societal attitudes toward specific forms of workplace dishonesty (for example, bribery is accepted as a normal part of doing business in many countries), and demand for goods that might be stolen from the workplace. The distinction between proximal and distal factors revolves around the extent to which they are unique to the immediate workplace (co-workers' norms, for example, represent proximal factors) or instead are part of the broader environment in which work takes place (for instance, the tightness of the job market is a distal factor).

The effects of situational variables are often complex, in part because different situational variables might interact. For example, efforts to tighten security might lead to increased perceptions of the risk associated with theft and other dishonest behaviors, but they might also heighten employees' awareness of the value of the merchandise, tools, and the like available in the workplace, thus increasing their temptation to attempt to defeat the security system. A second source of complexity is the presence of competing situational influences. It is likely that in most work settings, some situational variables encourage dishonesty (for instance, lax security), whereas others discourage dishonesty. For example, generally slow economic conditions together with poor security might tempt employees to steal, whereas group norms might deter theft. A third source of complexity is the variability in the strength of the various situational influences. Under normal conditions, most workers probably refrain from serious acts of dishonesty, but strong situational pressures (such as intense competition) may overcome the situational forces that usually deter dishonesty. Whether dishonesty actually occurs might depend on the combined strength of the other personal and situational factors that tend to discourage dishonest behavior.

A final source of complexity in describing situational effects is that situational variables are not completely distinct from the characteristics of the individuals who are part of the immediate or distal environment. Researchers interested in organizational climate have suggested that "the people make the place" (Schneider, 1987). In other words, through the processes of attraction, selection, and attrition, organizations tend to choose and retain specific types of individuals, who in turn define the climate, culture, norms, and other characteristics of organizations. Furthermore, individuals who fit the prevailing characteristics of the organization (those who are similar to other members of the organization in terms of their personality, beliefs, attitudes, and the like) are thought to be more likely to succeed than individuals who are substantially different from most of the other employees in the organization (Rynes & Gerhart, 1990). Therefore, research referring to situational factors is not necessarily limited to objective features of the external environment, or even to individuals' perceptions of those features, but must also consider the characteristics of the people already in the work force.

Situational Variables
Relevant to Workplace Honesty

The best way to organize research on situational variables likely to affect honesty is in terms of how these variables work, rather than in terms of the variables themselves. Figure 6-1 illustrates three distinct processes by which situational variables might affect honesty or dishonesty in the workplace. First, situational factors such as fear of failing in an important project or the need to compete with other organizations or individuals might lead to perceptions that dishonest behavior is necessary, which in turn will increase the likelihood that behavior of this sort will occur. In Chapter 2, I noted that economic need is occasionally, although not often, a factor in workplace dishonesty; economic factors constitute one of many groups of factors that might contribute to perceptions of necessity. Perceptions of necessity are probably more relevant in explaining serious acts of dishonesty, such as theft or misappropriation, than in explaining mild forms of production deviance.

Second, situational factors, such as prevailing societal attitudes toward particular forms of dishonesty and the norms of one's own work group toward those same acts, lead to perceptions that the behavior in question is either acceptable or unacceptable. Some individuals are more strongly affected than others by norms regarding acceptable behavior, but a clear consensus that particular dishonest behaviors are unacceptable to society in general and to the immediate work group should decrease the likelihood that anyone in the work group will engage in those behaviors. Third, factors such as the employer's security system and the consequences of being caught in the act of committing property or production deviance (for example, the employer's policies regarding enforcement and legal penalties for workplace crime) are likely to affect perceptions of the risks associated with specific acts of workplace dishonesty. As with perceptions of necessity, perceptions of risk are probably most relevant to the more serious forms of property deviance, such as theft. However, if an organization carefully monitors individual employees and enforces strict

Figure 6-1 *Ways Situational Factors May Affect Honesty in the Workplace*

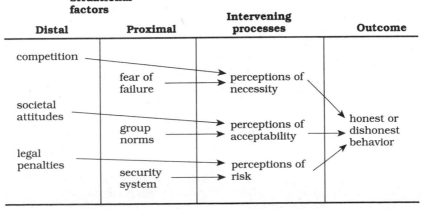

sanctions for acts of production deviance, individuals may see significant risks associated with taking long breaks, making long-distance calls from work, and so on and may avoid these acts.

Perceptions of necessity.   Dishonest behaviors are most likely to be seen as necessary in situations where important goals cannot readily be met through honest means *and* where dishonest behavior significantly increases the likelihood of meeting those goals. For example, in Chapter 2, I noted that one widely cited explanation for corporate corruption and white-collar crime is that managers and executives who face impossible demands or deadlines may see little likelihood of solving their problems without resorting to dishonest behavior. There is too little research to estimate the frequency with which this type of "unsharable problem" actually leads to dishonest behavior in the workplace, but case studies of corporate and white-collar crime often include references to perceptions of overwhelming necessity. Situational factors that lead to perceptions of necessity thus will probably also lead to increased levels of workplace dishonesty.

Perceptions of necessity may be more important in understanding white-collar crime and organizational misconduct than in explaining small thefts by individual employees. Whereas many acts of individual dishonesty are committed for reasons ranging from a desire for revenge against the organization to simple greed, a recurring theme in the anecdotal literature on white-collar crime and organizational misconduct is the idea that the particular dishonest act (for example, price-fixing or fraudulent labeling) was necessary for survival or to keep the organization or division competitive.

Vaughan (1983) cites competitive pressure as one key reason for several forms of organizational misconduct. In situations where a dishonest act, such as falsifying test results, seems to represent the difference between the survival and failure of an organization, the pressure to commit that act might be enormous. In general, when the situation is such that the consequences of *not* committing a dishonest act are grave, the act is likely to be seen as necessary, and if the opportunity arises the act may very well occur.

Perceptions of acceptability.   The belief that certain dishonest behaviors are common, justifiable, and entirely acceptable is a critical determinant of many forms of workplace dishonesty. The perception that a specific act is either acceptable or unacceptable is partly determined by the individual's beliefs, attitudes, and values. As noted in Chapter 5, one foundation for integrity testing is the fact that individuals who are most likely to commit thefts and other counterproductive acts seem to view those behaviors more favorably than do others. Although individual beliefs and attitudes are clearly important, the norms accepted by society in general and by one's immediate co-workers are probably equally important. In particular, there is evidence that informal sanctions from the work group are the single best deterrent to a number of forms of dishonest behaviors in the workplace (Hollinger, 1989; Hollinger & Clark, 1982b, 1983).

Research on attraction–selection–attrition processes (Schneider, 1987) suggests that the norms that characterize organizations and work groups may be highly stable and self-perpetuating, in the sense that there are substantial pressures to select and retain new group members who are similar to the present members of the group in important ways. This research suggests that assessment of the climate, culture, and norms of the organization and of various groups in the organization (through surveys, interviews, and so on) may be critical to controlling dishonesty in the workplace. Norms are resistant to change (although in Chapter 8, I will suggest some ways of encouraging norms that support honesty); therefore it may be very important to understand what behaviors are or are not viewed as acceptable by different sectors of the organization and to target efforts to control dishonesty at those groups who are most inclined to commit serious acts of workplace dishonesty.

Research cited in Chapter 2 suggests that individuals who have not yet learned or accepted the prevailing values and norms in an organization (such as new or younger employees) may be more likely to steal and perhaps to engage in other acts of property and production deviance than more seasoned employees are. This suggests that organizations should pay careful attention to the ways new employees are socialized into the organization. Later in this chapter, and also in Chapter 8, I will examine some of the processes by which norms regarding honesty in the workplace develop and affect behavior.

As in previous sections, it is important to distinguish between perceptions of acceptability and actual acceptance of dishonest behavior by co-workers. Chapter 5 reviewed research showing that individuals who believe that stealing is acceptable and approved by others are themselves more likely to steal. The fact that these beliefs may be misperceptions—in fact, most people strongly disapprove of theft—may not be all that relevant in determining their influence on the individual's behavior.

Perceptions of risk. The apparent risks associated with various forms of workplace dishonesty depend on two distinct sets of situational factors. First, there are factors related to the likelihood of detection. One role of security systems in organizations is to deter acts of property and production deviance by making the apparent risk of detection substantial (Carson, 1977). Highly visible security procedures (such as searches, the posting of uniformed guards, or surveillance by remote cameras) may be more useful in deterring theft and other forms of property and production deviance than in detecting them, whereas more sophisticated but less visible systems (for example, computerized inventory control systems) might be very useful for detecting violations but might not provide an effective deterrent unless employees can be kept aware of the capabilities of such systems.

Second, there are factors related to the consequences of detection. Many organizations are reluctant to prosecute employee theft, especially white-collar theft, and may even be reluctant to punish or sanction the individuals involved. In organizations where the apparent consequences of being caught committing theft or other dishonest acts are minimal, the deterrent value of security and monitoring systems might also be slight.[1]

The likelihood of dishonest behaviors is probably lowest when the perceived likelihood of detection is high *and* the perceived consequences of deception are substantial. However, if either of these factors is compromised (so that the likelihood of detection is low or penalties are minor), the risks associated with dishonest behavior may seem small, and if other personal and situational factors favor dishonesty (for example, if personal attitudes or work-group norms tolerate employee theft), those behaviors may indeed occur.

Situational Influences on Individual and Organizational Misconduct

Although many theories attempt to explain both individual dishonesty in the workplace and misconduct by entire organizations, researchers simply do not know enough about either to say definitely whether the causes of individual and organizational misconduct are similar or dissimilar. However, some features of organizational behavior suggest that the causes of individual versus organizational misconduct may differ. The key reason for this difference is that most forms of organizational misconduct require the active cooperation of many individuals and the passive assent (the refusal to blow the whistle) of many others. Although in isolated cases an individual or a small group of individuals can cause an organization to violate laws or regulations, most instances of organizational misconduct—such as price-fixing, fraudulent mislabeling of products, or alteration of test data (as in doctoring the X rays of welds in a construction project)—require that *many* individuals become involved in or at least accept dishonest acts. The cooperation of large numbers of individuals implies that the behaviors in question are likely to be viewed as acceptable (according to

---

[1] Once again, keep in mind that perceptions of risk may be more important than actual risk levels.

the prevailing norms) and that the perceived probability of detection or punishment is likely to seem low.

Vaughan's (1983) description of a case of Medicare fraud involving an entire chain of drugstores illustrates many of the situational and societal factors that make it possible for organizations to engage in large-scale, ongoing criminal activities. First, she notes that in this case many regulatory agencies were responsible for overseeing the activities of these stores, and competition and a lack of cooperation between these agencies made it unlikely that the illegal acts would be readily discovered. Indeed, the exposure of the fraudulent activities carried out at these stores was quite accidental. Second, economic competition between drugstore chains created pressure to inflate profits. Third, there was no real respect for the rules. Many of the legal rules and regulations governing the stores were not directly related to the norms or values of the organizations, but rather were regarded as arbitrary and pointless requirements. There was no consensus that the legal requirements in question were right and proper in and of themselves; instead it was believed that these requirements should be followed as long as the risks of detection were unacceptably high.

Vaughan's (1983) analysis of this particular case suggests that the relationship between the norms and values of the organization and the regulations that govern its activities is fundamental in understanding corporate wrongdoing. She notes that "as normative support for legitimate procedures erodes, organizations . . . resort to technically expedient but unlawful behavior" (p. 62); this behavior is especially likely when competitive pressures are intense. Her conclusion was that normative support for honest behavior is necessary to help resist the pressures to engage in dishonesty created by a combination of strong financial competition and lax regulation.

Normative Influences on Workplace Honesty and Dishonesty

The effects of the prevailing norms of society, the organization, and the work group on dishonesty in the workplace depends on two somewhat distinct facets of the norms themselves: their direction and their strength. First, norms might support all forms of honesty and discourage all forms of dishonesty. It is more likely, however, that norms will support most forms of honesty and tolerate some specific forms of dishonesty. Even among groups whose norms are likely to be especially strict (such as priests), probably some rules can be safely bent or broken without sanction from co-workers. Finally, even in the most corrupt organizations, it is unlikely that workplace norms will ever support or tolerate all forms of dishonesty; there is usually honor even among thieves.

Work-group norms define which behaviors are likely to be regarded as either truly honest or technically dishonest but in fact acceptable (taking long lunch breaks might be an example of the latter). Some technically dishonest behaviors will be accepted by most work groups, whereas other behaviors (such as stealing from co-workers) are likely to be viewed as unacceptable in virtually all circumstances. The range of behaviors regarded as acceptable and unacceptable will probably vary across organizations, divisions, and work groups; understanding the differences in norms across and within organizations might prove extremely useful for pinpointing areas that pose high risks of workplace dishonesty. All other things being equal, workplace dishonesty is most likely to occur when the prevailing norms imply that a wide range of dishonest behaviors are acceptable.

Second, a group's norms can have either a strong or a weak impact on the behavior of group members. At one extreme, the norms of cohesive, high-status groups might virtually dictate the behavior of most group members (Hackman, 1976; Sherif & Sherif, 1969). On the other hand, norms may have little impact, especially in cases where individuals do not identify with the group, where norms are unclear

Box 6-1   *The Hester Prynne Sanction*

One problem in dealing with corporate corruption is the difficulty in effectively punishing corporations. Corporate officers are rarely jailed, and fines are eventually passed on to consumers. As a result, the situational pressures regulation imposes on corporate corruption can be somewhat weak. French (1985) suggested that the "Hester Prynne sanction" be used to punish corporate offenses (see also Risser, 1989).

Hester Prynne, the heroine of Nathaniel Hawthorne's *The Scarlet Letter*, was unjustly condemned to wear a mark of shame (in the form of a large red "A" on her bosom) as a punishment for adultery. French (1985) suggested that a similar shame-based punishment be applied to corporations found guilty of corruption. In particular, he suggested that they be sentenced to finance and carry out a court-supervised advertising campaign publicizing their misconduct and the harm it had caused.

Although the suggestion has merit, the Hester Prynne sanction (along with most other proposals for punishing corporations) has the unfortunate feature of punishing the innocent as well as the guilty. Suppose you decided to invest your entire pension fund in stock of the XYZ corporation, and the next day you saw a commercial, produced and paid for by the XYZ corporation, advertising their wrongdoings—you would probably not think that the Hester Prynne sanction was such a good idea after all.

and inconsistent, or where groups have low status or cohesion. It is also likely that group norms have more influence on some group members than on others. In particular, individuals with high status in the group are usually subject to less scrutiny and control than those with lower status (Hackman, 1976; Sherif & Sherif, 1969). Finally, work groups are often characterized by two separate subgroups, an in-group and an out-group (Dansereau, Graen, & Haga, 1975; Linden, & Graen, 1980; Linville & Jones, 1980). In-group members receive more attention and rewards from group leaders and are given more responsibility and autonomy. More important, in-group members are given more slack, in the sense that their behavior is under less scrutiny and control than that of out-group members. It is likely that norms concerning workplace dishonesty have more influence on the behavior of members of the out-group than on members of the in-group.

A substantial amount of research on deviant behavior has examined the effects of anomie, or normlessness (Merton, 1964); this research suggests that deviant behavior is especially likely to occur when no clear countervailing norms exist. In theory, dishonest behavior might become even more prevalent when norms exist that strongly encourage it. However, it will be unusual for any group other than one made up of career criminals to have such norms. Although work-group norms might strongly support some types of production deviance that have become customary in the workplace (for example, if everyone takes long breaks and lunches, new workers might be strongly encouraged to do the same, even though the contract might call for shorter break periods), there are probably few examples of workplace norms that require work-group members to engage in serious acts of dishonesty.

Figure 6-2 illustrates the potential combined effects of the direction and strength of norms on dishonesty in the workplace. At one extreme, parish priests work in a context where strong norms support a high standard of honesty; one reason that incidents of institutional fraud in some churches make the news is that such incidents run so strongly counter to the norms expected for this workplace. At the other extreme, the prevailing norms might strongly support dishonesty. If the reports of longtime members of some police departments that are riddled with corruption can be believed, elaborate codes of conduct in these departments strongly regulate the "work" of the members and define the types of bribes, payoffs, and the like that are customary and expected.

In some cases, norms might be so poorly defined that they have little impact on the behavior of organizational members. For example, in a new plant, it might take some time for norms regarding honesty and dishonesty to develop, particularly if the plant is staffed primarily by new hires rather than by individuals transferred from some other part of the organization. Even after norms have developed, it may take more time for them to acquire any real force. However, as individuals start to identify with the work group and the organization, norms regarding honesty in the workplace may become increasingly important determinants of individual employees' behavior.

If the hypothesis described above is correct, you might expect to see a wide variation in workplace dishonesty at the outset in a startup plant, and it might take time for a stable pattern of honesty or dishonesty to develop. Once norms regarding theft and other forms of workplace dishonesty develop and achieve some strength, individual differences in workplace dishonesty may diminish. If the norms that do develop tend to discourage theft and other dishonest behaviors, it may be possible to substantially reduce the incidence and seriousness of workplace dishonesty. As I will suggest in Chapter 8, efforts to increase employees' commitment to and identification with the organization, and with its norms, might be useful in controlling workplace dishonesty, especially if norms that support honest behavior and discourage dishonesty can be instilled.

Finally, in some work groups, existing norms may generally support honesty, but the power of the norms to affect behavior may be minimal. For example, organizations that are faced with seasonal demands (such as tax preparation services) hire temporary employees during times of peak demand. The norms of the organization might very well support honesty, but because the temporary employees have little attachment to the organization, these norms may have little impact on the behavior of those employees.

Figure 6-2 *Influence of Direction and Strength of Norms on Workplace Dishonesty*

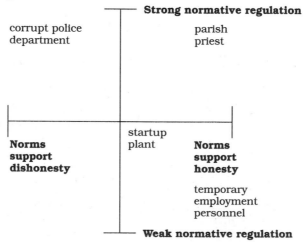

Development of Norms Supporting Dishonesty

Given the frequency and seriousness of employee theft and other forms of property and production deviance, it seems reasonable to conclude that the norms of many organizations and work groups must support or at least tolerate some forms of dishonesty. Although there are always some individuals willing to violate group norms, it is difficult to believe that behavior that is carried out at least occasionally by as much as 40 to 75% of the work force (see Chapter 1 for research on the frequency of property and production deviance) would nevertheless run counter to the prevailing norms. If the norms of organizations and work groups sometimes sanction dishonest behavior, why do they do so? If dishonesty is, in general, viewed negatively in society, how is it that norms sanctioning—and sometimes encouraging—dishonesty develop in the workplace?

Box 6-2   *Rate-Busting*

This chapter discusses a number of ways in which the norms of the organization could encourage either honesty or dishonesty. The norms of many work groups encourage production deviance—for example, doing as little work as possible short of getting fired. Other work groups' norms encourage a fair day's work for a fair day's pay. However, even these groups are likely to use their norms to restrict members' output.

Individuals who work at a frantic pace and substantially outproduce others are often labeled "rate-busters" and pressured to bring their production more closely in line with that of their colleagues (Sherif & Sherif, 1969). The academic equivalent of a rate-buster is the individual who "ruins the curve" by scoring extremely high on exams. My experience as a professor suggests that these students feel many of the same pressures as those applied to rate-busters in work settings, particularly when the class is small. In both academic and work settings, doing your absolute best is sometimes in conflict with another widely accepted norm—the belief that you shouldn't make your colleagues look bad.

Rate-busting is usually defined in relative terms (that is, out-producing your colleagues), which suggests that the rate-buster is not always the culprit. If most work-group members engage in extensive production deviance, the individual who gives a fair day's work for a fair day's pay may be treated as a rate-buster. It seems reasonable to believe that pressures to stop rate-busting will be more intense when everyone else is a slacker and the rate-buster is just doing his or her job than those pressures will be when the rate-buster is a better-than-average performer; but in both cases, variance from the average level of performance may lead to pressure to conform.

One possible answer is suggested by Schneider's (1987) research on the ways in which the types of people attracted to, selected, and retained by an organization define the climate and culture of the organization. It is possible that some organizations, for whatever reason, attract and select people with little regard for honesty. If Schneider's hypothesis is correct, these individuals could eventually set the tone for the organization, so that their personal shortcomings (here, their tolerance for many forms of dishonesty) eventually become part of the climate and culture of the organization. This type of organization will probably continue to seek out dishonest individuals and corrupt the few honest individuals who join the organization. In Trevino and Youngblood's (1990) terms, the selection of a few "bad apples" could eventually turn the organization into a "bad barrel."

While the process described above probably does explain how norms supporting dishonesty develop in some organizations, it clearly does not account for the widespread acceptance of several forms of workplace dishonesty. To understand how these latter norms develop, it is necessary to consider several characteristics of organizations that either encourage such norms or allow such norms to operate. It is likely that the organization's structure, rules and policies, and climate and culture all contribute to the development of these norms. Perhaps the most important reason for the development of such norms, however, is the widespread use of unofficial rewards, which tend to blur the distinction between acceptable and unacceptable forms of behavior in the workplace.

Effects of organizational structure.   Hosmer (1987) suggests that the structure of U.S. corporations might be partly to blame for the rash of fraud, misleading claims, and crime attributed to even the best managed corporations in the last decade (during 1985, *all* of the ten largest defense contractors faced federal criminal investigations). He notes that virtually all large corporations are diversified (that is, they operate in more than one industry) and that they are often organized into a number of semiautonomous strategic business units (SBUs), which represent related product divisions that act independently within a single industry. For example, in 1987, General Electric comprised 73 separate SBUs.

As the organization grows and diversifies, corporate management is likely to have less knowledge and understanding of individual SBUs. In the worst case scenario, corporate management may come to resemble an absentee landlord, who doesn't know or care about the properties or about how tenants come up with the rent money, as long as the bottom line continues to look good. This sort of management creates a condition that is highly conducive to ethical violations—a lack of awareness of the actual operations of the organization on the part of the people who are supposedly running things (Baucus, 1989; Finney & Lesieur, 1982).

The implicit competition between SBUs in many organizations creates further pressure for a wide variety of ethical violations. Organizations must make strategic decisions about which SBUs will receive or lose critical resources and support, and U.S. corporations are notorious for comparing SBUs primarily in terms of their short-term return on investment. As corporate management becomes more remote, it is likely to see and understand little other than the return achieved by each SBU, putting tremendous pressure on the managers of those SBUs to produce good numbers. Unfortunately, it is often easiest to produce those numbers by cutting corners or engaging in a variety of creative billing and accounting practices.

Gellerman (1989) suggests that upper management bears a heavy responsibility for the ethical behavior of employees, particularly lower-level managers, and that the executives of an organization are responsible for creating conditions that minimize the likelihood of ethical violations. This responsibility may become harder and harder to carry out as corporations become larger and more diverse, but the responsibility still remains. Corporate managers who demand results without creating conditions that substantially discourage the use of unethical methods to produce those results are ultimately answerable for the ethical violations that are bound to occur.

The same structural conditions (such as unmanageable size or diversification) that encourage unethical behavior in organizations will also encourage the development of dysfunctional norms. If executives and managers feel pressured to engage in unethical behaviors, they are likely eventually to rationalize their actions and come to believe that such behaviors are in fact acceptable. This process becomes a vicious cycle in which unethical behavior leads to norms tolerating or encouraging that sort of behavior, which in turn will lead to more unethical behavior.

Management theorists and consultants have expressed increasing interest in "flat" organizations, which are characterized by relatively few managers or levels of management and by work groups or functional units exhibiting high levels of autonomy. Although this type of structure is probably beneficial in many ways, it could also have several drawbacks related to the control of workplace dishonesty. In particular, such a structure could establish an environment where there is substantial pressure to behave dishonestly, and little corporate awareness of dishonesty, particularly if different units of the organization are in strong competition for important resources. Organizations that adopt flat structures should devote extra attention to efforts to monitor and maintain the ethical climate of the various business units that make up the corporation.

Effects of organizational policies, rules, and climate. It is virtually impossible to codify all forms of organizational behavior into a binding set of rules. Jansen and Von Glinow (1985) note that "the lay observation that an organization would come to a grinding halt if everyone narrowly followed the rules expresses the need for inconsistency and maneuvering room" (p. 815). However, ambiguity regarding the rules and standards that govern behavior in the organization can promote unethical behavior. The problem is particularly acute in organizations with reward systems that encourage behavior incongruent with the social and ethical norms espoused by the officers of the company. For example, an organization might publish a comprehensive code of ethics but might reward rather than punish individuals who violate that code, particularly if the violation results in a short-term gain for the organization.

Organizational reward systems often promote ethically questionable behaviors. Gellerman (1989) notes that there are strong inducements for unethical behavior in organizations where there are unusually high rewards for good performance, unusually severe punishments for poor performance, or both. Whether rewards are high or punishment is severe, there is strong pressure to report good results and therefore strong temptation to cut corners, misrepresent results, or use some dishonest means to enhance performance and minimize or hide mistakes. He cites examples from the stock and commodities markets in the 1980s, where vast fortunes could be made by relatively inexperienced individuals and where frauds and crimes of a gigantic scale were eventually revealed.

Ambiguous rules and policies can also indirectly support norms that tolerate employee theft or other forms of property and production deviance. Hollinger and Clark (1983) and others note that organizations often do not adequately define exactly what constitutes theft or what its consequences will be. For example, workers often feel it is within their rights to take scrap, spare materials, and other small, inexpensive objects (Horning, 1970). Organizations often fail to clarify their position regarding the use of materials, tools, company time, and so on for personal purposes. Similarly, organizations need to decide on the consequences of various forms of theft or deviance and to stick by their decisions. If workers see that managers who visibly pad their expense accounts never receive any sanction, they are likely to conclude that some forms of theft are indeed tolerated by the organization and to develop norms that tolerate these behaviors.

Cherrington and Cherrington (1985) present evidence that the climate of an organization can be related to the incidence of theft. They examined three retail chains and suggested that the climate of the chain with the lowest shortages could be characterized by a well-defined code of ethics, effective internal auditing controls, and a pleasant work environment. In contrast, the company with the highest shortages was characterized by a more negative climate, including higher levels of dissatisfaction, harsher systems of discipline, and more frequent checks on employees. Unfortunately, determining whether there is any causal relationship between climate and theft is difficult. It is possible that the positive climate helps to reduce theft and that the negative climate leads to theft. However, it is equally possible that frequent thefts make the climate more negative and that the negative features of the company with the greatest shortages are a response to rather than a cause of theft.

Organizational culture is cited as a potential cause of a variety of unethical behaviors in addition to theft. In particular, the culture of an organization is thought to be a critical influence on the ethical or unethical behaviors of managers and on violations carried out by the firm as a whole (for example, fraudulent cost overruns, knowing distribution of unsafe products; see Baucus, 1989; Trevino, 1986).

Victor and Cullen (1987) have shown that the ethical climate of organizations can be reliably measured, and that ethical climates vary extensively. However, empirical research linking ethical climates and cultures to organizational wrongdoing is still in its infancy. A number of compelling case studies suggest such a link (Baucus, 1989), but there have been too few studies to date to establish a firm causal link between the climate or culture of an organization and organizational wrongdoing.

It is likely that norms regarding honesty in the workplace represent an intervening variable that links the general climate and culture of an organization with specific incidents of dishonesty in the workplace. Organizational climate and culture could lead to work-group norms that tolerate or encourage dishonesty in two distinct ways. First, if the climate encourages competition and disregard for the rules, norms may develop that support organizational misconduct and personal dishonesty *on behalf of* the organization. In other words, employees may come to accept the implicit idea that winning is more important than honesty and may develop norms that encourage cutting corners or using dishonest means to succeed or to appear successful.

Second, if the climate leads to dissatisfaction and distrust, norms may develop that support forms of property and production deviance that constitute crimes and other dishonest acts *against* the organization. Chapter 2 discussed research demonstrating the link between job satisfaction, organizational commitment, and dishonesty (particularly theft). If the climate of the organization contributes to employees' feelings of distrust or dissatisfaction, ample evidence shows that acts of property and production deviance are likely to follow. It seems reasonable to conclude that norms tolerating these acts will also develop.

Unofficial Rewards

One source of difficulty in defining employee theft is the fact that almost all employees appear to get some of their compensation in the form of unofficial rewards (Ditton, 1977). These rewards represent privileges and the like that are not officially sanctioned but in fact are widely accepted as an employee's customary right. Perhaps the most common form of unofficial reward is payment in kind. Workers may take home materials or tools from the workplace, or may use company time, tools, and material to work on personal projects.

Dalton (1981) and others (for instance, Mars, 1973) present numerous examples of ways in which employees extract payment in kind. However, the practice of extracting unofficial rewards is not restricted to blue-collar workers. Managers and executives have a number of opportunities to obtain such rewards, ranging from padded expense accounts to the personal use of bonuses and such that airlines and other companies award to frequent business travelers.

It is widely believed that employee theft is partly a form of compensation for low wages (Ditton, 1977; Goode, 1978). Theft in low-paying jobs is not simply a matter of making up for the money that a higher-paying job would provide but is also a way to restore the worker's sense of equity. Because theft allows the worker to exact revenge, the value of employee theft to a worker who feels underappreciated may be considerably higher than the dollar value of the goods, materials, and time stolen. In a highly controversial paper, Zeitlin (1971) suggested that organizations should tolerate a certain amount of employee theft, because the dollar value of the amount stolen is less than it would cost to change the conditions that lead people to steal. For example, he suggested that an underpaid accountant might get as much satisfaction from stealing $2000 per year as he or she would get from from a $5000 raise. The opportunity to steal from one's employer might represent an important form of unofficial reward, and if the amount likely to be stolen is reasonably small, Zeitlin suggested that workers should have that opportunity. In Chapters 2 and 3, I noted a potential difficulty with Zeitlin's suggestion: once an organization develops a policy of tolerating a certain amount of theft, it may be difficult to draw the line that defines unacceptable theft. For example, an organization that has a policy of doing nothing about $200 thefts may be hard pressed to defend its decision to prosecute $210 thefts.

The availability of unofficial rewards varies substantially from job to job. Many executives and managers have opportunities to take advantage of a wide array of unofficial rewards that are virtually unavailable to nonmanagerial employees (such as padding their expense accounts). Nonmanagerial employees, on the other hand, often have more opportunities to steal materials, tools, and the like and to engage in so-called time theft. Jobs that present large numbers of opportunities for obtaining unofficial rewards (often through some form of workplace dishonesty) require a higher level of scrutiny than those in which the opportunity for this type of dishonesty is rare or nonexistent.

Norms and the invisible wage structure.   The widespread existence of pilferage and various forms of time theft in some particular jobs (such as that of a waiter) suggests that this form of unofficial reward is not the result of character flaws of the individuals employed or shortcomings in security and alarm systems. In a provocative paper, Ditton (1977) suggested that complex systems of perks and pilferage rights have evolved in many jobs and that these systems represent part of an invisible wage structure whose roots can be traced back to medieval times.[2] In most jobs, clear norms set out the amount and type of pilferage that is acceptable, and individuals who stay within those norms do not think of themselves as thieves (Altheide et al., 1978; Goode, 1978). Ditton (1977) and Mars (1973) describe the "fiddle" that represents a form of institutionalized pilferage practiced in many restaurants and hotels. In this system, pilferage from the organization is regarded as a customary part of a person's wages, whereas stealing money or valuables from customers is regarded as theft and is socially unacceptable.

Although norms regarding theft vary from organization to organization and from group to group, some theft may be predicted using the concept of "uncertain ownership" (Horning, 1970). In other words, some materials and property clearly belong to the workers (for instance, their car keys), and some clearly belongs to the organization (for example, the engine of the car coming down the assembly line). Other property that is small, copious, and inexpensive, such as scrap, nails, screws, and small parts often falls into the class of uncertain ownership, and depending on the norms of the work group, this property may be regarded as fair game for the taking, regardless of company rules to the contrary. Horning (1970) notes that stealing property that clearly belongs to other workers or to the company is usually forbidden by work-group norms, but that these same norms often allow or even encourage the theft of property whose ownership is seen as uncertain.

Granting unofficial rewards.   In the cases cited above, unofficial rewards are taken by the individual, often without the knowledge or approval of that person's superiors. However, in many circumstances, a manager or executive might want to go outside of official channels to

---

[2] Perks represent customary privileges, such as employee discounts. Pilferage can be thought of as a tacitly accepted perk that is technically a theft but is not sanctioned as one. The usual distinction between pilferage and theft is in terms of the consequences of getting caught. An individual caught pilfering usually must stop but is not punished.

grant some form of unofficial reward. Dalton (1981) presents several examples of situations in which unofficial rewards might be called for—in place of a promotion or raise, as a bonus for doing extra work, as a compensation for setbacks (such as a defeat in a matter being voted on), or to socialize the person being rewarded to understand the unofficial reward system. Especially if the official reward system is fairly rigid and inflexible, the ability to distribute unofficial rewards may be critical in encouraging the behaviors we refer to as "organizational citizenship," as in helping others with their work (see Bateman and Organ, 1983, and Brief and Motowidlo, 1986, for reviews).

Unofficial rewards and norms.   The unofficial reward system that exists in most organizations affects norms in two ways. First, if unofficial rewards are customary or are part of the invisible reward structure—for example, waiters may receive low pay based on the assumption that they pocket small amounts and do not report their tips on tax forms—such rewards will be regarded as the worker's right, not as unacceptable behaviors. It may be very difficult to stop workers from exercising such "rights," and any attempt to do so is likely to be met with indignation rather than remorse.

Second, the use of unofficial rewards by the organization as a way of bypassing official rules, policies, and restrictions creates ambiguity and a general disregard for those same rules. When managers or executives bend the rules to grant unofficial rewards, they probably encourage others to bend those same rules, and they make it difficult to punish some workers for taking unofficial rewards at the same time that higher-level employees are granting them.

Enforcement of Norms

Figure 6-2 suggests that the worst possible situation for an organization is when norms exist in the organization that support or tolerate many forms of dishonesty *and* these norms are strongly enforced—that is, individual employees are punished for *not* engaging in workplace dishonesty. Although this scenario may seem farfetched, it actually characterizes many cases of whistle-blowing, especially when the whistle-blower reports organizational wrongdoing to some external agency (see Chapter 2). Virtually every case study of external whistle-blowing presents examples of individuals being punished and shunned for refusing to engage in dishonest behavior. Returning to the example of corruption in police forces, the experiences of individuals such as Frank Serpico in the New York Police Department suggest that whistle-blowing can be downright dangerous.

The best case scenario for an organization is when the prevailing norms support honesty *and* these norms are strongly enforced. In such a case, work groups may provide their own informal security system. Because it is more difficult to deceive co-workers (especially in cases where acts of property or production deviance can be carried out only in their presence) than to deceive many security systems, the enforcement of norms supporting honesty may be the most effective method of controlling dishonest behavior in the workplace. It is useful, then, to understand the ways in which work groups enforce their norms and group and individual characteristics that lead to effective or ineffective enforcement.

Methods of enforcement.   The methods used to enforce group norms depend in part on whether the group is formally or informally structured. A formal group, such as the Elks or the Veterans of Foreign Wars, may employ formal sanctions—ranging from loss of status or privileges to expulsion from the group—to deal with serious violations of group norms. Informal groups, such as the group of co-workers in one's immediate work environment, do not have the power to apply such formal sanctions, but they nevertheless have a variety of highly effective means of enforcing their norms. Hackman (1976) suggests that the informal groups have power to enforce their norms through the control of both information and rewards.

First, work groups are critical sources of both task-related and social information. Many types of work require the active cooperation of co-workers, and the refusal of co-workers to give someone the assistance and information needed to do his or her job can be a powerful means of enforcing group norms. Groups are also the source of many rewards, ranging from work-related rewards, such as production bonuses, to the social rewards of group membership itself and the liking and approval of group members. The ability and willingness of the group to withhold or dispense these rewards provides a potentially powerful means of norm enforcement.

The method of enforcement may depend on the seriousness of the violation. Clear violation of a well-accepted and important group norm (for example, the norm that you do not steal from group members) may result in serious deliberation by the group, with a formal decision to apply sanctions. Violation of a less important norm, or a norm that is less clearly defined, may result in the informal application of sanctions by some group members, with no concerted effort by the group to force compliance. As was noted earlier, the method of norm enforcement will also depend in part on characteristics of both the individual involved and the group whose norms have been violated.

Effects of characteristics of groups and their members.   Group norms have their strongest effect on individual members when groups are: (1) attractive, (2) cohesive, and (3) powerful (Festinger, Schachter, & Back, 1950; Sherif & Sherif, 1969). For example, an organization such as the Marine Corps has very high status in the eyes of many individuals, and engages in a variety of activities that increase the organization's cohesiveness. An example is that the stress of boot camp tends to increase graduates' sense of cohesiveness and identification with the Corps. The organization has the power to impose a wide range of formal and informal sanctions on members who violate norms. As a result, the norms of this particular group have a powerful influence on the behavior of most of its members.

The power of informal groups such as a work group is partly a function of its attractiveness and cohesiveness. In other words, the sanctions that might be imposed by the work group on members who violate its norms are most potent when the individual identifies strongly with the group. If you have no interest in and little interaction with your co-workers, their norms regarding honesty in the workplace are likely to have little impact on your behavior.

Two types of individual characteristics affect the degree to which group norms regulate individual behavior. First, as noted earlier, the individual's position in the group affects the degree to which specific norms apply. High-status individuals are not subject to the same regulations as apply to others, and behaviors that are forbidden to low-status individuals may be tolerated if the individual has achieved formal or informal rank and position in the group (Sherif & Sherif, 1969). In general, the higher an individual's status in the group, the wider the range of behaviors defined as acceptable (Hackman, 1976).

Second, a number of individual differences, such as personality traits (for example, need for affiliation) and gender, may affect one's tendency to comply with rules and norms. For example, there is evidence that females are, on the whole, more compliant, and that a few personality traits are reliably linked with compliance (Lippa, 1990). However, in the case of both gender and personality, the links are generally weak. On the whole, the available research suggests that one's role and status within the group have a greater influence on compliance with norms than do individual difference variables.

Controlling Honesty and Dishonesty by Manipulating the Situation

Several strategies organizations use to encourage honesty or discourage dishonesty involve changing critical features of the situation. The most obvious example is provided by security and monitoring systems, which are designed in part to increase the apparent risks associated with dishonest behaviors such as theft or production deviance. There are, however, many other ways in which a situation might be changed in order to decrease dishonesty or increase honesty. For example, when employees encounter severe financial problems such as gambling losses or catastrophic illness, they may turn to theft if no other means of coping with the problem is available to them. Organizations might reduce the perceived necessity of theft by providing services such as financial counseling, low-cost loans, or insurance to help reduce the pressures created by financial problems. In fact, many organizations include these types of services in their Employee Assistance Programs.

In addition to security systems, this section discusses three specific programs designed to reduce employee theft by manipulating situational variables. The first of these attempts to increase awareness of employee theft; the second provides incentives to report thefts; and the third is designed to provide less costly and destructive alternatives to the types of property and production deviance common in many organizations.

Security Systems

Carson (1977) notes that the major goal of security systems in organizations should be deterrence rather than apprehension of thieves. A wide array of procedures are used to enhance security in organizations, including guards and uniformed security personnel; perimeter security (fences, lighting, and security patrols); locks and barriers; checkpoints and key controls (such as time clocks and key and card-entry systems); badges, passes, and identification systems; physical separation of distinct functions or areas through which material assets must pass; periodic audits of company assets; cargo seals; and counter-espionage systems to guard against unwanted disclosure of trade secrets (Carson, 1977; Curtis, 1973; Fennelly, 1989; Finnerman, 1981; Keogh, 1981; Strobl, 1978; Walsh & Healy, 1973).

Sapse, Shenkin, and Sapse (1980) present an interesting history of police forces and guard services. Although the use of guards and uniformed security personnel is common, this approach is not without its risks, especially if unqualified individuals are hired. Carson (1977) notes that at one point, the New York Port Authority reported that they caught guards stealing more often than the guards caught others stealing. When you consider the nature of the guard's job, perhaps this phenomenon is understandable: guards often are poorly paid and have few co-worker contacts (particularly if they work during hours when the shop floor is inactive), and their jobs can be extremely boring. This type of job is not likely to promote a high level of commitment, satisfaction, or other attitudes that help to minimize employee theft.

Security audits.   The first step in designing a security system is a thorough audit of potential security risks. This assessment includes a wide range of factors, often starting with the architecture and site layout (Burstein, 1986). Both the physical setting (including such things as fences and lighting) and the nature of the work itself are considered in identifying points at which crimes of various sorts are most likely to occur or to be deterred.

Security experts often use questionnaires, checklists, and flow-charts to identify security risks (Broder, 1984; Carson, 1977; Tweedy, 1989). After analyzing the proper flow of materials, cash, documents, and individuals through the organization, potential trouble spots and optimal checkpoints can be located.

The most basic task of security systems is to monitor and control the movement of people and materials. Security audits assess the flow of both people and materials, and suggest appropriate points for either restricting unnecessary movement (for example, by separating production facilities from offices to reduce movement between the two) or for keeping track of necessary movements.

Computer applications.   Computers are playing an increasing role in both the commission and prevention of acts of workplace dishonesty. On the one hand, the use of computers has either spawned or facilitated several types of crime, such as the theft of information and the unauthorized transfer of funds, both of which are more easily done by computer than through other media. On the other hand, computers form the backbone of many advanced security systems and often play a critical role in processing information regarding inventory shortfalls, breaches of physical security, unauthorized access, and the like.

Most crimes committed with the help of computers involve theft or improper transfer of money, property, or services (Tweedy, 1989). Other threats include theft of information, alteration or unauthorized access to data stored in the computer, or the loss of computer services (for example, through computer viruses). Schweitzer (1987) described several classes of computer programs or programming techniques used in committing computer crimes. Examples include such exotic-sounding threats as (1) a trojan horse, or a covert program embedded in a normal operating program that causes changes in the data base, system shutdowns, or other similar problems; (2) a salami, or a small program change that causes problems unlikely to be noticed at a single point in time but that, over time and taken together, become substantial (such as deducting one cent from everyone else's paychecks and transferring it to one's own); (3) a logic bomb, or a code inserted into a program that causes catastrophic failure (such as erasing a hard drive) when triggered; and (4) a masquerade, or a program that convinces the computer that the programmer is someone else, usually as a way of gaining unauthorized access to the computer.

Tweedy (1989) discusses the use of computers in security. First, there are a number of specialized programs and applications designed to enhance the security of computers themselves, ranging from password protection systems to programs that detect and remove specific computer viruses. Second, computers make it easier to create integrated security systems that link perimeter sensors, inventory controls, entry control systems, and other methods used to track the movement of people and objects in and out of the premises.

Surveillance and spies.   The practice of using in-house surveillance, often by employing undercover operatives to help uncover various forms of theft and property deviance, has a long and varied history. The systematic use of undercover operatives in U.S. organizations can be traced to the employment of Pinkerton detectives to infiltrate labor unions and to investigate quasi-criminal organizations such as the Molly Maguires, who allegedly terrorized coal mining operations in Pennsylvania during the 19th century. Today, the use of spies and undercover operatives is widely recommended (Carson, 1977; Fennelly, 1989) and is thought to be increasing (Kovach, 1985; Peterson & Carlson, 1987).[3]

Employees working at computer terminals, at high-tech cash registers, or on the phone are increasingly subject to electronic surveillance (Cook, 1988). It has become more common for organizations to use computers and video cameras to monitor attendance, lateness, speed of work (for example, number of computer keystrokes a worker performs per minute), length and frequency of breaks, and so on, leading to the widespread feeling that "Big Brother is watching" (Brophy, 1986; Stone & Stone, 1990). In retail stores, the same technology used to deter shoplifting can be used to detect internal theft and, possibly, to monitor individual salespeople's performance (Abend, 1989). Concern about electronic monitoring of employees has led to the introduction of federal legislation substantially limiting electronic monitoring and other similar forms of surveillance, such as the proposed Privacy for Consumers and Workers Act.

Surveillance methods may involve searches of employees' desks, lockers, or work areas. Such searches raise a number of potentially complex legal issues because of the potential for violations of privacy.

---

[3] Kovach's (1985) article illustrated some of the difficulties involved in determining exactly how widespread the practice of using undercover operatives actually is. He notes that 54% of the companies responding to one survey employ or have employed professional undercover operatives posing as workers. However, little detail is given regarding the number or type of companies surveyed or the response rate. Thus, it is difficult to tell whether the figure of 54% corresponds at all to organizations' actual usage of undercover operatives.

The complexity of these issues is magnified by the fact that states vary widely in the extent to which they recognize the privacy rights of employees (Mendelsohn & Morrison, 1988). For example, a search of an employee's desk—which is, after all, the employer's property—may or may not be permissible, depending on the applicable state laws and the customary practices in the workplace regarding privacy.

Using Signs, Reminders, and Feedback to Reduce Theft

Glasscock, Deckner, and Mahan (1991) reviewed several studies in which signs were used as part of a program to combat employee theft. For example, studies showed that posting signs identifying what merchandise had been stolen in the previous week, or how much cash was missing, seemed to reduce theft substantially. There are several possible explanations for the effectiveness of this technique, including the possibility that it heightens all employees' awareness of theft, or that the thieves learn that management knows what is stolen and possibly which employees are likely to be involved in the thefts. In any case, this technique seems to be highly cost-effective. Its effectiveness may be enhanced when it is combined with positive feedback and incentives. Gaetani and Johnson (1983) found that posting graphs praising employees for progress in reducing shrinkage, together with modest incentives for good performance in this area, seemed to lead to considerable reduction in apparent theft.

Although it is likely that signs providing feedback about the amount of shrinkage, theft, and wastage helps to reduce these drains on an organization, it is not necessary to incorporate such information in the sign to affect the rate of theft. A number of communities in the United States, Great Britain, and Japan have experimented with innovative techniques to remind potential thieves or violators that they run substantial risks. The simplest technique is to display cardboard cutouts or mannequins dressed as police or security officers. Substantial evidence demonstrates that this technique can reduce speeding— several Japanese cities post such mannequins near highways—and shoplifting.

The use of signs and other forms of public feedback probably affects both the apparent risks of theft, property deviance, and so on and the apparent acceptability of these behaviors. For example, by posting a sign each week tracking the amount of shrinkage, management is reminding employees that (1) it is sufficiently concerned about this behavior to take steps to reduce it and (2) it is paying attention to the amount and type of shrinkage. In contrast, an organization that does nothing about shrinkage is sending the message that it is not overly concerned with theft or waste (which implies that these behaviors may be acceptable) and that it is not carefully monitoring the sources of shrinkage (which implies that the risk of engaging in these behaviors is minimal).

Rewards for Reporting Dishonesty

Although employees are often aware of theft by their co-workers, they often have no incentive to report it. Indeed, given the fairly universal norm against "tattling," employees may have a fairly strong incentive to keep quiet. One way to increase employees' willingness to report incidents of production and property deviance is to provide fairly substantial rewards for doing so. For example, Glasscock, Deckner, and Mahan (1991) report that some stores provide cash rewards for employees who report thefts by co-workers. These rewards seemed to reduce theft, acting as both a deterrent and as a direct means of catching and disciplining thieves.

The act of reporting a co-worker's theft or other dishonest behavior entails some risk. Even if the act receives general approval from the work group, as might happen if an employee reported thefts by an individual who is generally disliked, repercussions from the individual who was turned in are always possible. Thus, rewards for reporting dishonesty will be effective only when the rewards are substantial and reliable. An organization that provides a small cash reward only upon conviction is likely to have few takers. Research on decisions that involve a mix of positive and negative outcomes (here, a possible cash reward but a certain conflict with a co-worker) suggests that positive outcomes may have to substantially outweigh potential negative ones before individuals will actually report thefts and other acts of workplace dishonesty (Kahneman & Tversky, 1979).

Providing Alternatives to Theft

Taylor (1986) suggests that employers provide an alternative to theft by giving employees items that they might take anyway, especially dated, partially damaged, or nonsalable merchandise. This tactic will probably help prevent some types of thefts—when people steal because they want or need an item or the cash they might get from selling that item. It is clear, however, that many people steal for other reasons, such as getting revenge, restoring equity, asserting power, or simply for the thrill of it (Hogan & Hogan, 1989; O'Bannon, Goldinger, & Appleby, 1989). In order to deal with thefts of this sort, very different alternatives may be necessary.

Assume that a large number of thefts were committed by individuals who wanted to express their frustration, or "blow off steam." It would probably be worthwhile to do two things: (1) determine the source of their frustrations and, if possible, do something about it, and (2) provide less destructive ways for employees to blow off steam. For example, employees sometimes construct dart boards featuring their supervisor's likeness as a bull's-eye. Although this method of blowing off steam hardly encourages respect for management, it is probably less harmful than employee theft. It might make more sense to encourage such relatively harmless ways of venting frustration than to discourage them.

Evaluating Situational Interventions

This section has reviewed a number of suggestions for changing the organizational situation in ways that may encourage honesty or discourage dishonesty. With few exceptions, however, the effectiveness of these changes is unknown; none of these strategies has been adequately evaluated. Although the idea of changing the situation makes sense, the jury is still out on the effectiveness of most situational approaches.

The evaluation of any organizational change is a complex and daunting task (for recent statements of the difficulty of designing evaluation research, see Cook, 1990; and Cook, Campbell, and Peracchio, 1990). A number of technical issues must be addressed in attempting to assess the impact of interventions of this sort, and a thorough examination of the technical literature on program evaluation is beyond the scope of this book. However, a few principles of program evaluation deserve some comment.

The first step in evaluating any of the suggestions described in this section is to identify an appropriate set of outcome measures. Identifying outcome measures in turn requires a detailed knowledge of the goals of the intervention and at least some speculation about why a particular intervention works. For example, the use of signs to provide feedback about employee theft is designed to reduce theft by heightening employees' awareness of the amount of theft *and* of management's determination to reduce theft. This example suggests that an evaluation should examine at least three outcomes: (1) actual theft, (2) theft awareness, and (3) awareness of management's concerns regarding theft. An examination of the process components of this theft-reduction program—in this case, outcomes (2) and (3)—is especially useful if the feedback program does not seem to affect actual theft levels. Feedback that is not noticed or that is misinterpreted may be ineffective, and an examination of the processes by which feedback is supposed to reduce theft may suggest ways of improving the feedback program.

The second step in evaluating any intervention is to design a study that eliminates as many alternative explanations for the intervention's effects as possible. For example, it is well known that virtually any change in a work situation that represents a novel break in the daily routine affects workers' behavior—sometimes referred to as a Hawthorne effect. This effect suggests that virtually any theft-reduction program might seem to work in the short term, simply because it is new and different. Long-term assessments are often necessary. Second, changes in theft, dishonesty, and so on may be caused by factors that have nothing to do with a theft-reduction program. For example, the Senate Judiciary Committee recently finished highly publicized hearings dealing with sexual harassment. Any program for curbing sexual harassment in the workplace that was put into place shortly before the hearings began probably now seems to be a stunning success.

Eliminating alternative explanations is partly an issue of research design but is also a function of understanding why the intervention works. This is the second reason for paying attention to the process components alluded to earlier. If the intervention seems to work, but none of the processes supposedly responsible for that intervention's success actually occurs, this result may indicate that the apparent change in theft, dishonesty, and so on is due to something other than the intervention itself. Returning to the example of using signs to reduce theft, if the signs resulted in a decrease in actual theft but no change in employees' awareness of theft or of management's efforts to reduce theft (maybe because employees don't pay any attention to the signs), it might be reasonable to conclude that the apparent reduction in theft was not caused by the signs.

SUMMARY

We are still far from understanding the various ways in which situational factors affect employee theft and other forms of dishonesty in the workplace. Nevertheless, by identifying the processes that probably link situational variables with dishonesty, it is possible to pull together several lines of relevant research. In this chapter, I suggested three ways in which situational variables might influence workplace dishonesty—by affecting the perceived necessity of the behavior in question, by affecting the acceptability of that behavior, and by affecting the apparent risks associated with that behavior. For example, security systems affect the perceived risks associated with workplace dishonesty, whereas the norms of the organization or the work group affect the acceptability of these behaviors.

A substantial portion of this chapter was devoted to norms concerning workplace dishonesty for two reasons. First, there is evidence that norms are the best single predictor of workplace dishonesty and the best single method of control (Hollinger & Clark, 1983). Second, normative control of workplace dishonesty is uniquely cost-effective. If the prevailing norms discourage dishonest behavior, work groups may monitor their own behavior and enforce the norms when workers try to violate them. As I will suggest in Chapter 8, virtually anything that a company can do to encourage norms that support honesty in the workplace may be worthwhile.

Several features of organizations and their environments that affect the development of dysfunctional norms—that is, norms that tolerate or encourage dishonesty—were discussed. These features include the structure, policies, and climate of the organization. The use of unofficial reward systems, both as a matter of custom and as a matter of organizational policy, and the possible effects of these rewards on norms regarding honesty in the workplace were noted.

The final section of this chapter discussed several strategies for changing the situation in ways that decrease the apparent necessity of dishonest behavior, decrease its acceptability, or increase the risks associated with that behavior. These strategies range from security systems to programs that provide employees with less expensive and destructive alternatives to theft in the workplace. The need to evaluate these programs and some difficulties in conducting those evaluations were noted.

With the exception of installing security systems, few large-scale attempts have been made to date to alter organizational situations in ways likely to increase honesty or decrease dishonesty in the workplace. It often seems easier to change people (through the use of integrity tests in personnel selection, for example) than to change situations. It is likely, however, that the most effective strategies for dealing with honesty in the workplace will be those that pay attention to both personal and situational causes and correlates of dishonesty and that attempt to change both people and situations.

CHAPTER SEVEN

Encouraging Honesty in Organizations

Chapters 4, 5, and 6 suggested that a number of methods might be used to detect and deter dishonesty in the workplace. More evidence supports the use of some methods than others, but on the whole a reasonable body of research shows that it is possible to decrease dishonesty in the workplace. The present chapter examines several methods that attempt to achieve the same general end using the opposite strategy—that is, rather than attempting to deter and decrease dishonesty, these methods are designed to encourage honesty in the workplace.

Many of the methods developed to increase honesty in the workplace are designed to heighten managers' and executives' awareness of the ethical dimensions of the decisions they must make. For example, McDonald and Zepp (1990) discuss a number of methods currently used by corporations, including training programs, mentoring schemes, the use of group decision making in ethically sensitive areas, the development of codes and ethical policy statements, and the appointment of an ethics ombudsperson. Several of these methods will be discussed in this chapter.

This chapter starts with a discussion of the relationships between efforts to either decrease dishonesty or increase honesty, integrity, or ethical awareness. Next, three strategies for increasing honesty are outlined. The first involves the age-old principle that leaders must set an example for their followers. Theories of observational learning and organizational socialization shed some light on the ways subordinates model the behavior of their superiors and are useful for understanding how examples from the top can be either effective or ineffective in encouraging honesty. The second strategy involves efforts to teach business ethics. There is considerable controversy over the proposition that ethics can be reasonably defined or successfully taught; definitions of business ethics, methods of ethics training, and the evaluation of the effects of ethics training are all examined in this section. The third and final strategy uses a variety of structures and policies in organizations to encourage honesty. Examples range from codes of ethics to mentoring programs.

At first glance, strategies aimed at increasing honesty seem to reflect an optimistic view of human nature, whereas efforts to decrease dishonesty seem pessimistic. If you are a pessimist, you might assume that human nature is corrupt and that people will be dishonest unless they are somehow deterred. If you are an optimist, you might assume that human nature is perfectible and that what is needed are efforts to encourage people's basic honesty. In fact, as you will see in the text, the relationship between these two approaches to dealing with honesty in the workplace is more complex than that implied by the optimist/pessimist dichotomy.

Discouraging Dishonesty versus Encouraging Honesty

In theory, efforts to discourage dishonesty and efforts to encourage honesty should be complementary rather than mutually exclusive alternatives. However, the precise relationship between the two strategies probably depends on individuals' reactions to the specific methods used. If the reaction to each of the two programs considered alone is positive, the two strategies will probably complement one another. Well-designed efforts to discourage dishonesty (for example, drug testing in jobs such as airline pilot or bus driver) will probably enhance the effectiveness of equally well-designed programs to encourage honesty (for instance, a training curriculum that integrates ethical discussions into virtually all modules). By removing some of the conditions conducive to dishonesty (such as the presence of drug-abusing pilots), you make it easier for everyone to behave in an honest fashion. Theologians refer to this type of joint strategy as ensuring virtue by removing the occasion of sin.

If both are well designed, programs to enhance honesty and to deter dishonesty probably enhance one another. Programs that successfully control theft or other forms of dishonesty can also help create a climate in which honesty can flourish. However, if either is poorly designed, one might undercut the other. For example, if employees are hostile to the programs used to deter dishonesty (for example, polygraph exams in drug laboratories are sometimes permissible but are not always well accepted by employees), they may be suspicious and cynical about your efforts to develop higher ethical standards. Similarly, if employees view an ethical training program as a ridiculous waste of time, they might view other programs, including those aimed at decreasing dishonesty, similarly.

Effects of Organizational Environment and Culture

Effective and sensible programs to deter dishonesty also help to establish an environment in which it is possible to effectively encourage honesty. By removing obvious sources of temptation and frequent examples of dishonest behavior from the work environment, an organization can help to create conditions in which honest behavior is easier and is viewed as more appropriate. Many methods of decreasing dishonesty were discussed in the preceding chapters; one potentially effective strategy, from the viewpoint of creating an environment in which honesty is possible, is to do a careful job in selecting and screening employees.

Both theoretical and empirical support exists for the proposition that hiring people who place a high value on honesty helps to establish a climate of honesty in the organization (McDonald & Zepp, 1990; Schneider, 1987; Trevino, 1986). This climate can be further enhanced by removing sources of ethical ambiguity, which requires that you establish and stick to consistent standards regarding honesty in the workplace. Gellerman (1989) claims that people strongly prefer to work in environments where there is little ambiguity regarding ethical standards and that, in these environments, people are more likely to abide by strict standards of ethics and honesty.

Organizations That Encourage Dishonesty

Both the structure and culture of many organizations promote dishonesty. Most organizations are hierarchical, result-oriented, failure-averse, and promotion-oriented. The military is an outstanding example of an organization in which promotions are extremely important—officers who are passed over for promotion must eventually leave the service—and in which a single failure or mistake can destroy one's chance of further career progress. The result of this system is that too many career-minded officers avoid situations in which they might make mistakes and cover up the mistakes they do make (Hackworth, 1989, gives an insightful account of his experiences in this system). A system that was somewhat more tolerant of minor mistakes would make it easier for military officers and their supervisors to be more honest in conducting performance reviews.

Excessive pressure to be a team player is also conducive to dishonesty (Argyris & Schon, 1988; Janis, 1972). This pressure may account for the fact that large numbers of employees, managers, and executives often go along with various forms of organizational misconduct (see Chapter 6) , even if they personally disagree with the organization's actions. Srivastva and Barrett (1988) suggest that to encourage honesty in organizations, the norms of the organization should (1) legitimate members' inquiry into all realms of organizational activity, (2) accept dissent, and (3) value diversity of outlook.

Modeling Honesty

One fairly obvious strategy for encouraging honesty in others is to be honest yourself. This strategy is particularly effective for individuals who are closely watched and whose behavior is likely to be admired and imitated. Whenever a sports figure, actor, or public figure gets in trouble, you will probably hear some commentator bemoan the fact that he or she is not providing a good role model. The implication is that others may imitate that person's destructive or dysfunctional behavior. The same is true in organizations; the process of learning one's role in the organization, which includes learning the norms regarding honesty, depends largely on the behavior of the individuals who serve as models. If influential role models in organizations demonstrate high standards of honesty, others may follow. On the other hand, if these role models are dishonest in the workplace, their behavior may trigger dishonesty in their co-workers and subordinates.

Role models influence the behavior of individuals in organizations in two distinct ways. First, every member of an organization learns his or her role partly by direct observation and imitation of other organization members' behavior. Second, models have an indirect influence by affecting the climate and culture of the organization. Most employees of a large organization will rarely, if ever, see the CEO, but his or her behavior nevertheless serves as a model through its effect on the norms, traditions, rituals, and other facets of the organization's culture. Executives who are willing to bend the rules in the pursuit of profit probably set a different ethical climate than those who are willing to forgo profit in order to avoid ethically questionable transactions.

Example from the Top

A number of researchers and commentators have suggested that the example set by upper management is critical in determining the ethical culture of an organization (Cherrington & Cherrington, 1985; Gellerman, 1989; Mathews, 1988; McDonald & Zepp, 1990; Serpa, 1985). Cherrington (1986) suggests that in a large organization, where employees have little contact with top management, the ethical example of both upper management and the immediate manager or supervisor is critical to the development and maintenance of an ethical culture. Unless the ethical behavior of the immediate supervisor, whose behavior can be observed by the individual, is consistent with that of upper management, the ethical standards embraced by upper management are unlikely to have an impact on the individual.

One way to make the example set by upper managers especially relevant is to require them to abide by the same procedures for ensuring ethical behavior as other employees have to follow. For example, J. C. Penney requires management to submit to package inspection on the same basis as everyone else (Zemke, 1986). Similarly, the drug testing program followed by the U.S. Navy requires all officers and enlisted personnel, from recruits to fleet admirals, to submit to random drug tests. Including everyone in the program demonstrates two things. First, it suggests that ethical requirements are more important than rank; the same standards apply to employees at low and high levels in the organization. Second, it suggests that the ethical requirements themselves are not an unreasonable infringement on the individual. Unfortunately, many organizations impose ethical restrictions, constraints, or tests on their lower-level employees but exempt their executives or managers (examples include drug tests and integrity tests; see Chapters 4 and 5). In doing so, organizations probably send the wrong message to both executives and employees.

Although the behavior of the CEO and other executives is probably quite important, it is likely that the popular and scientific press has placed too much emphasis on example from the top, and too little on the example of individuals at lower levels in the organization. With the exception of Cherrington's (1986) paper, most discussions of role models in organizations seem to focus on the top of the hierarchy. However, there is clear evidence that norms, values, and beliefs about appropriate behavior in organizations are formed quite early in one's career, when an individual is likely to have little or no contact with executives and upper-level managers (Feldman, 1976; Van Maanen & Schein, 1979). Thus, senior members of work groups and second-level supervisors may have the greatest impact on the socialization of new nonexempt and managerial employees. Their role may be analogous to that played by sergeants in the army. Students of military history agree that generals are somewhat important, but sergeants are absolutely critical; it is the sergeants who socialize new recruits and who form the traditions, norms, and rituals of military life. Similarly, a new employee's first supervisor or first mentor might have a much stronger effect on his or her honesty than the rather indirect example set by the CEO.

Applications of Learning Theory

Although many researchers have used learning theory to help understand crime and other deviant behavior (Akers, 1985; Burgess & Akers, 1966; Sutherland & Cressy, 1978), few have attemped to examine how individuals learn honesty in organizations. There are a wide range of theories of learning, ranging from those that deal with simple conditioning to those dealing with the acquisition of complex skills (Weiss, 1990, reviews applications of learning theory in organizations). Of these, social learning theory seems most relevant to understanding the processes involved in modeling honest or dishonest behaviors in organizations.

Social learning theory.   Social learning theory (Bandura, 1977, 1986; Rotter, 1982) deals with the ways we learn by observing and imitating the behavior of others. The process of behavior modeling involves four interrelated steps (Weiss, 1990). First, the observer must attend to the model's behavior. The attention devoted to specific behaviors depends on a number of variables, including the salience and functional value of the behavior and the observer's expectation that future benefits will result from observing the behavior. Second, the observer must store the behavior in memory. Memory researchers have shown that what is stored in memory is not a mirror image of what has been observed but rather is affected by the cognitive processes and structures of the individual (Underwood, 1983; Wyer & Srull, 1986). Thus, the same behavior may be encoded and represented in memory in different ways by different individuals. Third, what is remembered must be translated into behaviors; cognitive knowledge of what you want to do must be translated into concrete performance. Because behaviors are affected by a wide range of environmental cues and conditions, the behavior that you exhibit might not be exactly the same as the one you observed, especially if the two situations differ in important ways. Finally, the individual must be motivated to exhibit the behavior; this motivation might involve a mix of external and internal incentives.

The application of social learning theory to modeling honest behavior in organizations is best illustrated with an example. First, the role model must perform some behavior that demonstrates honesty and that captures the observer's attention. For example, an executive who rewarded a whistle-blower rather than shunning or punishing him or her would probably be noticed, in part because that behavior is apparently so unusual (thus increasing its salience). Next, the observer must appropriately interpret and cognitively represent that behavior. Subordinates who interpret this behavior as an insincere attempt to mollify regulatory agencies will probably come away with a different idea of what they should do than will individuals who interpret it as sincere. At a less conscious level, the way that each individual categorizes the behavior will depend in part on existing cognitive structures (such as schema; see Lord & Maher, 1991, for a review of research on cognitive representation). Two different individuals who interpret the behavior in similar ways might store somewhat different images in memory.

Once the behavior is stored in memory, the observer must, before exhibiting the behavior, recognize situations in which it is possible and appropriate and be motivated to exhibit it. If the observer identifies strongly with the model, the incentives to exhibit the behavior might be intrinsic. Alternatively, the observer might expect that the behavior will be directly rewarded, or indirectly rewarded to the extent that it enhances his or her career prospects.

Characteristics of observers, models, and acts that affect learning.   The most widely replicated finding in research on social learning is that observation of a model being reinforced increases modeling, whereas observation of a model being punished decreases modeling (Bandura, 1986; Rotter, 1982; Weiss, 1990). In addition to the rewards and punishments associated with the act itself, several critical variables affect modeling. First, some acts are more readily modeled than others. Acts that require highly specialized skills, that are predominantly mental (such as composing poetry), or that depend on specific situational conditions (for example, you cannot reward whistle-blowing until someone blows the whistle) are more difficult to model than acts that are easily observed, that can be easily carried out with some practice, and that can be carried out in a variety of circumstances.

Weiss (1990) describes several characteristics of the observer and the model that affect social or observational learning; some of these are presented in Table 7-1. Several of the characteristics in Table 7-1 suggest that the heavy emphasis that the popular literature on modeling honesty places on example from top managers and executives may

Table 7-1   *Some Characteristics of Model and Observer That Affect Observational Learning*

Model characteristics
  Status
  Competence
  Control over resources
Observer characteristics
  Self-esteem
  Perceptual and cognitive skills
  Existing cognitive structures
  Similarity to the model

be appropriate after all. Individuals at the top of the hierarchy have high status, as well as control over resources, and are likely to be seen as highly competent. All three of these variables are directly related to the likelihood of modeling. However, the distance between top executives and lower-level employees may be an important factor limiting their influence on the behavior of many members of the organization. A great deal of research documents the importance of the similarity between the observer and the model in observational learning. Although upper-level managers and executives have many characteristics, such as power and control over resources, that make them desirable models, the substantial gulf that sometimes separates senior managers and executives from lower-level employees may limit the effectiveness of example from the top in defining the ethical climate of an organization.

Weiss (1990) suggests that self-esteem is a key variable in determining whether an observer will attempt to model others' behavior. Individuals with low self-esteem seem more willing to draw cues from others' behavior and may be more easily influenced. However, regardless of one's self-esteem, one's ability to successfully model others' behavior also depends on a variety of observational and performance-related skills, as well as on the existing knowledge and cognitive structures in place at the time the behavior is observed.

Effects of exposing dishonesty.   Organizations are often reluctant, for a number of reasons, to expose workplace dishonesty by prosecuting or punishing offenders. However, a policy to closely monitor and ruthlessly expose dishonest behavior could have the quite unexpected effect of reinforcing most workers' basic honesty, not simply deterring their dishonesty. There is evidence that most workers and managers believe that they are significantly more honest than their peers (Trevino, 1986). This belief may result from self-serving distortions of one's own level of honesty, but another possibility is that most managers and employees greatly overestimate the dishonesty of their peers. It is possible that a very strict policy of investigating and publicizing workplace dishonesty would help workers to develop a more realistic idea of the actual level of honesty and dishonesty in their organization. Research discussed in Chapters 2 and 5 suggests that individuals who believe that dishonesty is common are themselves more likely to engage in dishonest behavior. Perhaps if organizations could make it clear that serious forms of dishonesty are actually, in many organizations, somewhat rare, this information would help employees to follow the honest course in situations requiring ethical decisions.

Although the exposure of dishonesty may not, at first glance, seem like a method of modeling honesty, in fact it is just that. Organizations that conceal or fail to deal with the inevitable dishonesty that is always present in the workplace are not themselves being honest. Willingness to face up to incidents of dishonesty serves to reinforce the basic organizational policy of valuing integrity at all levels.

Organizational Socialization

The socialization process refers to the transition from the status of a newcomer, who knows little about the organization and its norms or about his or her role in the organization, to that of a knowledgeable insider, who understands the nuances of his or her role as well as the relationship between that role and the roles of others in the organization (Fisher, 1986). Much of this socialization occurs by means of informal interactions, in which persons with a vested interest in how well you perform your role evaluate and comment on your behavior (Graen, 1976). Behaviors that are consistent with the prevailing norms and the employee's role are met with approval, and behaviors inconsistent with the norms and the role are not. The role socialization process can be intensive during the initial period that an individual occupies a job; the critical experiences in organizational and job socialization typically occur during the first year (Buchanan, 1974).

Feldman (1976) suggests that organizational socialization occurs in several distinct steps. First, some anticipatory socialization occurs before an individual enters the job; individuals are likely to start with expectations about their role as well as the behaviors appropriate for that role. In the current context, individuals come into the organization with some expectations regarding the norms regarding honesty in the workplace. Socialization itself begins with the process of accommodation, which involves initiation to both the task and the group, role definition, and the development of congruence between one's standards and the prevailing standards of the organization. Individuals who remain in the work group and the organization usually develop norms and beliefs increasingly similar to those of other members of the organization. Next comes role management, which involves resolution of conflicts between the work role and other roles (such as family roles), as well as resolution of conflicting demands presented by the work role. One particularly difficult area in role management may be the potential for conflicts between personal ethics and the ethical standards that characterize the workplace.

The precise content of what is learned in role socialization will vary from job to job, but some broad categories of learning are likely to be present in most jobs (Fisher, 1986). First, and most obvious, the individual must learn how to do the job (Wanous, 1980). Thus, training activities, both formal and informal, are one component of socialization. Second, the individual must learn the values and norms of the immediate work group. Third, the individual must learn the values, culture, goals, and norms of the organization, which are not always the same as those of the work group. As was noted earlier, these norms, values, and so on probably develop through observing others' behavior (Weiss, 1978). Finally, the individual must incorporate the new role into his or her identity or self-image. One implication of this final category of learning is that a fully socialized individual will not only learn the role, but will also internalize at least some aspects of the role.

Whereas research on social learning suggests that powerful, high-status members of the organization (such as the CEO and high-level executives) may be potent models, research on organizational socialization argues for the importance of co-workers and supervisors who are encountered early in one's tenure. This research suggests that an individual's norms, work values, and the like are modeled partly on those of influential members of the organization encountered early in that individual's career.

One way to reconcile the apparent conflict in emphasis of the research in these two areas is to remember that examples from the top have both a direct and indirect effect. The norms and values demonstrated by individuals at the top of the hierarchy affect the culture of the organization, which in turn affects the behavior of other organizational members. The most important role of top-level managers, at least with regard to modeling honesty in the workplace, may be to establish a climate in which organization members lower in the hier-

Box 7-1 *Liar's Poker: A Corporate Culture Gone Crazy*

In his book *Liar's Poker*, Michael Lewis (1989) provides a hilarious but troubling description of the corporate culture of Salomon Brothers, a leading bond-trading firm. Lewis served as a bond salesman and detailed his impressions as a trainee and salesman in London and New York.

The culture described by Lewis is characterized by the macho swaggering of the successful salesmen and traders. The trading floor was the site of idiotic feats of gluttony (for example, guacamole was ordered in five-gallon drums), practical jokes and horseplay (such as throwing telephones at trainees), and childish (except for the scale) bravado. The book's title refers to a legendary game of liar's poker (a sort of card game played using serial numbers on dollar bills) in which the stakes were $1 million.

The organization described in Lewis's book is not one in which examples from the top contributed to the honesty of lower-level employees. Subsequent to the publication of *Liar's Poker*, the firm admitted to serious financial improprieties, replaced several executives, and promised to change its ways. It is too soon to tell whether such promises can be kept (Norris, 1991).

archy will be likely to provide positive role models for one another and for new members of the organization.

Socialization tactics and honesty. Van Maanen and Schein (1979) described a wide variety of strategies for socializing members into organizations or into specific roles within organizations. First, they noted that the socialization process might involve either groups that are socialized together (as, for example, in basic training in the military) or individuals who are socialized on their own. Second, socialization might involve either formal activities (such as training programs or ceremonies) or informal activities (for example, when co-workers "show you the ropes"). Third, socialization activities might proceed according to a fixed schedule (for instance, the first-year activities of entrants in the service academies) or on a variable schedule. Fourth, socialization might follow either a serial or a disjunctive strategy. Serial processes involve instruction from direct role models (an example would be placing rookie police officers with veterans), whereas disjunctive processes involve learning from individuals, such as instructors, who hold very different roles from the one you are about to enter.

It is likely that much of the socialization involving norms regarding honesty in the workplace is individual, informal, unplanned, and serial in nature—that is, norms regarding honesty in the workplace are probably learned from peers and other direct role models through informal interactions. Furthermore, it is unlikely that these informal processes will ever be completely replaced by socialization programs designed by the organization. This does not mean, however, that organizations are powerless to influence the norms or the socialization processes of their employees. The research reviewed by Van Maanen and Schein (1979) and others for instance, Feldman, 1976) suggests that organizations can design socialization programs that are likely to significantly affect workers' norms and beliefs regarding honesty in the workplace.

As noted earlier, early socialization is most critical, indicating that organizational socialization efforts might most profitably be directed at new employees. Van Maanen and Schein (1979) suggest that collective socialization activities are particularly appropriate for and influential with new entrants in the organization. They cite examples such as boot camp and procedures for initiating new members into secret societies, religious orders, and even fraternities; such collective socialization efforts can be quite stressful but can also have a profound effect on behavior. To institute boot camps for new employees would be going a bit too far, but the idea of structured collective socialization activities for new employees should be considered carefully. Before employees join their work group, they might be exposed to activities designed to heighten their awareness and understanding of ethical issues in the organization. Such activities might include detailed coverage of the organization's code of ethics, ethical discussion groups, or any of the other methods of increasing ethical awareness that are discussed in the following section.

Business Ethics

The topic of business ethics is broader than the topic of honesty in the workplace, although honesty underlies many of the ethical dilemmas faced in business. Any definition of business ethics must include discussion of the rights and obligations of the various stakeholders in the organization, such as managers, stockholders, employees, suppliers, customers, and the public, and of the sources and limitations of those rights and obligations (Freeman, 1990). In particular, ethical behavior in business does not require or imply absolute honesty or candor. In negotiation, bargaining, and the determination of prices and profits, it is well accepted that both parties (sellers and buyers) operate with partial information, and that a tactic such as stating, "this is my final offer," when in fact some less favorable offer might be accepted, is well within the "rules of the game" (Carson, Wokutch, & Murrmann, 1982). Similarly, in many situations, such as job interviews, individuals are expected to "put their best foot forward," and self-serving deviations from absolute candor are not treated as lies. Finally, a supervisor who turns in a mildly flattering performance appraisal rather than facing the interpersonal stress that would accompany a less favorable one or a subordinate who shows enthusiastic support for a project he or she does not really want to do is not really being deceptive. Rather, all of these deviations from absolute truthfulness represent socially acceptable behaviors that can, in some circumstances, contribute to the smooth functioning of the organization.

Although ethics and honesty are not synonymous, they are clearly related. In particular, unethical behavior in complex organizations almost always requires some level of dishonesty and deception, at least in the form of covering up misconduct. Ethical behavior, on the other hand, requires both honesty and integrity (see Chapter 1 for a discussion of the distintion between honesty and integrity). Therefore, programs designed to increase sensitivity to ethical issues in business often involve efforts to increase or encourage honesty in the workplace.

Theories of Ethical Behavior

The wide range of theories and approaches for defining ethical and unethical conduct are often broken down into three basic types: (1) utilitarian theories, (2) rights-based theories, and (3) justice-based theories (Fritzche & Becker, 1984). Utilitarian approaches focus on an act itself and its consequences. Rule utilitarianism states that an act is ethical if it conforms with established rules. Act utilitarianism states that an act is ethical if its outcomes or consequences are beneficial. Rights-based theories suggest that an act is ethical to the extent that it ensures or does not detract from basic human rights (such as the right to free consent or to due process). Justice-based theories suggest that an act is ethical to the extent to which the decision process involved is fair and impartial.

There is evidence that this categorization of ethical theories is useful in describing actual decision making. A study by Fritzche and Becker (1984) suggests that managers use utilitarian rules to define ethical conduct in a wide variety of simulated decisions. For example, in making ethical judgments in a laboratory task, managers seemed to consider both the extent to which acts conform with organizational policy, legal requirements, and so on and the immediate consequences of their acts.

While this three-level classification of ethical theories is useful, it does not offer any immediate suggestions for increasing honesty. Drawing heavily from the work of developmental psychologists such as Piaget, Kohlberg (1969, 1981) developed a theory of the development of moral reasoning that has substantially influenced the thinking behind many programs designed to increase honesty in the workplace.[1] The seven stages of moral reasoning central to Kohlberg's theory are illustrated in Table 7-2.

Kohlberg's theory suggests that most individuals develop their understanding of what is right and wrong over a long period of time and that the eventual definition of right and wrong adopted by the individual reflects his or her progression through a well-defined hierarchy of types of moral reasoning. Young children operate at a preconventional level, in which the definition or right and wrong depends on rules set down by others. As they mature, children move to a conventional level, in which they adopt and internalize rules and start to recognize some acts as right or wrong regardless of the rewards and punishments that might immediately accompany the act. At a postconventional level, the definitions of right and wrong flow from the set of general ethical principles the individual has chosen to follow.

Within each of the three general levels, there are a number of stages of moral development, in which right and wrong are successively defined in slightly different terms. In general, the stages proceed from self-oriented to other-oriented thinking and from a punishment/reward orientation to an abstract principle orientation. Each successive stage represents a higher level of reasoning regarding the

---

[1] Although Kohlberg's theory is widely cited by practitioners, it has largely fallen out of favor among researchers who study ethical behavior.

Table 7-2   *Stages in Kohlberg's Theory of the Development of Moral Reasoning*

I. Preconventional level

Stage 1—*punishment and obedience orientation:* The physical consequences of an act determine whether it is good or bad.

Stage 2—*instrumental relativist orientation:* Things that satisfy your needs, and sometimes the needs of others, are good.

II. Conventional level

Stage 3—*"good boy/good girl" orientation:* Behavior that pleases others and earns approval is good.

Stage 4—*"law and order" orientation:* Respect for authority, order, and doing one's duty determine what is right.

III. Postconventional level

Stage 5—*Social contract orientation:* The consensus of society, which can change, defines what is right.

Stage 6—*Universal ethical principle orientation:* Right is defined in terms of self-chosen universal principles of good and bad.

Stage 7—*Cosmic ethical principle orientation:* Right is defined in terms of the oneness of the universe, leading to principles that are cosmic rather than strictly people- or world-oriented

---

definition and nature of right and wrong. A number of studies suggest that the moral reasoning of most adults is similar to that described in Stage 4 of Kohlberg's theory (Colby, 1978) and that moral reasoning at Stage 5 or beyond is relatively rare, even in educated groups such as managers (Trevino, 1986).

Kohlberg's theory might be applied to the problem of unethical behavior in organizations in two ways. First, it is possible that the selection of employees, particularly managers, whose moral reasoning is at higher rather than lower stages in the hierarchy might help increase ethical behavior in organizations (Blasi, 1980; Trevino, 1986). Several studies demonstrate a modest relationship between one's stage of moral development and various types of ethical behavior (see Trevino, 1986, for a review). Second, it might be possible to increase the sophistication of an individual's moral reasoning through training or education (Baxter & Rarick, 1987).

Unfortunately, there are difficulties with both these suggestions. Attempts to select individuals whose moral reasoning is at one of Kohlberg's higher stages (especially at Stages 5 to 7, which define the postconventional level) will be problematic because of the relative scarcity of individuals at these higher stages. If there are very few qualified managers at Stages 5 to 7, it will be impossible for every company to use selection as a strategy for increasing the sophistication of moral reasoning—the pool will quickly dry up.

Training is problematic for a number of reasons. First, Kohlberg's theory deals with a way of viewing the world that develops over a very long period of time. The process of developing a style of moral reasoning spans a person's entire childhood and much of his or her early adulthood. It may be very difficult to substantially change views that are developed and reinforced over such long periods. Second, the issue of transfer of training might be particularly relevant in the context of moral reasoning. Even if you succeed in training a person to think about moral problems in a different way, there is no guarantee that changes in behavior will result. As Trevino (1986) points out, ethical behavior reflects both individual and situational influences, and among the individual influences, the style of moral reasoning might not be the most important factor. A variety of other individual characteristics, including locus of control and ego strength, might be important in determining whether an individual translates his or her judgment about what is right or wrong into ethical behavior at work. I will return to the question of training as a method of increasing ethical behavior later in this section.

Levels of analysis.   The theories illustrated above deal with the process of moral or ethical decision making. It is also useful to consider the content of such decisions. Freeman (1990) suggests that ethical issues in organizations can be described and analyzed at four different levels of analysis. First, there are a number of societal issues that involve relationships between business and the most basic institutions of society. For example, the recent Catholic Bishops' Pastoral Letter on the U.S. Economy questioned the morality of materialism and unbridled capitalism and suggested that more attention needed to be paid to the human dignity of workers. Second, there are a number of issues that involve stakeholders (individuals and groups who have a stake in the organization). Stakeholders include employees, suppliers, customers, financiers, and the community. Many ethical questions, such as the ethical issues involved in closing an outdated plant with little prior notice, require that decision makers consider the effects of their decisions on several groups of stakeholders.[2]

Third, there are ethical decisions that deal with employee policy, many of which involve the definition of the mutual rights and responsibilities of employees and organizations. For example, organizations must consider the balance between privacy rights and their concerns over the problems associated with drug use in deciding whether to institute a program of drug testing. Finally, there are ethical decisions that involve interpersonal issues that arise as a function of the relationships among individuals in the organization. These include issues such as sexual harassment and discrimination on the basis of gender or race.

---

[2] The identification of stakeholders is an important step in application of several decision theories (Edwards & Newman, 1982). Balzer and Sulsky (1990) and Murphy and Cleveland (1991) applied this process in evaluating performance appraisal systems.

Ethical issues at any of these four levels could have implications for honesty in the workplace. For example, food manufacturers are currently under fire from the Food and Drug Administration for advertising claims implying that their products are fresh, wholesome, and healthy when this is not necessarily the case. A company that decides to adopt completely honest advertising must consider several sets of potential consequences. An honest advertising policy might be good for society but very bad for the stakeholders of the organization; an admission on the part of a cereal manufacturer that its product is a tasteless amalgam of sugar and overprocessed ingredients rarely found in nature would probably spare consumers from the ill-advised use of its product, but the organization would not survive long.

Ethics and Business

In part because of increasing public disclosure of ethical violations, the widespread attention focused on the topic of business ethics may make concern for business ethics appear to be a fairly recent phenomenon (Brenner & Molander, 1977). In fact, business ethics has been an important topic for much of the history of U.S. business, and beliefs regarding business ethics and assumptions about the social and ethical responsibilities of corporations have evolved considerably over the course of this century.

In the earlier stages of capitalism, business's concern for ethics and social responsibility was best summed up in J. P. Morgan's famous statement, "I owe the public nothing."[3] Prior to 1960, discussions of ethics in business were conducted mainly by religious leaders; examples include a number of papal encyclicals issued during the 1870s, dealing with questions of just wages and the morality of capitalism (DeGeorge, 1987). In the 1960s discussions of social issues in business focused mainly on legal issues. In the 1970s business ethics began to emerge as a separate field of inquiry, and the notion that businesses had responsibilities beyond maximizing profits became widely accepted. The early 1980s represented a period of consolidation, in which business ethics emerged as a standard part of business training (Cooke & Ryan, 1988). As DeGeorge (1987) notes, by 1985 three separate professional societies were dedicated to business ethics (the Society for Business Ethics, the Society for Professional Ethics, and the Social Issues in Management Section of the Academy of Management); more than 20 textbooks, 10 casebooks, and at least five journals dealt with the topic; and more than 500 courses at colleges, universities, and

---

[3] Teitelman (1989) discusses business ethics during that period and shows that although attitudes toward social responsibility were different then, probably that period and the present do not differ substantially in terms of the tendency for corporations and businesspeople to act in an ethical manner.

schools of business were offered on business ethics. A business ethics bibliography covering the years 1981 to 1985 contains more than 4000 titles (Jones & Bennett, 1986).

Defining business ethics.   The question of exactly what *business ethics* means has received a good deal of attention. Drucker (1981) suggests that there is no such thing as "business ethics"; to him, the phrase usually implies that some ethical standard applies to business-people that is more rigorous than the standard applied to everyone else. He suggests that the same ethical rules and standards that apply outside of business should also define business ethics, and that there is little need for the examination of business ethics as a special field of inquiry. His critics (for example, Hoffman & Moore, 1982) agree that the same ethical principles apply to businesspeople as to everyone else; but they go on to observe that special problems arise in business that do not occur outside the business setting (such as the question whether a corporation has the same ethical responsibilities as a person) and that the phrase *business ethics* is nothing more than a simple extension of general ethical principles to the unique problems that arise in this particular setting.

There is also considerable disagreement over whether business ethics can be taught (Cooke & Ryan, 1988). In part, the answer to this question depends on precisely what is meant by *business ethics*. If this phrase denotes little more than knowledge of right and wrong, the critics are probably correct (Axline, 1990). An individual who does not know right from wrong prior to getting his or her M.B.A. will probably not learn the distinction from a few courses on business ethics; ethical values develop over one's lifetime and are resistant to change (Pocock, 1989). However, it does seem reasonable that courses in business ethics can help individuals to recognize and diagnose ethical prob-lems in business and to apply ethical principles in analyzing alter-native courses of behavior. The aim of courses, seminars, and the like developed to enhance business ethics should not be to teach ethics per se, but rather to teach the application of ethical principles to real business problems. Axline (1990) describes this effort as encouraging "an environment in which the right questions are asked at the right time" (p. 88).

Business ethics and personal ethics.   As noted earlier, some critics believe no real distinction can be drawn between business ethics and personal ethics. Unfortunately, many employees, managers, and ex-ecutives appear to believe and act as if such a fundamental distinction can be made; that is, it often appears as if individuals leave their personal ethics at the office door and engage in a variety of behaviors in their roles as employees or businesspeople that would be unthinkable in their private lives (Cooke & Ryan, 1988; Freeman, 1990; Mathews, 1988).

It is useful to consider some aspects of an individual's role in a complex organization that might cause him or her to act in ways that would be clearly unethical outside of the work setting. First, an individual in the workplace has a specific role (for example, as a research scientist or sales manager) that conveys obligations and implies constraints that do not impinge on that same individual outside of his or her work role. Acting as an autonomous individual, I may not care whether my unit reaches its quota, but acting as the unit's manager, I should care very much. Second, and perhaps most important, various roles in organizations are highly interdependent. If I decide to take an ethical stand regarding a questionable decision made by the organization, I affect not only myself, but possibly others as well. Many unethical decisions are probably made by generally honest individuals who don't want to let the company or the unit down.

Third, as has already been noted several times, there are pressures in organizations to show results, avoid mistakes, please the boss, and so on that are not present outside the organization. Because of the combinations of role obligations, individual pressures, and the simple need to get the task done, it may be that high personal standards are not sufficient to guarantee ethical behavior in one's organizational role. However, one consideration that is very relevant for organizations may provide the extra support needed to translate personal ethics into ethical behavior in the workplace—that is, the possibility that good ethics make good business.

Ethics and the bottom line.   One of the more radical changes in attitudes toward business ethics is the growing belief that ethics are good for profits (Axline, 1988, 1990; Harrington, 1991). Evidence regarding the true relationship between business ethics and profitability is somewhat mixed, but on the whole it seems to show that ethical practices are positively correlated with profits (Axline, 1988, 1990; Becker & Fritzche, 1987; Cooke & Ryan, 1988). A great deal of anecdotal evidence also exists for the links between ethics and profits. Several popular books have examined highly successful organizations; examples of such books include Peters and Waters's *In Search of Excellence,* Peters and Austin's *A Passion for Excellence,* and Kanter's *The Change Masters.* One characteristic common to many of these successful organizations is a culture that encourages ethical sensitivity and that does not allow ethical questions to be sidestepped in the pursuit of short-term gain.

Unfortunately, it is difficult to make sensible statements about the direction of the causal relationship, if any, between ethics and profits.

One possibility is that ethical acts create profit. However, another, perhaps more credible, possibility is that competition and economic hard times lead to unethical behaviors. Organizations that are doing well may be able to "afford" to behave in an ethical fashion but may fall prey to dishonesty as soon as profits decline. The correlation between profits and ethics cannot, by itself, be taken to indicate that an organization can expect to be more profitable if it becomes more ethical.

Even if they are not convinced that ethical business practices contribute to profits, many executives have become aware of the potential costs of unethical business practices, especially if enforcement agencies are vigilant and aggressive; they have also come to believe that unethical business practices are bad for the long-term relationships between organizations and their customers, suppliers, and other stakeholders. This attitude toward business ethics is in sharp contrast to the one expressed by many of the "robber barons" who built the great monopolies (and also the great railroads, utilities, and industries) in the 1880s and 1890s, who seemed to believe that ethics were for suckers.

Training in Business Ethics

Training in business ethics now occurs in both academic and business settings (Cooke & Ryan, 1988). Weber (1990) noted that nearly 50% of all business schools offer courses on social responsibility and business ethics. Although the content of these courses varies greatly, the best programs seem to focus on ethical awareness (that is, increasing sensitivity to ethical dilemmas at work) and ethical reasoning (that is, learning strategies for solving ethical dilemmas). Harrington (1991) notes that 30 to 45% of the companies he surveyed have in-house ethics training. As in academic settings, the content varies considerably, but this training often involves statements from the CEO emphasizing ethical business practices, discussions of the corporate code of ethics, and descriptions of procedures for dealing with or reporting unethical behavior.

The most common method of ethical training is a stand-alone course in a business school. However, there is a growing trend toward educational curricula that integrate ethics into many or most facets of the academic or training curriculum (Cooke & Ryan, 1988). Also, an increasing number of institutes and research centers are now devoted to the study and advancement of business ethics. Training programs usually include exposure to ethical theories (often Kohlberg's theory), together with practice in applying the principles to typical business situations. The question whether training of this sort works depends in part on the criteria and the methods used to evaluate such training.

Evaluating ethics training.   Training researchers have proposed a number of different criteria and frameworks for evaluating training. For example, Goldstein (1986) suggests that training be evaluated in terms of whether change occurs, whether change is due to training, whether the change is related to organizational goals, and whether similar changes are likely to occur with new participants in the same training program. Cascio (1987) notes the relevance of the time frame and suggests that different criteria and research designs might be appropriate for evaluating short-term and long-term changes that result from training.

Kirkpatrick (1977, 1983) proposed that training programs should be evaluated against four distinct types of criteria: reactions, learning, behavior, and results. First, it is useful to examine individuals' reactions to the content and delivery of the training. If individuals see the training as irrelevant or contrary to the norms of the organization, it is unlikely that the training will change their behavior. Second, individuals' learning might be tested. If individuals never learn or retain critical information in the training program, they will not be able to apply it. Third, you might look for changes in behavior. If the goal of training is to increase the incidence of ethical behavior, it seems logical to attempt to measure this behavior and compare behavior after training to behavior prior to training (for discussions of research designs employed in these comparisons, see Cascio, 1987; Cook & Campbell, 1979; Cook, Campbell, & Peracchio, 1990). Finally, you might examine the results of training. It is possible that the training can be successful in teaching ethical principles and in changing the behavior of the individuals who receive training, but the results of those changes might not be relevant, worthwhile, or quite what the organization expected. For example, an organization plagued by employee theft might put all its employees through ethical training. If the training is successful in changing the behavior of 90% of all employees, but leaves the 10% who were doing most of the stealing untouched, the results might be disappointing. If the other 90% are now more willing to question authority, to blow the whistle, or to put ethical issues before any considerations of profit, the net result of this "successful" training program might not look so good to the organization after all.

There is evidence that training in ethical principles can be effective, at least in terms of learning criteria. For example, Penn and Collier (1985) trained business students in the principles that underlie Kohlberg's theory of moral development and observed significant changes in levels of moral reasoning, with substantial numbers of students showing a higher level of moral analysis after the training than before. There is also some evidence that ethical training can affect behaviors. Mentkowski (1988) described the curriculum of Alverno College, in which issues related to ethical values are explicitly considered in many of the courses taken by students. There is evidence that this level of exposure to ethical concerns can indeed affect both knowledge of ethics and actual decision making. However, it is not clear whether this level of near-total immersion in ethical debates is needed or whether instead behavioral effects might result from less intensive curricula.

Applying Ethical Principles: Decision Aids

Although managers and executives may accept high ethical standards in principle, they often find it difficult to apply these theories of ethics to the problems they face daily in business. It is one thing to read and study Aristotle's *Nichomachean Ethics,* and quite another to apply the principles expounded in that book to business decisions. What is often needed to translate a general understanding of ethical principles to everyday application is a set of decision aids, or tools that can be used to apply the principles to actual business decisions. For example, Nash (1986) suggests that a set of twelve questions, shown in Table 7-3, be considered in determining whether an action or policy is ethical.

Many organizations use decision schemes that parallel some aspects of the strategy presented in Table 7-3. For example, McDonald and Zepp (1990) describe the "Light of Day" decision strategy in use in some parts of IBM. This strategy encourages managers to ask whether any part of a recent decision would embarrass them or the organi-

Table 7-3 *Questions to Consider in Determining the Ethical Status of Business Decisions*

1. Have you defined the problem accurately?
2. How would you define the problem if you stood on the other side of the fence?
3. How did this situation occur in the first place?
4. To whom and what do you give your loyalties as a person and as a member of the corporation?
5. What is your intention in making this decision?
6. How does your intention compare with the likely results?
7. Whom could your decision or action injure?
8. Can you engage the affected parties in a discussion of the problem before you make your decision?
9. Are you confident that your position will be as valid over a long period of time as it appears now?
10. Could you disclose without qualm your decision or action to your boss, your CEO, your family, or society as a whole?
11. What is the symbolic potential of your action if understood? If misunderstood?
12. Under what conditions would you allow exceptions to your stand?

SOURCE: Adapted from Nash (1986).

zation if it came into the open. If the answer is yes, the action may be at least ethically questionable. This strategy is a variation on the "*New York Times* strategy" sometimes used in diagnosing cases of sexual harassment—that way, if you would feel embarrassed to find your behavior described on the front page of the *New York Times*, avoid that behavior.

Structural Approaches to Increasing Honesty

The third strategy for increasing honesty in the workplace is to change the rules, policies, procedures, or structure of the organization in ways that make honest behavior both easier and more likely. The most widespread structural change of this type is the adoption of a formal code of ethics. To supplement these codes, many organizations employ discussion programs and seminars to clarify the code, as well as mentoring programs to provide individual advice and monitoring of ethical decisions.

A growing number of organizations use either committees or individuals, often in the role of an ethics ombudsperson, to help assure that important decisions conform to ethical principles and rules and to provide some neutral forum for questions and advice on ethical issues in organizations.

Codes of Ethics

Recent surveys suggest that virtually all large firms have formal codes of ethics (Center for Business Ethics, 1986). The trend toward developing such codes began in earnest in the late 1970s (Dinitz, 1982), and it is now routine for companies to include codes of ethics in employee handbooks, operating manuals, and so on. Codes of ethics are more common in the United States than in Japan or Western Europe (Berenbeim, 1987), and they are increasingly likely to cover a wide range of specific topics rather than offering only glittering generalities. Examples of topics most frequently covered by such codes include employee conflicts of interest, gifts to corporate personnel, sexual harassment, unauthorized payments, affirmative action, employee privacy, and relations with U.S. and foreign governments and with customers and competitors (Berenbeim, 1987; Cressy & Moore, 1983; Mathews, 1988).

The emergence of codes of ethics is a welcome sign of increasing awareness of ethical issues in business. More than three-quarters of the organizations participating in a fairly recent Conference Board survey had written codes of ethics; nearly half of these also had some sort of ethics discussion program to supplement the code (Berenbeim,

1987). However, there appears to be little relationship between the establishment of codes of ethics and ethical or unethical behavior in organizations (Cressy & Moore, 1983; Mathews, 1988)—that is, codes by themselves do virtually nothing to decrease the frequency or severity of ethical violations. Trevino (1986) notes that codes are most likely to work when they are enforced and consistent with the organization's culture. Unfortunately, codes of ethics sometimes seem to be little more than public-relations gestures, which fail to either reflect or affect the actual behavior of organizational members.

Ethics discussion programs.   It is unlikely that much can be accomplished by simply publishing and distributing a code of ethics. Many organizations have created programs to assure that their employees read and understand their codes and to help employees apply the codes in their day-to-day activities. Ethics discussion programs, ranging from structured seminars put on by outside consultants to informal peer discussions, are widely used for this purpose.

Ethics discussion programs often use case studies to illustrate the meaning and application of ethics codes. These case studies can range from formal presentations of actual events (for example, the case study series developed by the Harvard Business School) to discussions of hypothetical problems that managers or employees might encounter in their jobs. When they are done well, case studies help clarify the meaning of a code of ethics and provide employees with a standard frame of reference for determining when different parts of the code apply. The potential drawback of the case method, however, is that it is easy to focus on the concrete details of the immediate case and to lose your focus on the meaning or the message (that is, fail to see the forest for the trees). The success of this method may depend on both the cases themselves and on the skills of the discussion leader.

As with many other programs in organizations, the success of ethical discussions may depend partly on the orientation of the participants. If participants view these discussions as irrelevant, because of the cases themselves or because of their cynicism regarding the ethics program itself (employees might, for instance, view the code as self-serving and hypocritical), ethical discussion will probably accomplish little. This method is probably most useful for individuals who accept the code as a reasonable and realistic standard for their behavior in the workplace and who are interested in understanding the code and its application.

Ethical ambiguity of codes.   Several authors have suggested that far from showing a higher concern for ethical behavior, the emergence of ethical codes actually represents an attempt by organizations to distance themselves from important ethical issues. First, as Gellerman

(1989) notes, written codes seem to "pass the buck" from the organization to the individual. When misconduct is detected in or by an organization, the executives of that organization can point to the code and claim that because the misdeed is forbidden in the code, it represents an individual aberration that is not the organization's fault or responsibility. Second, codes seem to show more concern for actions against the company than for illegal or unethical acts committed on behalf of the company (Berenbeim, 1987; Cressy & Moore, 1983; Mathews, 1988). Issues such as conflicts of interest (as when an employee divulges trade secrets for personal profit) are routinely addressed in many codes, but there is little consensus about what organizational misdeeds, if any, should be proscribed in a code.

Cressy and Moore's (1983) analysis of 119 codes suggests that organizations are substantially more concerned with ethical violations that decrease profit, such as employee theft, than with ethical violations that tend to increase profits, such as misleading advertising or price-fixing. Although the term *code of ethics* implies a high standard of integrity, these codes may sometimes be little more than a gimmick to discourage some behaviors that seem to erode profits and to limit the organization's liability when a member of the organization is caught in some dishonest act.

Box 7-2   *What Codes of Conduct Might Tell You about Organizations*

The codes of conduct published by various organizations differ substantially in both their content and tone. Some codes read like the Ten Commandments—they are first and foremost a list of things you should not do. Others take a more positive tone, going out of their way to explain why certain rules are in place and what options short of dismissal exist for dealing with various violations. It is tempting to draw generalizations about the management style of the organization from the tone and content of the code. Consider the policies regarding substance abuse in two codes described by Manley (1991, pp. 128–129). One organization's code notes that the organization's "concern with alcohol and drug-related problems is limited to their effects on work performance" and goes on to encourage early use of employee assistance programs. Another organization's code makes it clear that all drug use is forbidden and that any involvement in the sale or solicitation of drugs will lead to immediate discharge.

The second organization's code suggests a more punitive, authoritarian attitude. It is not clear, however, whether a generalization of this sort is valid or fair. There is no clear evidence at this point that differences in codes of conduct tell you anything worthwhile about differences in management style or philosophy. However, the idea is a plausible one that deserves empirical examination.

Individuals and Groups
Responsible for Encouraging Honesty

Many organizations give specific individuals or groups the responsibility of encouraging honesty in employees. This responsibility might be a formal part of one's job description (for example, an individual with the job title "ethics ombudsperson") or it might be an informal but widespread understanding (for instance, that individuals who help train and socialize a new employee are responsible for ethical development as well as for teaching the newcomer the tasks included in the job). Three examples are presented below.

Ombudspersons.   Many organizations have one or more individuals with job titles something like "ethics ombudsperson." In theory, persons in this job are independent, neutral, and credible individuals. Their functions include investigation, advice, and counseling in ethical matters of all sorts (McDonald & Zepp, 1990). They are supposed to field inquiries and complaints, monitor and investigate the ethical aspects of the organization's dealings, and provide a safe, neutral outlet for employees and other stakeholders to deal with their concerns about ethical issues in the organization. In fact, an ombudsperson who is too much of a gadfly can experience trouble in an organization; being overly aggressive in this role can harm a person's later career progress (Srivastva & Barrett, 1988).

The best ombudsperson is probably an individual who has extensive experience in an organization and who has reached the peak of his or her career. This individual has less to fear than a newer employee and also is more likely to be both knowledgeable and credible. The disadvantage of using such a person is that he or she is probably well socialized into the existing policies and practices of the organization and may be less enthusiastic in investigating the ethical aspects of long-standing policies than in investigating more recent developments in the organization.

Ethics committees.   Several organizations now use committees that are specifically charged with examining the ethical aspects of major decisions in the organization. For example, before deciding to close a plant, the CEO of an organization might ask for a report from such a committee. There is no guarantee that the committee's recommendations will be followed, but this structure does help ensure that someone considers the full range of ethical issues and at least brings them to the attention of decision makers.

The composition and tasks of ethics committees vary tremendously across organizations. Some organizations even employ philosophers, sometimes referred to as ethicists, who serve either as committee members or as resource persons for such committees. Others are made up of members who serve rotating terms and who might be drawn from many of the different functional divisions of the organization.

The overall effect of such a committee may depend substantially on the type of decisions they are asked or allowed to review. At one extreme, the use of the committee might be completely voluntary, with no clear norm supporting or discouraging referral of decisions to this committee. At the other extreme, this committee might be required to consider every proposal put forth in the organization.[4] Most ethics committees are probably somewhere between these extremes; in general, the higher the likelihood that important decisions will be examined by the committee, the greater the impact of the committee on the conduct of the organization.

The mere existence of an ethics committee, particularly one that is used for most or all important decisions, may encourage honesty in the workplace, almost regardless of the specific deliberations or recommendations of the committee itself. The fact that important decisions are subject to formal ethical scrutiny suggests that ethical considerations are indeed important and that honesty and integrity are valued by the organization. Of course, this effect would not occur if a committee examined many decisions, but its recommendations are routinely ignored. If the organization is likely to continue unethical practices, the existence of an ethics committee probably only makes matters worse, because it implies that the organization is knowingly violating ethical standards.

Mentoring.   The role of a mentor has received tremendous attention in both the popular and the research literature. Briefly put, a mentor is a more senior employee, often considerably older than you, who takes a personal role in your development (such phrases as "show you the ropes" and "take you under his or her wing" abound in the mentoring literature). Mentors often voluntarily invest their time and energy in the development of specific individuals, but in many organizations senior employees are assigned to act as mentors to individual employees.

McDonald and Zepp (1990) suggest that mentors might aid in the ethical development of the employees with whom they work. This suggestion is probably sound, provided that ethical behavior is consistent with the culture of the organization. In organizations where the typical method used to achieve success is to find creative ways to bend the rules, most mentors will probably teach their charges crea-

---

[4] Similar committees exist at virtually all universities to review potential ethical violations in research involving human subjects or captive animals.

tive ways to bend the rules. Indeed, if you accept the premise that a mentor's role is to give you advice and guidance that will help you succeed in the organization, it is likely that the mentors in an unethical organization are a major force in keeping the organization unethical. However, if the organization is one in which honesty and ethical behavior will contribute to success, good mentors will probably encourage the development of norms and behaviors that are highly consistent with honesty in the workplace.

SUMMARY

This chapter began by comparing two distinct strategies for dealing with honesty in the workplace—discouraging dishonesty and encouraging honesty—and noted that these strategies can either complement or interfere with each other, depending largely on the specific methods used to implement each strategy. If both are carried out well, these two strategies reinforce one another. However, if poorly designed methods are used to carry out either strategy, particularly methods likely to be resented or viewed as ineffective by employees, both approaches are probably hurt.

Three strategies for increasing honesty were discussed. First, the use of modeling was discussed. Modeling is probably an excellent technique for encouraging either honesty or dishonesty in organizations. If workers observe influential, well-respected individuals behaving in dishonest or ethically ambiguous ways, they will probably learn the same types of dishonesty. However, if managers and executives hold themselves to high ethical standards, they may serve as models who affect the behavior of other members of the organization through both direct observational learning and through their effects on the climate and culture of the organization.

Second, techniques for defining and increasing business ethics were discussed. There is still some controversy over the proposition that ethics can be taught, but this controversy seems to be subsiding. The more pressing issue may be whether programs that teach ethics also affect the behavior of members of the organization. Some scattered evidence suggests that behavioral changes are possible with a fairly extensive and intensive ethics curriculum, but it is not at all clear that the types of ethics programs currently in place in organizations or business schools will have substantial effects.

A third strategy for encouraging honesty is to change the policies, rules, and structures of an organization. The types of structural changes that seem most popular include codes of ethics, ethical discussion programs, and ethics committees and ombudspersons. While these changes probably do some good, they are relatively minor, given the apparent seriousness of problems caused by dishonest and unethical behaviors in organizations. In the chapter that follows, possibilities for more extensive changes in the structure and style of U.S. organizations will be discussed.

CHAPTER EIGHT

Pitfalls and Promise in the Pursuit of Honesty in Organizations

This final chapter has two purposes. First, I will identify important gaps in our knowledge, or in the application of our knowledge, about honesty in the workplace. Many practices, ranging from business education to integrity testing, are based at least in part on theories and explanations of workplace dishonesty that have not been fully examined or tested. Second, I will suggest several particularly promising new directions for future research and application.

Three problems seem particularly important when one considers the current state of our knowledge and practice in areas related to honesty in the workplace. First, in many areas, both our knowledge and understanding of the data are either incomplete or unreliable. The most obvious example is provided by the extensive disagreement over the amount of workplace theft. Second, a fairly narrow range of strategies has been heavily relied on in discouraging dishonesty and encouraging honesty. Person-oriented strategies, such as integrity testing, are common, whereas situation-oriented strategies, such as changing norms related to honesty, have received scant attention, especially if you exclude security-oriented approaches to discouraging dishonesty. Strategies that consider interactions between persons and situations are virtually unheard of. Third, the unwanted side effects of various strategies to increase honesty or decrease dishonesty are often left unconsidered.

Three areas for future research and application are identified in this chapter. First, methods of developing high levels of commitment to the organization are discussed. Considerable evidence demonstrates that committed individuals are less likely to engage in behavior destructive to the organization or to support norms that tolerate these behaviors. If high levels of commitment can be encouraged, there may be less need to worry about dishonesty in the workplace. Second, methods of assessing both personal and situational characteristics—and their interactions—that are relevant to honesty in the workplace are examined. Third, ongoing assessments of integrity, as opposed to one-shot screening tests, are suggested as an important component of understanding honesty in the workplace.

The final section of this chapter deals with changes in organizational structure and culture that may be necessary to build and sustain high levels of honesty in the workplace. These changes will require employees, managers, and executives to think about their roles in very different ways; they may prove very difficult to fully implement. Nevertheless, the final section of this book suggests that it may be impossible to achieve high levels of honesty in the workplace without fundamental changes in the way American organizations work.

Gaps in Our Knowledge
about Honesty in the Workplace

The research presented in Chapters 1 through 7 leads to two very general conclusions. First, dishonesty in the workplace is a serious problem. Second, a number of methods exist that are at least somewhat effective for encouraging honesty and discouraging dishonesty in the workplace. However, a number of serious problems still need to be addressed in both research on honesty in the workplace and applications of that research. In particular, there are a number of critical gaps in our knowledge, as well as a failure to consider the total range of strategies for dealing with honesty or to fully consider the interactions between and the unwanted side effects of different methods for encouraging honesty and discouraging dishonesty in the workplace.

Estimating the Frequency
and Seriousness of Workplace Dishonesty

Chapters 1, 3, and 4 discussed the surprising imprecision of estimates of the extent and seriousness of employee theft, drug use, production deviance, and so on. After examining the figures themselves and the processes by which these estimates are obtained, it is clear that anyone who quotes a particular figure as an accurate picture of the amount lost to theft, the extent of white-collar crime, the effects of employee drug use on productivity, or the like simply doesn't know what he or she is talking about. A more skeptical attitude toward the widely quoted figures for losses due to theft, production deviance, and other forms of workplace dishonesty is clearly warranted.

Social scientists often use confidence intervals to express the precision of their results; application of this practice to research on honesty in the workplace would help to inject a healthy dose of realism into the field. For example, instead of saying that $40 billion is lost annually to employee theft, it might be more realistic to say something like, "The amount lost to employee theft each year is somewhere in the range of $5 billion to $200 billion; the best guess is somewhere in the ballpark of $40 billion." If nothing else, statements such as these would focus everyone's attention on the dubious validity of the multibillion dollar figures that are so often quoted to justify various interventions such as employee drug testing, preemployment integrity tests, sophisticated and expensive security systems, and the like. All these interventions may be worthwhile, but none of them is likely to be as good or as important as its proponents claim.

Our ignorance of the true cost of theft, production deviance, and so on represents an obvious problem, but it may not be the most critical gap in our understanding of workplace dishonesty. Even if you accepted the lowest reasonable estimate of the seriousness of property and production deviance, drug use, white-collar crime, and so forth (for example, $5 billion for employee theft), you would still probably reach the same conclusion—that workplace dishonesty is a serious problem and that efforts to encourage honesty and discourage dishonesty are worthwhile. A much more serious gap in our knowledge and understanding of workplace dishonesty is in the area of estimating and interpreting base rates.

Understanding the Meaning and Measurement of Base Rates

It is often tempting to think of honesty in the workplace in terms of simple dichotomies, such as honest versus dishonest employees, or employees who commit some production deviance versus those who commit no production deviance. This way of thinking is not only simple, it also allows you to apply a wide range of analytic tools to the problem of analyzing the effects of various interventions and strategies for dealing with honesty. For example, the type of decision theory presented in Chapter 3, which classifies decisions as true positives, false positives, true negatives, and so on, requires that the outcome variable be dichotomous. Similarly, most discussions of base rates encourage this type of dichotomous thinking.

For example, suppose that an organization has 120 workers, and that the base rate for production deviance is estimated to be .75. This is usually taken to mean that 75% of all employees (that is, 90 employees) engage in some form of production deviance and 25% (that is, 30 employees) refrain from acts of production deviance. The problem with thinking about the world in terms of dichotomies such as honest/ dishonest is that you can lose a great deal of potentially important information by fitting everyone or everything into one of two categories. In this example, knowing that 75% of all employees engage in production deviance doesn't tell you (1) what specific types of deviance are most common, (2) the frequency of different types of deviance, (3) differences in individuals' patterns of deviance, and so on. The statement that 75% of your employees engage in production deviance could mean anything, ranging from the finding that most employees take an occasional long lunch to the finding that most employees sabotage production on a regular basis.

While information about base rates is useful, we clearly need to go beyond the base rate to understand the true extent and nature of workplace dishonesty. Two critical dimensions of workplace dishonesty that can be masked by quoting the overall base rate are its frequency and its severity. Returning to the example of the base rate for production deviance, knowing that 75% of all employees engage in this form of behavior simply doesn't tell you enough. A two-way contingency table, such as that presented in Table 8-1, would provide a compact way of describing the variations of dishonest behavior among those who are classified as having committed some form of production deviance.

The two-way table tells you a number of things, including the relationship between frequency and seriousness. Based on the figures shown in Table 8-1, you could conclude that most acts of production deviance are both infrequent and relatively minor and that serious acts are rare (however, keep in mind that definitions of "minor" or "serious" might be highly subjective). Furthermore, in this example, there is a small but potentially important relationship between frequency and seriousness; the correlation between frequency and seriousness, expressed as a contingency coefficient, is .08. Alternatively, you might want to combine the two dimensions into a single index of overall involvement in production deviance, which could be constructed

Table 8-1   *Two-Way Contingency Table Displaying Frequency and Seriousness of Production Deviance*

		Seriousness		
	TRIVIAL	*MINOR*	*MODERATE*	*SERIOUS*
RARE	17.5%[a]	9%[a]	3%[b]	2%[b]
OCCASIONAL	15.5%[a]	8%[a]	2%[c]	2%[c]
FREQUENT	14.5%[b]	5%[c]	1.5%[d]	1%[d]
CONSTANT	13.5%[b]	4%[c]	1%[d]	.5%[d]

Frequency (label for rows)

[a] Least serious

[b] Somewhat serious

[c] Moderately serious

[d] Most serious

NOTE: Figures in the table indicate the proportion of all individuals who commit production deviance who fall in each category. For example, in this case, 5 of every 1000 workers who commit production deviance are constantly involved in serious acts.

Figure 8-1   *Distribution of Involvement in Production Deviance Category*

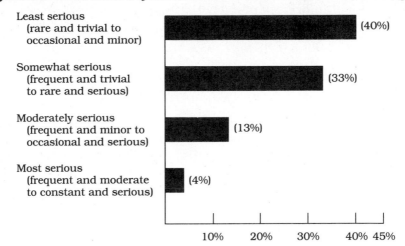

by considering both seriousness and frequency. For example, an individual who committed a few acts of truly serious production deviance has a higher level of involvement than an individual who commits a few, or even several, acts of a trivial nature.

To illustrate the process of combining information about seriousness and frequency, the data from Table 8-1 were grouped into four categories, reflecting a combination of frequency and seriousness. The first category (least serious) included acts that ranged from rare and trivial to occasional and minor. The second category (somewhat serious) included acts that ranged from frequent and trivial to rare and serious. The third category (moderately serious) included acts that ranged from frequent and minor to occasional and serious. The fourth category (most serious) included acts that ranged from frequent and moderate to constant and serious. The bar graph shown in Figure 8-1 illustrates the percentage of individuals involved in production deviance who fall into each of the four categories.

This figure suggests that nearly three-quarters of the individuals in this example fall into the two less serious categories, indicating relatively low levels of involvement in production deviance. It is important to note here that the figures used to generate Table 8-1 and Figure 8-1 are completely hypothetical; not enough is known about the true frequency and seriousness of production deviance to completely fill the cells of Table 8-1 (however, data presented by Hollinger and Clark, 1983, suggest that the figures used here are realistic). It is also important to note that contingency tables and frequency figures do not exhaust the range of methods that might be used to present information on the various behaviors that are collapsed into a category such as honest or dishonest. Rather, the methods illustrated in Table 8-1 and Figure 8-1 suggest some very simple graphic displays that could convey critical information about the frequency and seriousness of workplace dishonesty, which is lost by simply citing a base rate.

Importance of People and Situations in Determining Honesty

A second critical gap in both research and practice in the area of honesty in the workplace is our limited understanding of the relative importance of persons, situations, and particularly the interactions between personal and situational variables as determinants of honest or dishonest behaviors. Strategies aimed predominantly at either the person (such as integrity testing) or the situation (such as security systems) can undoubtedly help, but each approach attacks only part of the problem. While it is tempting to argue about which part of the problem—persons or situations—is more important, the question is probably moot. Persons affect situations and situations affect persons; what is needed is more research, and more applications of this research, dealing with the interaction between personal and situational variables (Sackett, 1985; Trevino, 1986). However, for a number of reasons, this type of research may be very difficult to do and even more difficult to apply.

In Chapter 1, I noted that situations can be classified as strong or weak and that the relative importance of personal characteristics as predictors of behavior is highest in weak situations and lowest in strong situations. Although the general characteristics of strong situations are well known (that is, they provide strong cues regarding appropriate behavior and strong incentives to follow those cues), the exact situational characteristics likely to lead to strong or weak situational influences on honesty are difficult to determine. One reason for this difficulty is that, as Schneider (1987) notes, the characteristics of the situation are in part determined by the people involved. A person who is thrown in with dishonest co-workers faces a dramatically different situation than does a person in the same organization, and in the same material situation, whose co-workers are generally honest. If nothing else, norms regarding honesty will certainly differ in the two groups.

Another difficulty in research on person × situation interactions and honesty, first suggested by Aristotle, is that the effects of honesty may not be symmetrical. Aristotle suggested that honest individuals behave the same way in a wide range of situations, whereas dishonest individuals are often impelled by the situation to hide their dishonesty and are dishonest only when the situation permits. I know of no empirical research testing the implicit hypothesis that honest individuals are better equipped to resist situational pressures, but it is an interesting possibility.

An alternative hypothesis is that Aristotle was only partly right; that is, there may be individuals at either extreme of the honesty continuum whose behavior is rarely if ever affected by situational forces. I would label this the "sociopaths and saints" hypothesis. The relatively small influence of situational pressures on individuals who are extremely dishonest (sociopaths) or extremely honest (saints) can be explained by noting that these individuals rarely encounter situational pressures that are as strong as their personal inclinations to either lie or adhere to the truth. True interactions between personal and situational factors might be confined to those individuals who are nearer to the middle on the continuum from sociopaths to saints.

This alternative hypothesis suggests that situational factors become more important when personal inclinations toward honesty in a particular group of people are clustered around the middle range (that is, the group has very few sociopaths or saints and lots of moderately honest people). If everyone is in that ethically ambiguous state in which they can easily be influenced toward either honesty or dishonesty, it is obviously important to remove situational pressures toward dishonesty and put into place situational incentives for honest behavior. On the other hand, if everyone is either a saint or a sinner, there may be little you can do about honesty other than to install a good alarm system and hope for the best.

Unanticipated Side Effects of Honesty Interventions

A third gap in our knowledge is the failure to fully consider the unwanted side effects of many of the interventions designed to decrease dishonesty or increase honesty in the workplace. Earlier, I noted that the use of integrity tests that ask specifically about theft and other dishonest behaviors (that is, overt or clear-purpose tests) could lead to more dishonesty as a result of (1) heightening applicants' and employees' awareness of theft and opportunities for theft, (2) suggesting that theft is common, which can lead to greater tolerance of theft, and (3) relaxing the vigilance of managers, who may think that the test solves all of their problems with workplace dishonesty. Similarly, the use of intrusive procedures such as polygraph testing, drug testing through urinalysis, computerized monitoring of workers, or periodic searches of the workplace could create more problems than they solve, by creating the perception that the workplace is a hostile environment and that management is distrustful and suspicious.

Clear evidence shows that employees' satisfaction with their jobs and commitment to the organization are critical determinants of both property and production deviance; in the section that follows, I will review methods that might be used to increase organizational commitment. It follows from this research that organizational policies and actions that lead to dissatisfaction, distrust, lack of commitment, and so on can raise the potential for a wide variety of acts against the organization.

Research on reaction to employee drug testing (for example, Murphy & Thornton, 1992; Murphy, Thornton, & Prue, 1991; Murphy, Thornton, & Reynolds, 1990) suggests that it may not be what the organization does so much as how it does it that determines employees' reactions to various efforts to control dishonesty and encourage honesty. Policies that seem arbitrary, unrealistically restrictive, or unduly invasive of employees' privacy seem to provoke negative reactions. On the other hand, if the same policies are carefully explained or justified, reactions seem substantially more positive. This explanation probably needs to go beyond a simple statement that the policy in question has been put into place to deal with employee theft; elements such as prior consultation with employees or their representatives and procedural guarantees of employee rights (such as a system for appealing adverse decisions) contribute to employee acceptance of policies designed to deal with honesty in the workplace.

While the goal of encouraging honesty seems widely accepted, programs that are truly effective can have the unanticipated consequence of encouraging honesty in circumstances where a little dishonesty would probably be preferred. For example, suppose you convinced all supervisors to be completely honest in their annual performance appraisals. If instead of receiving the usual inflated appraisals everyone received exactly what he or she deserved, the consequences would probably be high levels of dissatisfaction, diminished motivation, and lower commitment to the organization (Murphy & Cleveland, 1991). It is not clear whether the benefits of absolute honesty would in this case outweigh the costs. Similarly, an organization that commits itself to encouraging honesty might experience more incidents of whistle-blowing, which immediately put the policy of organizational honesty to the test. If you really want honesty, you will not only have to put up with whistle-blowing, you might have to reward and encourage this type of behavior.

Organizations that attempt to encourage honesty will at some point have to face the difficult question of how much honesty they really want or can stand. As long as an organization doesn't do anything to encourage honesty, it can get away with the sort of platitudes found in typical organizational mission statements, but as soon as an organization gets serious about encouraging honesty, it will also have to be serious about the consequences.

Future Directions for Research and Application

The research reviewed in this book suggests a number of avenues for future research and application that hold significant promise for encouraging honesty and discouraging dishonesty in the workplace. First, given the importance of job satisfaction and organizational commitment as possible causes of honest or dishonest behavior in the workplace, it seems obvious that efforts to increase employees' satisfaction and commitment should have a substantial impact on honesty. A number of books in the popular and scientific press have suggested ways of developing high-involvement organizations, which supposedly are more productive, efficient, and profitable than organizations in which employees are not involved in their work. Whether the claims of proponents of high-involvement organizations will turn out to be correct is a question beyond the scope of this book. However, many of the strategies used to develop such organizations are likely to have a substantial impact on honesty in the workplace, and even if they do nothing else, they may be worthwhile for that reason.

Second, methods of assessing both persons and situations, with the goal of matching persons and situations in ways that minimize dishonesty while also minimizing some of the side effects noted above, may have a significant impact on the workplace. Finally, programs for the ongoing assessment of integrity, as opposed to assessments with a single preemployment test, hold promise for encouraging honesty at work.

Organizational Commitment and Honesty in the Workplace

Individuals react in very different ways to the organizations in which they work. Some workers give little thought to the organization, whereas others have very strong feelings, ranging from contempt and disgust to a high degree of loyalty to and identification with the organization. Social scientists and organizational researchers have devoted considerable attention to the concept of organizational commitment and to understanding its nature, causes, and consequences.

A variety of definitions of organizational commitment have been suggested (Eisenberger et al., 1986; Etzioni, 1975; Kanter, 1968; Salancik, 1977; Staw, 1977), many of which include concepts such as identification with the goals and values of the organization; an exchange of regard, rewards, and attachment between the organization and the individual; and an attachment to co-workers and other social relations at work. Mowday, Porter, and Steers (1982) define organizational commitment as a multidimensional construct that includes three distinct components: (1) a desire to maintain membership with the organization, (2) belief in and acceptance of the values and goals of the organization, and (3) a willingness to exert effort on behalf of the organization.

Several authors have noted that commitment is strongly related to theft and other forms of dishonesty (Frank, 1989; Mowday, Porter, & Steers, 1982; Schein, 1968); Hollinger and Clark (1983) suggested that one way to reduce theft might be the use of preemployment screening tests or interviews designed to predict commitment to the organization. As Frank (1989) notes, people are more likely to steal from strangers and from people or organizations with whom they have formed no bonds than from family, friends, and groups with which they identify. This tendency suggests that one method of reducing employee theft and other forms of dishonesty harmful to the organization is to increase the commitment of employees to the organization.

As is true of so many other qualities, organizational commitment is affected by both personal and situational variables. There is evidence that personality characteristics, such as conscientiousness, are positively related to organizational commitment (Kozlowsky & Moaz, 1988; Mowday, Porter, & Steers, 1982; Weiner, 1982). There is also evidence that older employees and employees with more tenure show higher levels of commitment, whereas education is negatively correlated with commitment (Mowday, Porter, & Steers, 1982).

Situational variables thought to affect commitment include the level of job stress (stress is negatively correlated with commitment; see Morris & Sherman, 1981; Stevens, Beyer, & Trice, 1978), job scope, opportunities for interesting work, and autonomy (all are positively correlated with commitment; see Mottaz, 1988; Steers, 1977; Stevens, Beyer, & Trice, 1978). Pay equity and the extent to which the organization values the individual's work are also positively correlated with commitment (Eisenberger et al., 1986; Steers, 1977). Finally, systems that provide employees with some feeling of ownership (either actual ownership or psychological identification with the organization), such as stock option plans, seem to lead to higher levels of commitment (Tucker, Nook, & Toscano, 1989).

Perceived organizational support. The concept of "perceived organizational support" is critical for understanding the conditions under which individuals are likely to show high or low levels of commitment to the organization. Eisenberger, Fasolo, and Davis-LaMastro (1990) define perceived support as the extent to which employees believe that the organization values their contributions and cares about their well-being. Organizations that pay fairly; make efforts to guarantee the safety, health, and comfort of their workers; are willing to recognize and reward extra-role behaviors (behaviors not required by the job but beneficial to the organization); and show concern over equity in dealing with their employees are more likely to be seen as supportive than organizations that do not. Rewards, praise, and approval are also important components of organizational support (Eisenberger et al., 1986). Organizations that reward excellence and that make efforts to convey praise and approval in circumstances where it is deserved are more likely to be seen as supportive than organizations that do not.

Perceived organizational support is directly related to both the attitudes and behaviors of workers. First, there is evidence that support from the organization increases the likelihood that employees will identify with and internalize the values and norms of the organization (Eisenberger et al., 1986; Eisenberger, Fasolo, & Davis-LaMastro, 1990). In particular, individuals who believe that the organization values them and cares about them tend to perceive the organization's gains and losses as their own, in the sense that what is good for the organization is also seen as good for them and what harms the organization is seen as bad for them. It seems clear that employees who identify with the organization in this way will be less likely to engage in dishonest behaviors that hurt the organization than will employees who do not identify with the organization. Second, there is evidence that perceived organizational support is directly related to both job performance (Eisenberger, Fasolo, & Davis-LaMastro, 1990, report a positive correlation ($r = .33$) between support and performance) and absenteeism (here, the correlation is negative ($r = -.40$); see Eisenberger et al., 1986, and Eisenberger, Fasolo, & Davis-LaMastro, 1990). Finally, perceived organizational support is associated with a variety of prosocial acts on behalf of the organization (Brief & Motowidlo, 1986; Mowday, Porter, & Steers, 1982).

Increasing organizational commitment. If one accepts the hypothesis that employees who show high levels of commitment and loyalty to the organization are unlikely to engage in dishonest behavior at work (especially when this behavior is harmful to the organization), it seems clear that one strategy for dealing with dishonesty at work will entail attempts to increase employees' commitment to the organization. There are some reasons to believe that this strategy will work. For example, Frank (1989) noted that employee theft is relatively rare in Japan and suggested that one reason for this low level of theft is that Japanese workers are highly loyal and committed to the organizations in which they work. He attributed this high level of commitment to a combination of cultural factors and extensive efforts on the part of Japanese corporations to socialize members of their organizations.

The fact that organizational commitment is a product of both the characteristics of the individual and of the situation suggests two strategies for increasing commitment to the organization. First, an organization might select individuals who are most likely to become committed to the organization. Second, conditions within the organization might be created that foster commitment. I will focus on the latter strategy, in part because little is known about the feasibility of identifying and selecting people who are more likely to commit to a specific organization.

Mathieu and Zajac's (1990) review identifies three ways in which the organization might affect employees' level of commitment: through characteristics of the job, through the relationship between work groups and their leaders or superiors, and through the definition of each employee's role in the organization. First, the job must provide autonomy, challenge, scope, and opportunities for intrinsic rewards (Mathieu & Zajac, 1990; Mottaz, 1988). If most jobs are boring, simple, and repetitive, it is unlikely that high levels of commitment will develop. Second, relations between work groups and their leaders must be effective (DeCotiis & Summers, 1987; Luthans, Baack, & Taylor, 1987). Leaders must communicate well with their subordinates, seek out and make use of participation, provide appropriate guidance and structure for critical tasks, and look after the welfare of their subordinates (Mathieu & Zajac, 1990). Third, employees' roles in the organization must be clearly and consistently defined. There is substantial evidence that role ambiguity, role conflict, and role overload all detract from commitment to the organization (DeCotiis & Summers, 1987; Mathieu & Zajac, 1990).

In his book on high-involvement management, Lawler (1986) reviewed a number of interventions that have been applied in organizations to increase employees' level of participation, commitment, and involvement in the organization. These interventions include quality circles, survey feedback, job enrichment, the design of semiautonomous work teams, gainsharing, and joint union–management programs to improve the quality of work life. There is evidence that all these approaches can improve productivity and organizational effectiveness, although the precise mechanisms responsible for the success of these programs in different organizations are not yet fully understood. Although the research and practice reviewed by Lawler does not deal directly with honesty in the workplace, it is reasonable to believe that any or all of these interventions could help reduce dishonesty, at least to the extent that the interventions increase commitment to the organization. A good deal of research will be needed before the effectiveness of interventions such as these in reducing dishonesty, increasing honesty, or both can be determined.

Adler and Adler (1988) discuss the ways in which intense loyalty to organizations might develop. Elements that contribute to loyalty, which might be defined as an extreme form of commitment, include a dominating leader, identification with the group or organization (developed, for example, through opportunities to publicly represent the organization), cohesion, and goal alignment (the belief that an individual's ultimate ends are served by advancing the goals of the organization). Research on identification with groups (for example, Sherif & Sherif, 1969) suggests that another key to loyalty might be shared hardship or adversity. Individuals who weather difficult times in organizations might develop high levels of commitment and loyalty, particularly if the organization shows continuing loyalty to them.

Unanticipated side effects of commitment.   High levels of commitment and loyalty are not sure cures for all types of dishonesty at work. Although they may tend to reduce the number of crimes against

Box 8-1   *How Japanese Organizations Build Commitment*

It is widely believed that the success of Japanese organizations in manufacturing high-quality goods is partly due to the high levels of commitment shown by their workers. Although this commitment is partly due to cultural factors, there is evidence that it is also a product of the way in which Japanese organizations are structured and managed (Lincoln & Kalleberg, 1990).

Two aspects of Japanese organizations have received the most attention. First, these organizations are more likely to seek consensus and input from lower levels in the organization (the *ringi* system) than their U.S. counterparts are. Second, and perhaps more important, large employers sometimes provide an extraordinary array of services and benefits. These range from permanent employment to company housing and health care; sex education and family planning classes; classes for women in flower arranging, cooking, and dance; clubs dedicated to art, chess, or the tea ceremony; and schools for employees' children. Some organizations offer religious services at company shrines, and many sponsor frequent outings, festivals, and contests.

Although some of the benefits of such "company welfarism" are attractive, this strategy also has its dark side. Critics of Japanese organizations complain that this extensive involvement of the organization in all phases of its employees' lives illustrates a stifling, paternalistic attitude. Lincoln and Kalleberg (1990) also suggest that younger Japanese, who are growing up in a more affluent society, may be less willing to subordinate their concerns to those of the organization. It may be that the very success of Japanese organizations is planting the seeds for a society in which it will be difficult to sustain current high levels of commitment to the organization.

the organization, commitment and loyalty may increase the number of crimes on behalf of the organization. Research on white-collar crime (for example, Dinitz, 1982; Meier & Short, 1982) suggests that the individuals engaged in these activities often take substantial risks even though they expect relatively little in the way of personal benefit. It may be that their loyalty to the organization encourages them to take actions that seem to benefit the organization, even when those actions are illegal or otherwise sanctionable.

Commitment to and loyalty to the organization is also likely to inhibit behaviors such as whistle-blowing and to increase the likelihood that individual employees, managers, or executives will cooperate with various forms of organizational misconduct, especially if that misconduct appears to have the support of respected and powerful role models. High levels of commitment may also give additional strength to organizational norms, and if those norms encourage or tolerate dishonest behavior, commitment to the organization could increase the incidence of such behavior.

The net effect of commitment on honesty in the workplace probably depends on the norms and values that are part of the organization's culture. If dishonest behavior is rewarded, commitment can have a disastrous effect, turning honest individuals into dishonest employees. On the other hand, if the organization truly values honesty, commitment to that organization may provide a strong incentive for honest behavior.

Matching Persons and Situations

The "sociopaths and saints" hypothesis discussed earlier suggests that some individuals are largely immune to situational pressures for either honest or dishonest behavior, but that most individuals are to some degree affected by situational characteristics, ranging from security procedures to the prevailing norms regarding honesty. The fact that most individuals are neither sociopaths nor saints suggests that organizations should pay careful attention to the situational variables that may encourage either honest or dishonest behavior in their employees.

One strategy for dealing with situational variables is to prepare for the worst case scenario—that is, to start with the assumption that everyone is basically dishonest and must be deterred from committing acts of property and production deviance and to arrange the situation accordingly. This strategy has two drawbacks: it is expensive, and it creates an atmosphere of hostility and suspicion, which is likely to negatively affect satisfaction, commitment, and eventually honesty. An alternative is to prepare for the best case scenario, based on the optimistic assumption that everyone is basically honest. This assumption will save money on security systems and will preclude some of the problems caused by tight or intrusive security and control measures, but it also gives less honest employees a virtual license to steal.

The best compromise between preparing for the worst case, by installing elaborate security and other situational controls, and hoping for the best case, by paying little attention to situational factors, might involve matching individuals to situations. Some individuals are near the "saints" end of the continuum and would be unlikely to engage in dishonest behavior in most situations. Placing those individuals in situations where there are few substantial efforts to control dishonesty or to encourage honesty would probably be a safe bet; they will probably be honest in any case. On the other hand, some individuals need constant supervision, as well as substantial incentives, to remain honest. Placing these individuals in situations that strongly discourage dishonesty and strongly encourage honesty may be your only hope.

Assume for a moment that personal and situational characteristics could be measured on the same scale (see Chatman, 1989, and O'Reilly, Chatman, & Caldwell, 1991, for examples of such measurement). Given such measures, the matching process described above would work in the way illustrated in Figure 8-2. Individuals whose personal inclinations toward honesty are relatively weak should be placed in situations where strong measures are taken to deter dishonesty and encourage honesty. Individuals whose personal inclinations toward honesty are relatively strong require less in the way of situational pressure.

Figure 8-2 suggests that mismatches between individuals and situations can cause problems in two ways. First, they lead an organization

Figure 8-2   *Matching the Characteristics of People and Situations*

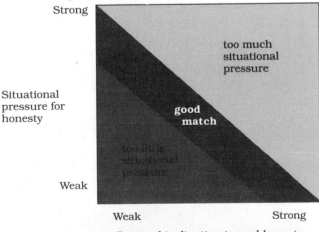

to waste resources by putting into place situational pressures that are entirely unnecessary (for example, strong deterrents and expensive ethical training for individuals who would behave honestly without those pressures). Second, a mismatch may cause the organization to risk exposure to production and property deviance by putting individuals into situations that tempt them beyond their power to resist. Good matches between individual characteristics and situational pressures may make possible a high degree of efficiency in efforts to manipulate situational variables that affect honesty in the workplace.

Barriers to implementation.   Although the idea of matching individuals to situations has clear appeal, there are a number of practical barriers to its immediate implementation. First and most obvious, there is no good method for measuring the characteristics of persons and situations on comparable scales. Most measures of honesty, conscientiousness, and other relevant personality traits employ normative scales, in which each individual's score is interpreted in relation to some normative group or population. For example, a personality inventory might indicate that an individual is in the 95th percentile on the scale labeled "honesty," which means that his or her score is as high as or higher than 95% of the population for which this test was designed, or on which it was normed. There are few standardized instruments for measuring situations, but these would probably also report scores in a normative fashion, this time comparing this particular situation to the range of all possible situations. Thus, if the pressures for honesty in a particular situation were in the 95th percentile, this would mean that compared to other situations, this one exhibited strong pressures for honesty. Even if such a measure could be obtained, there would be no reasonable way to compare the scores from person-oriented and situation-oriented normative measures. That is, a score that represents the 95th percentile for persons cannot be sensibly compared to a score that represents the 95th percentile for situations.

Item response theory (Drasgow & Hulin, 1991) provides an idea of how this dilemma might be solved. This theory is used to understand the meaning of test scores and responses. One of the many differences between this theory and the classical theory of reliability that dominated psychological testing for most of its history is that item response theory defines the difficulty of a test item in terms of the amount of ability needed to respond correctly, rather than in terms of how many people choose the right or wrong answer. An analogous strategy might be applied to the problem of matching persons and situations. That is, personal characteristics and situational characteristics may not represent two distinct variables, but rather two different ways of thinking about the same variable—the likelihood of dishonest behavior.

One way to define an honest person is to note that he or she behaves honestly in a wide range of situations, whereas a dishonest person behaves honestly only when the situation permits; this is Aristotle's definition. One way to define a situation conducive to honesty is to note that in such a situation, most persons are honest. In a situation conducive to dishonesty, more people are dishonest. The concept that links persons and situations in this case is the probability or likelihood of dishonest behavior.

It might be possible to express a person's honesty in terms of the percentage of all reasonable situations in which he or she would exhibit honesty. For example, a person who is honest in 98% of the situations in which he or she might reasonably be found is more honest than another who exhibits honest behavior in only 40% of all situations. Similarly, you might express the situational pressures for honesty in terms of the percentage of all individuals who behave honestly in that situation. A situation in which 90% of all people are honest exhibits stronger pressure than a situation in which 50% of all people are honest.

It is not clear whether matching persons and situations in terms of these percentages (for example, a person who is honest 70% of the time might be best placed in situations where 30% of all individuals are honest) would be optimal, but it would provide a good starting point and a probable basis for finding the best tradeoff between personal inclinations and situational pressures best suited to ensure honesty in the workplace.

Ongoing Assessment of Honesty and Integrity

Although integrity tests are quite useful, they are not always used in the optimal way. For example, the most common use of integrity tests is in preemployment testing, when individuals are tested once and either hired or rejected, partly on the basis of test scores. This use of the tests makes sense from the perspective of personality research, which suggests that the personality traits that seem most related to honesty are relatively stable. However, a case can be made for the ongoing assessment of honesty and integrity, as opposed to the current one-shot assessment technique.

Research reviewed in several earlier chapters suggests that the norms, climate, and culture of an organization affect the beliefs, attitudes, and behaviors of employees. An individual who joins the organization with a strong belief in honesty and integrity may soon find himself or herself acting in ways inconsistent with those beliefs. Some people learn to live with this inconsistency, whereas others simply leave the situation. However, many people adapt to the situation by slowly changing their perceptions, attitudes, and beliefs. Knowing what a person believes at the point of entering the organization may not tell you much about his or her beliefs a few months or years down the road. Even if you hire individuals whose current attitudes, beliefs, and personalities are indicative of honesty, there is no guarantee that they will not change.

Ongoing assessments of honesty and integrity might yield a variety of benefits. First and most obvious, it helps determine whether individuals who were hired partly because of beliefs, attitudes, and personality characteristics related to honesty have changed. Second, it provides an indirect way of assessing the effects of socialization into the organization. If individuals hired into a particular division or unit routinely become more tolerant of dishonesty after a few months in the unit, this pattern is a clear indication of trouble with the unit. Third, this type of ongoing assessment might be useful for assessing the overall drift of the organization. Consistent negative changes could indicate changes in the culture of the organization—or of society in general. On the other hand, if the organization is engaged in systematic efforts to increase honesty, trends in scores on integrity tests might provide one useful measure for assessing the effectiveness of those efforts.

As with any other assessment program, it is important to consider the actions that might be taken on the basis of assessment outcomes. In particular, you need to decide what to do about an individual who passes an integrity test at the point of hire but fails a similar test at some later date. It is clear that you should not fire or discipline an otherwise satisfactory employee on the basis of a single test score. On the other hand, there is no point in doing an ongoing assessment if you plan to ignore the results. The results of later assessments may indicate the need for careful monitoring of employees whose scores seem to indicate an increased risk of theft or other forms of workplace dishonesty, especially if the employees in question are placed in situations that present opportunities to commit acts of production or property deviance.

Ongoing assessments of integrity might include anything from regular assessments of shrinkage rates in different work areas to periodic administration of integrity tests to individual employees. Strategies that involve repeated testing present a variety of practical and technical problems that deserve close attention. For example, if the same exact test form is administered at regular intervals to each employee, you must be concerned with carryover effects—that is, the effects of previous test administrations on responses to the current test. Carryover effects can be reduced to some extent by using alternative forms of the test at each administration, but relatively few integrity tests provide alternative forms (O'Bannon, Goldinger, & Appleby, 1989). Another strategy might be to use different tests at different times, but this makes the comparison of test scores difficult. Different integrity tests measure different factors and employ different measurement strategies (for example, clear-purpose and veiled-purpose tests differ in important respects), and scores may not be directly comparable. Finally, you must always consider the effects of measurement error on comparisons between test scores. All tests, including integrity tests, are affected by errors in measurement, and seemingly large changes in test scores may reflect nothing more than measurement error. This point is discussed further in the section that follows.

Measuring and interpreting change.   It is surprisingly difficult to determine whether people's attitudes and beliefs have changed over a set period of time. The most immediate obstacle to making this assessment is the lack of alternative forms for many questionnaires and scales that might be used to assess integrity and honesty. If individuals are asked to respond to the same exact questionnaire many times, eventually their responses to the current form must become contaminated by their responses to the earlier versions. For example, suppose I came by every month and asked you if you were satisfied with your job. Eventually, you might start to wonder why I keep asking the same question, and what is so wrong with the job that I keep raising the question.

The technical literature on the measurement of change is large and diverse (although dated, Harris, 1963, is still the best single reference). One particularly difficult problem is that the most obvious method of measuring change—that is, by calculating the simple difference between scores at Time 1 and scores at Time 2—is probably the worst. Difference scores are highly unreliable, particularly when they are based on administrations of the same scale at two different points; they are plagued by a host of statistical problems that make their interpretation extremely difficult (Cronbach, 1990; Murphy & Davidshofer, 1991).

In addition to the statistical and psychometric problems encountered when measuring change, substantive questions about the meaning of change often arise. Golembiewski, Billingsley, and Yeager (1976) suggested that many organizational interventions can lead to different types of change, which may not all have the same meaning. For example, sending managers to a seminar on business ethics might simply make them more honest. However, it might also change their conception of how honest they actually are. If the seminar makes them aware of ethical violations that previously went unnoticed, managers might report that they are less honest after attending the seminar than they would have reported that they were before. Finally, the seminar might change managers' understanding of exactly what is meant by honesty in the workplace; for example, they might now regard production deviance as dishonesty, whereas they once thought of it as simple laziness. Any of these changes could affect their responses to ongoing assessments of honesty in the workplace.

The framework developed by Golembiewski, Billingsley, and Yeager (1976) does not exhaust the set of possibilities, but it does provide a starting point for asking questions about what kind of change might occur over time in the attitudes, beliefs, norms, and personal characteristics that contribute to honesty, rather than focusing solely on how much change occurred. It is possible that any or all of the types of change described in this framework could occur as the result of interventions by the organization, such as publishing and discussing a code of ethics; events outside of the organization, like news reports of organizational misconduct; or the simple passage of time.

Can Honesty Thrive in the American Workplace?

The structures, cultures, products, and management styles of American corporations very tremendously. Nevertheless, a number of features are common to most corporations that, taken together, make it difficult to envision high levels of honesty among employees, managers, or executives. Some of these features were discussed in earlier chapters (for example, diversification and "absentee ownership"). In this final section, I will focus on three features of American corporations that probably contribute to dishonesty at all levels: (1) the formal and informal reward systems, (2) the system of status differentiation, and (3) the time frame for defining success.

Compared to similar organizations in other countries, U.S. corporations typically have more levels of management and faster career progression. They are more likely to use promotion as a reward and failure to receive promotion as a punishment, to distribute substantial rewards for success and substantial punishments for failure, to overpay their managers and executives, and to emphasize outcomes (such as third-quarter sales) more than processes (for example, if those sales were attained by depleting stocks needed elsewhere). Certainly, there are exceptions, but these themes repeatedly emerge from cross-cultural research on organizations. The important point here is that *all* of these features contribute to dishonesty in the workplace, particularly at the managerial and executive level. They also probably influence honesty at the shop-floor level, because the behavior of managers and executives affects the norms and behaviors of all employees, both through direct observational learning and through their effects on the culture of the organization.

The hierarchical structure of U.S. corporations also contributes to dishonesty at all levels of the organizations. In many organizations, wide status differences exist between labor and management, and similar differences between top executives and lower-level managers. This gap probably contributes to a sense of alienation among nonexempt employees, and it may contribute to delusions of grandeur among executives. News stories about employees' concerns with uncaring organizations and about executives' abuse of privileges are depressingly familiar. It is likely that the sometimes excessive gap between different levels in the organization contributes to both the sense of alienation and the inflated sense of worth of employees and executives, respectively, and that these in turn increase the likelihood of a number of forms of dishonest behavior. Employees who feel alienated are probably more likely to engage in production deviance than are those who feel connected to the company. Executives who overestimate their power, importance, and worth are probably more likely to bend the rules than those with less exalted standing in the organization.

Finally, the legendary American obsession with short-term results creates both opportunities and pressures to commit a variety of dishonest acts. Some of the best minds in law, accounting, and management are devoted to the art of creating paper profits, systems for juggling resources, creative tax shelters, and a variety of other dodges to make this quarter's figures look especially good. Even if you ignore the basic dishonesty of much of this activity, the diversion of so much talent away from the potentially useful work it could be doing instead is a clear waste.

Managers who don't (or can't) cook the books to make their short-term profits look good still have at their disposal a variety of other profit-maximizing strategies that are, in the long run, both dishonest and bad for the organization. For example, if you are the boss of the third shift in an underground coal mine, you might be tempted to let the other two shifts take care of maintenance, and tell your workers to dig as much coal as possible without worrying about fixing leaks, installing timbers, and so on. In the short term, this will be very good for you, even though in the long run the mine will probably collapse.

Structures That Promote Honesty

In the last ten years, several books on organizational excellence have been published ranging from those that incorporate substantial amounts of research (for example, Lawler, 1986) to those drawn largely from interviews and anecdotes. A recurring theme in those books is that the organization of the future will be flatter (have fewer levels of managment) than current corporations are, will be more participative and less authoritarian, and will focus on quality and long-term relations with suppliers, customers, and other stakeholders. This type of organization may or may not thrive in the global economy; it is too soon to tell. However, this seems exactly the type of organization likely to achieve high levels of honesty.

Organizations of this type would foster honesty in many ways. First, they would tend to remove both the incentive for and the possibility of committing many forms of organizational misconduct. Actions that jeopardize the relationships between the organization and various stakeholders are less likely to be rewarded and more likely to be monitored in such an organization. As noted earlier, this type of organization is also more likely to foster commitment and satisfaction, both of which contribute to norms that discourage dishonesty and encourage honesty in the workplace. Because these organizations would also allow employees more opportunities to directly observe the behavior and norms of high-status individuals, they would also provide enhanced opportunities for behavioral modeling.[1]

Finally, this type of organization may attract different types of employees. Individuals who have no desire to identify with the job or the organization may gravitate to more traditional organizations, whereas individuals predisposed to commitment and involvement may gravitate to these newer organizations. Research reviewed in several earlier chapters suggests that someone who is predisposed to commitment is exactly the type of person who is most likely to be honest, all other factors being equal.

Although this style of organization is now widely recommended, it is not clear whether American organizations will in fact move in this direction. Organizational change is usually a slow and painful process, and the expected gain may not be worth the pain to all managers, executives, or shareholders. Nevertheless, if organizations of this type can develop and thrive, they may provide the best chance to achieve and sustain high levels of honesty in the workplace.

SUMMARY

This chapter highlighted both problems and promising directions for future research and application in the area of honesty in the workplace. First among the problem areas cited here were the critical gaps in our knowledge about the extent and seriousness of workplace dishonesty. Perhaps the most important gap is in our understanding of

---

[1] However, as I noted in Chapter 7, modeling could work against you if the individuals who serve as models are more dishonest than the observers who are modeling their behavior.

the true meaning of the various figures that are so widely quoted for the base rates and the amounts lost to various forms of property and production deviance. Second, limitations in our understanding of person × situation interactions and their implications for honesty in the workplace were discussed. On the whole, too little attention is paid to the joint effects of persons and situations. Most strategies for increasing honesty or decreasing dishonesty in the workplace focus on the person or on the situation; strategies that consider both dimensions together are rare.

Third, the unanticipated effects of programs to discourage dishonesty or encourage honesty were discussed. It is critical to think through two issues that seem to be ignored in many interventions: (1) the reactions of employees and job applicants to these interventions, and (2) the way the organization might look if these interventions actually work. Several researchers and commentators (for example, Murphy & Cleveland, 1991; Zeitlin, 1971) have suggested that a little dishonesty is good for you, and that an organization in which everyone was honest about everything would encounter a wide range of problems.

Three areas for future research and application were identified. First, efforts to increase employees' commitment and loyalty to the organization seem worthwhile for a number of reasons, including the strong possibility that high levels of commitment will lead to lower levels of dishonesty. However, it is also important to watch for the possibility that high levels of commitment will lead to more dishonesty in situations where dishonest behavior appears to benefit the organization. Without loyal, committed employees, many forms of organizational misconduct would be impossible.

A second promising idea is matching individuals to situations. Several practical and technical problems have to be solved, but if you can determine the optimal level of situation pressure needed to maintain honesty in different individuals or groups, it may be possible to achieve a high level of efficiency—without the unintended side effects noted earlier—in a program designed to increase honesty or decrease dishonesty. A third suggestion is that assessments of integrity should be ongoing; to assess integrity only once is to assume that the beliefs, attitudes, norms, and so on that encourage honesty in the workplace never change.

The final section of this chapter discussed features of corporations and other organizations that appear to encourage workplace dishonesty and suggested ways the workplace must change if we are ever to achieve high levels of honesty. These changes overlap considerably with those called for by a number of organizational theorists and experts on organizational excellence. It may be that in organizations of the future, honesty will be easier to achieve and sustain.

References

Abend, J. (1989, June). More deterrents to theft. *Stores, 71*, 61–65.

Adler, P. A., & Adler, P. (1988). Intense loyalty in organizations: A case study of student athletes. *Administrative Science Quarterly, 33*, 401–417.

Akers, R. L. (1985). *Deviant behavior: A social learning approach* (3rd ed.). Belmont, CA: Wadsworth.

Altheide, D. L., Adler, P. A., Adler, P., & Altheide, D. A. (1978). The social meanings of employee theft. In J. M. Johnson & J. D. Douglas (Eds.), *Crime at the top: Deviance in business and the professions* (pp. 90–124). Philadelphia: Lippincott.

Anglin, D. (1988). *Monitoring drug abuse prevalence in the workforce*. Presented at NIDA Conference on Drugs in the Workplace. Washington, DC.

Angoff, W. H. (1988). Validity: An evolving concept. In H. Wainer & H. Brown (Eds.), *Test validity* (pp. 19–32). Hillsdale, NJ: Erlbaum.

APA Task Force. (1991). *Questionnaires used in the prediction of trustworthiness in pre-employment selection decisions: An A.P.A. Task Force Report.* Washington, DC: American Psychological Association.

Argyris, C., & Schon, D. A. (1988). Reciprocal integrity: Creating conditions that encourage personal and organizational integrity. In S. Srivastva (Ed.), *Executive integrity* (pp. 197–222). San Francisco: Jossey-Bass.

Arvey, R. D., & Faley, R. H. (1988). *Fairness in selecting employees* (2nd ed.). Reading, MA: Addison-Wesley.

Ash, P. (1976). The assessment of honesty in employment. *South African Journal of Psychology, 6*, 68–79.

Ash, P. (1991). *The construct of employee theft proneness.* Park Ridge, IL: SRA/London House.

Axline, L. L. (1988). Ethics: Good for business? *Communications, 2* (9), 86–89.

Axline, L. L. (1990). The bottom line on ethics. *Journal of Accountancy, 170* (12), 87–91.

Bacas, H. (1987). To stop a thief. *Nation's Business, 75* (6), 16–23.

Balzer, W. K., & Sulsky, L. M. (1990). Performance appraisal effectiveness and productivity. In K. Murphy & F. Saal (Eds.), *Psychology in organizations: Integrating science and practice* (pp. 133–156). Hillsdale, NJ: Erlbaum.

Bandura, A. (1977). *Social learning theory.* Englewood Cliffs, NJ: Prentice Hall.

Bandura, A. (1986). *Social foundations of thought and action: A social cognitive theory.* Englewood Cliffs, NJ: Prentice Hall.

Bar-Hillel, M., & Ben-Shakhar, G. (1986). The a priori case against graphology. In B. Nevo (Ed.), *Scientific aspects of graphology.* Chicago: Charles C Thomas.

Barland, G. H. (1988). The polygraph test in the USA and elsewhere. In A. Gale (Ed.), *The polygraph test: Lies, truth and science* (pp. 73–95). London: Sage.

Baron, R. A., & Byrne, D. (1991). *Social psychology: Understanding human interaction* (6th ed.). Boston: Allyn & Bacon.

Barrick, M. R., & Mount, M. K. (1991). The big five personality dimensions and job performance: A meta analysis. *Personnel Psychology, 44*, 1–26.

Bateman, T. S., & Organ, D. W. (1983). Job satisfaction and the good soldier: The relationship between affect and employee "citizenship." *Academy of Management Journal, 26*, 587–595.

Battan, D. (1984). *Handwriting analysis: A guide to personality.* San Luis Obispo, CA: Padre Productions.

Baucus, M. S. (1989). Why firms do it and what happens to them: A re-examination of the theory of illegal corporate behavior. In J. Poste (Ed.), *Research in corporate social performance and policy* (vol. 11, pp. 93–118). Greenwich, CT: JAI Press.

Baxter, G. D., & Rarick, C. A. (1987). Education for the moral development of managers: Kohlberg's stages of moral development and integrative education. *Journal of Business Ethics, 6*, 243–248.

Becker, H., & Fritzche, D. (1987). Business ethics: A cross-cultural comparison of managers' attitudes. *Journal of Business Ethics, 6*, 289–295.

Bem, D. J., & Allen, A. (1974). On predicting some of the people some of the time: The search for cross-situational consistencies in behavior. *Psychological Review, 81*, 506–520.

Bem, D. J., & Funder, D. D. (1978). Predicting more of the people more of the time: Assessing the personality of situations. *Psychological Review, 85*, 485–501.

Ben-Shakhar, G. (1989). Non-conventional methods in personnel selection. In P. Herriot (Ed.), *Assessment and selection in organizations.* Chichester, UK: Wiley.

Ben-Shakhar, G., Bar-Hillel, M., Bilu, Y., Ben-Abba, E., & Flug, A. (1986). Can graphology predict occupational success? Two empirical studies and some methodological ruminations. *Journal of Applied Psychology, 71*, 645–653.

Ben-Shakhar, G., & Furedy, J. J. (1990). *Theories and applications in the detection of deception.* New York: Springer-Verlag.

Berenbeim, R. E. (1987). *Corporate ethics.* New York: The Conference Board.

Berman, K. (1989). Banks advised to screen employees. *Business Insurance, 23* (7), 26.

Binning, J. F., & Barrett, G. V. (1989). Validity of personnel decisions: A conceptual analysis of the inferential and evidential bases. *Journal of Applied Psychology, 74*, 478–494.

Blasi, A. (1980). Bridging moral cognition and moral action: A critical review of the literature. *Psychological Bulletin, 88*, 1–45.

Blau, P. M., & Scott, W. R. (1962). *Formal organizations.* San Francisco: Chandler.

Bowers, K. (1973). Situationalism in psychology: An analysis and critique. *Psychological Review, 80*, 307–363.

Brenner, S. R., & Molander, E. A. (1977). Is the ethics of business changing? *Harvard Business Review, 55*, 57–71.

Brief, A. P., & Motowidlo, S. J. (1986). Prosocial organizational behavior. *Academy of Management Review, 11,* 710–725.

Broder, J. F. (1984). *Risk analysis and the security survey.* Boston: Butterworth.

Brophy, B. (1986, September 29). New technology, high anxiety. *U.S. News and World Report,* pp. 54–55.

Buchanan, B. (1974). Building organizational commitment: The socialization of managers in work organizations. *Administrative Science Quarterly, 19,* 533–546.

Buckley, D. M. (1988). Turning the tables. *Security Management, 32* (4), 103–105.

Buckley, J. P. (1987). Nobody's perfect. *Security Management, 32* (5), 77–82.

Buckley, J. P. (1989). The integrity interview: Behavioral analysis interviews for job applicants. *The Investigator, 5* (3), 9–12. Chicago: John E. Reid & Associates.

Burgess, R. L., & Akes, R. L. (1966). A differential association-reinforcement theory of criminal behavior. *Social Problems, 14,* 128–147.

Burstein, H. (1986). *Industrial security management.* New York: Praeger.

Burton, R. V. (1963). Generality of honesty reconsidered. *Psychological Review, 70,* 481–499.

Butcher, J. N. (1991). Screening for psychopathology: Industrial applications of the Minnesota Multiphasic Personality Inventory. In J. Jones, B. Steffy, & D. Bray (Eds.), *Applying psychology in business: The handbook for managers and human resource professionals* (pp. 835–850). Lexington, MA: Lexington.

Byrne, R. W. (1991, May/June). Brute intellect: Understanding the animal mind. *The Sciences,* 42–47.

Caldwell, R. G. (1968). A re-examination of the concept of white-collar crime. In G. Gies (Ed.), *White-collar criminal.* New York: Atherton Press.

Carson, C. R. (1977). *Managing employee honesty.* Los Angeles: Security World Publishing.

Carson, R. C. (1989). Personality. *Annual Review of Psychology, 40,* 227–248.

Carson, T., Wokutch, R. E., & Murrmann, K. F. (1982). Bluffing in labor negotiations: Legal and ethical issues. *Journal of Business Ethics, 1,* 13–22.

Carter, R. (1987, July). Employee theft often appears legitimate. *Accountancy, 100,* 75–77.

Cascio, W. F. (1987). *Applied psychology in personnel management* (3rd ed.). Englewood Cliffs, NJ: Prentice-Hall.

Cascio, W. F., Alexander, R. A., & Barrett, G. V. (1988). Setting cutoff scores: Legal, psychometric, and professional issues and guidelines. *Personnel Psychology, 41,* 1–24.

Center for Business Ethics (1986). Are corporations institutionalizing ethics? *Journal of Business Ethics, 5,* 85–91.

Chadwick-Jones, J. K., Nicholson, N., & Brown, C. (1982). *The social psychology of absenteeism.* New York: Praeger.

Chapman, S. N., & Carter, P. L. (1990). Supplier/customer inventory relationships under just in time. *Decision Sciences, 21,* 35–52.

Chatman, J. A. (1989). Improving interactional organizational research: A model of person-organization fit. *Academy of Management Review, 14,* 333–349.

Cherrington, D. J. (1986). *Testimony before the Committee on the Judiciary.* U.S. Senate. 99th Cong., 2d sess. Serial J-99-893.

Cherrington, D. J., & Cherrington, J. O. (1985). The climate of honesty in retail stores. In W. Terris (Ed.), *Employee theft* (pp. 51–65). Chicago: London House Press.

Cleveland, J. N., & Murphy, K. R. (1992). Analyzing performance appraisal as goal-directed behavior. In G. Ferris & K. Rowland (Eds.), *Research in personnel and human resource management* (vol. 10, pp. 121–185). Greenwich, CT: JAI Press.

Clinard, M. B. (1990). *Corporate corruption.* New York: Praeger.

Cohen, J. (1990). An early warning system to control inventory shrinkage. *Supermarket Business, 45* (9), 25.

Colby, A. (1978). Evolution of a moral development theory. In W. Damon (Ed.), *Moral development.* San Francisco: Jossey-Bass.

Conway, L. G., & Cox, J. A. (1987). Internal business shrinkage. *Baylor Business Review, 5* (2), 8–11.

Cook, M. F. (1988, April). What's ahead in human resources? *Management Review, 4,* 41–44.

Cook, T. D. (1990). The generalizability of causal connections: Multiple theories in search of clear practice. In L. Secrest, E. Perrin, & J. B. Bunker (Eds.), *Research methodology: Strengthening causal interpretations of non-experimental data.* (PHS Pub. No. 90-3454). Rockville, MD: Agency for Health Care Policy and Research.

Cook, T. D., & Campbell, D. T. (1979). *Quasi experimentation.* Skokie, IL: Rand-McNally.

Cook, T. D., Campbell, D. T., & Peracchio, L. (1990). Quasi experimentation. In M. Dunnette & L. Hough (Eds.), *Handbook of industrial and organizational psychology* (2nd. ed., vol. 1. pp. 491–576). Palo Alto, CA: Consulting Psychologists Press.

Cooke, R. A., & Ryan, L. V. (1988). The relevance of ethics to management education. *Journal of Management Development, 7* (2), 28–38.

Crant, J. M., & Bateman, T. S. (1989). A model of employee responses to drug-testing programs. *Employee Responsibilities and Rights Journal, 2,* 173–190.

Crepieux-Jamin, J. (1909). *L'écriture et le caractère.* Paris: Alcan.

Cressy, D. R. (1970). Violators' vocabularies of adjustment. In E. O. Smigel & H. L. Ross (Eds.), *Crimes against bureaucracy* (pp. 65–86). New York: Van Nostrand Reinhold.

Cressy, D. R. (1986). *Testimony before the Committee on the Judiciary.* U.S. Senate. 99th Cong., 2d sess., Serial J-99-893.

Cressy, D. R., & Moore, C. A. (1983). Managerial values and corporate codes of ethics. *California Management Review, 25* (4), 53–77.

Cronbach, L. J. (1988). Five perspectives on the validity argument. In H. Wainer & H. Brown (Eds.), *Test validity.* Hillsdale, NJ: Erlbaum.

Cronbach, L. J. (1990). *Essentials of psychological testing* (5th ed.). New York: Harper & Row.

Cronbach, L. J., & Gleser, G. C. (1965). *Psychological tests and personnel decisions* (2nd ed.). Urbana: University of Illinois Press.

Cronbach, L. J., Gleser, G. C., Nanda, H., & Rajaratnam, N. (1972). *The dependability of test scores: Theory of generalizability for scores and profiles.* New York: Wiley.

Crown, D. F., & Rosse, J. G. (1988). A critical review of the assumptions underlying drug testing. *Journal of Business and Psychology, 3,* 22–41.

Cunningham, M. R. (1989). Test–taking motivations and outcomes on a standardized measure of on-the-job integrity. *Journal of Business and Psychology, 4,* 119–127.

Cunningham, M. R., & Ash, P. (1988). The structure of honesty: Analysis of the Reid Report. *Journal of Business and Psychology, 3,* 54–66.

Curtis, R. (1973). *Security control: Internal theft.* New York: Chain Store Age Books.

Dalton, M. (1981). The interlocking of official and unofficial reward. In O. Grusky & G. A. Miller (Eds.), *The sociology of organizations: Basic studies* (2nd ed., pp. 324–345). New York: Free Press.

Dansereau, F., Graen, G., & Haga, W. J. (1975). A vertical dyad linkage approach to leadership within formal organizations: A longitudinal investigation of the role-making process. *Organizational Behavior and Human Performance, 13,* 46–78.

Davis-Blake, A., & Pfeffer, J. (1989). Just a mirage: The search for dispositional effects in organizational research. *Academy of Management Review, 14,* 385–400.

DeCotiis, T. A., & Summers, T. P. (1987). A path analysis of a model of the antecedents and consequences of organizational commitment. *Human Relations, 40,* 445–470.

DeGeorge, R. T. (1987). The status of business ethics: Past and future. *Journal of Business Ethics, 6,* 201–211.

DePaulo, B. M., Stone, J. I., & Lassiter, G. D. (1985). Deceiving and detecting deceit. In B. Schlenker (Ed.), *The self and social life* (pp. 323–370). New York: McGraw Hill.

DePaulo, P. J. (1988). Research in deception in marketing communication: Its relevance to the study of nonverbal behavior. *Journal of Nonverbal Behavior, 12,* 253–273.

DePaulo, P. J., & DePaulo, B. M. (1989). Can deception by salespersons and customers be detected through nonverbal behavioral cues? *Journal of Applied and Social Psychology, 19,* 1552–1577.

DePaulo, P. J., DePaulo, B. M., Tang, J., & Swaim, G. W. (1989). Lying and detecting lies in organizations. In R. Giacalone & P. Rosenfeld (Eds.), *Impression management in the organization* (pp. 377–396). Hillsdale, NJ: Erlbaum.

Digman, J. M. (1990). Personality structure: Emergence of the five-factor model. *Annual Review of Psychology, 41,* 417–440.

Dinitz, S. (1982). Multidisciplinary approaches to white-collar crime. In H. Edelhertz & T. Overcast (Eds.), *White collar crime: An agenda for research* (pp. 129–152). Lexington, MA: Lexington.

Ditton, J. (1977). Perks, pilferage and the fiddle: The historical structure of invisible wages. *Theory and Society, 4,* 39–71.

Downey, J. E. (1919). *Graphology and the psychology of handwriting.* Baltimore: Warwick & York.

Dozier, D. B., & Miceli, M. P. (1985). Potential predictors of whistle-blowing: A prosocial behavior perspective. *Academy of Management Review, 10,* 823–836.

Drasgow, F., & Hulin, C. L. (1991). Item response theory. In M. Dunnette & L. Hough (Eds.), *Handbook of industrial and organizational psychology* (2nd ed., vol. 1, pp. 577–636). Palo Alto, CA: Consulting Psychologists Press.

Drucker, P. (1981, September). Ethical chic. *The Public Interest, 63,* 18–36.

Druckman, D., & Swets, J. A. (1988). *Enhancing human performance: Issues, theories and techniques.* Washington, DC: National Academy Press.

Dudycha, G. J. (1936). An objective study of punctuality in relation to personality and achievement. *Archives of Psychology, 29,* 1–53.

Edwards, W., & Newman, J. (1982). *Multiattribute utility theory.* Newbury Park, CA: Sage.

Eisenberger, R., Fasolo, P., & Davis-LaMastro, V. (1990). Perceived organizational support and employee diligence, commitment, and innovation. *Journal of Applied Psychology, 75,* 51–59.

Eisenberger, R., Huntington, R., Hutchinson, S., & Sowa, D. (1986). Perceived organizational support. *Journal of Applied Psychology, 71,* 500–507.

Ekman, P. (1973). *Darwin and facial expression: A century of research in review.* New York: Academic Press.

Ekman, P. (1975). *Telling lies: Clues to deceit in the marketplace, politics, and marriage.* New York: Norton.

Ekman, P., & O'Sullivan, M. (1991). Who can catch a lie? American Psychologist, 46, 913–920.

Ethical principles of psychologists, as amended on June 2, 1989 (1989). *American Psychologist, 45,* 390–395.

Etzioni, A. (1975). *A comparative analysis of complex organizations.* New York: Free Press.

Feldman, D. (1976). A contingency view of socialization. *Administrative Science Quarterly, 21,* 433–452.

Feliu, A. G. (1990, Winter). Whistle blowing while you work. *Business and Society Review,* 65–67.

Fennelly, L. J. (1989). *Handbook of loss prevention and crime prevention.* (2nd ed.). Boston: Butterworth.

Festinger, L., Schachter, S., & Back, K. (1950). *Social pressures in informal groups: A study of human factors in housing.* New York: Harper.

Finnerman, E. D. (1981). *Security supervision: A handbook for supervisors and managers.* Boston: Butterworth.

Finney, H. C., & Lesieur, H. C. (1982). Contingency theory of organizational crime. In S. Bacharach (Ed.), *Research in the sociology of organizations* (vol. 1, pp. 255–299). Greenwich, CT: JAI Press.

Fisher, C. D. (1986). Organizational socialization: An integrative review. In K. Rowland & G. Ferris (Eds.), *Research in personnel and human resource management* (vol. 4, pp. 211–242). Greenwich, CT: JAI Press.

Fisher, J. D., & Baron, R. M. (1982). An equity based model of vandalism. *Population and Environment, 5,* 182–200.

Frank, F. D., Lindley, B. S., & Cohen, R. A. (1981). *Standards for psychological assessment of nuclear facility personnel.* Washington, DC: U.S. Office of Nuclear Regulatory Research.

Frank, R. F. (1989, summer). How passion pays: Finding opportunities in honesty. *Business and Society Review*, 20–28.

Freeman, R. E. (1990). Ethics in the workplace: Recent scholarship. In C. L. Cooper & I. T. Robertson (Eds.), *International review of industrial and organizational psychology*. (vol. 5, pp. 149–167). Chichester: Wiley.

French, P. A. (1985). The Hester Prynne sanction. *Business and Professional Ethics Journal, 4* (2), 19–32.

Friedman, M. (1970, September 13). The social responsibility of business is to increase profits. The *New York Times Magazine*, pp. 32 ff.

Fritzche, D., & Becker, H. (1984). Linking management behavior to ethical philosophy: An empirical investigation. *Academy of Management Journal, 27*, 166–175.

Furedy, J. J., & Liss, J. (1985). Countering confessions induced by the polygraph: Of confessionals and psychological rubber hoses. *Criminal Law Quarterly, 29*, 91–114.

Gaetani, J. J., & Johnson, C. M. (1983). The effects of data plotting, praise, and state lottery tickets on decreasing cash shortages in a retail beverage chain. *Journal of Organizational Behavior Management, 5*, 5–15.

Gellerman, S. W. (1989). Managing ethics from the top down. *Sloan Management Review, 30* (2), 73–79.

Gies, F. L., & Moon, T. H. (1981). Machiavellianism and deception. *Journal of Personality and Social Psychology, 41*, 403–416.

Glasscock, S. G., Deckner, C. W., & Mahan, T. F. (1991). The use of signs to control shoplifting and employee theft. In J. Jones, B. Steffy, & D. Bray (Eds.), *Applying psychology in business: The handbook for managers and human resource professionals* (pp. 862–870). Lexington, MA: Lexington.

Glenn, J. J. (1988). Business students and ethics: Implications for professors and managers. In C. C. Walton (Ed.), *Enriching business ethics* (pp. 213–232). New York: Plenum Press.

Goldman, P. (1983). A sociohistorical perspective on performance assessment. In F. Landy, S. Zedeck, & J. Cleveland (Eds.) *Performance measurement and theory* (pp. 337–352). Hillsdale, NJ: Erlbaum.

Goldstein, I. (1971). The application blank: How honest are applicants? *Journal of Applied Psychology, 55*, 491–492.

Goldstein, I. (1986). *Training in organizations: Needs assessment, development, and evaluation* (2nd ed.). Pacific Grove, CA: Brooks/Cole.

Golembiewski, R., Billingsley, K., & Yeager, S. (1976). Measuring change by OD designs. *Journal of Applied Behavioral Science, 12* (2), 133–157.

Goode, E. (1978). *Deviant behavior: An interactionist approach*. Englewood Cliffs, NJ: Prentice-Hall.

Goodenough, D. R. (1976). The role of individual differences in field dependence as a factor in learning and memory. *Psychological Bulletin, 83*, 675–694.

Graen, G. (1976). Role-making processes in complex organizations. In M. D. Dunnette (Ed.), *Handbook of industrial and organizational psychology* (pp. 1201–1246). Chicago: Rand-McNally.

Greenberg, J. (1990). Employee theft as a reaction to underpayment inequity: The hidden cost of pay cuts. *Journal of Applied Psychology, 75*, 561–568.

Gust, S. W., & Walsh, J. M. (1989). *Drugs in the workplace: Research and* evaluation data. NIDA Research Monograph 91. Rockville, MD: National Institute on Drug Abuse.

Guthrie, J., & Olian, J. (1989, April). *Drug and alcohol testing programs: Influence of organizational context and objectives.* Presented at Annual Conference of Society for Industrial and Organizational Psychology, Boston.

Hacker, A. (1978). Loyalty and the whistle blower. *Across the Board, 15,* 4–9, 76.

Hackman, J. R. (1976). Group influences on individuals. In M. Dunnette (Ed.), *Handbook of industrial and organizational psychology* (pp. 1455–1526). Chicago: Rand-McNally.

Hackworth, D. H. (1989). *About face.* New York: Touchstone.

Hagan, J. (1989). *Structural criminology.* New Brunswick, NJ: Rutgers University Press.

Hale, M. (1980). *Human science and the social order.* Philadelphia: Temple University Press.

Hampson, S. E. (1988). What are truthfulness and honesty? In A. Gale (Ed.), *The polygraph test: Lies, truth and science* (pp. 53–64). London: Sage.

Harrington, S. J. (1991). What corporate America is teaching about ethics. *Academy of Management Executive, 5,* 21–30.

Harris, C. W. (1963). *Problems in measuring change.* Madison: University of Wisconsin Press.

Harris, M. M., & Sackett, P. R. (1987). A factor analysis and item response theory analysis of an employee honesty test. *Journal of Business and Psychology, 2,* 122–135.

Hartshorne, H., & May, M. A. (1928). *Studies in deceit.* New York: Macmillan.

Hegarty, W. H., & Sims, H. P (1978). Some determinants of unethical behavior: An experiment. *Journal of Applied Psychology, 63,* 451–457.

Hoffman, W. M., & Moore, J. M. (1982). What is business ethics? A reply to Drucker. *Journal of Business Ethics, 1,* 293–300.

Hogan, J., & Hogan, R. (1989). How to measure employee reliability. *Journal of Applied Psychology, 74,* 273–279.

Hollinger, R. C. (1989). *A manager's guide to preventing employee theft.* Park Ridge, IL: London House Press.

Hollinger, R. C., & Clark, J. P. (1982a). Employee deviance: A response to the perceived quality of the work experience. *Work and Occupations, 9,* 97–114.

Hollinger, R. C., & Clark, J. P. (1982b). Formal and informal social controls of employee deviance. *The Sociological Quarterly, 23,* 333–343.

Hollinger, R. C., & Clark, J. P. (1983). *Theft by employees.* Lexington, MA: Heath.

Horgan, J. (1990). Test negative: A look at the evidence justifying illicit-drug tests. *Scientific American, 262* (3), 18–22.

Horning, D. N. (1970). Blue-collar theft: Conceptions of property, attitudes toward pilfering, and work-group norms in a modern industrial plant. In E. O. Smigel & H. L. Ross (Eds.), *Crimes against bureaucracy* (pp. 45–64). New York: Van Nostrand Reinhold.

Hosmer, L. T. (1987). The institutionalization of unethical behavior. *Journal of Business Ethics, 6,* 439–447.

Hough, L. M., Eaton, N. K., Dunnette, M. D., Kamp, J. D., & McCloy, R. A. (1990). Criterion-related validities of personality constructs and the effect of response distortion on those validities. *Journal of Applied Psychology,* 75, 581–595.

Hovarth, F. (1978). An experimental comparison of the Psychological Stress Evaluator and the galvanic skin response in the detection of deception. *Journal of Applied Psychology,* 63, 338–344.

Hovarth, F. (1979). The effects of differential motivation on detection of deception with the Psychological Stress Evaluator and the galvanic skin response. *Journal of Applied Psychology,* 64, 323–330.

Hunter, J. E., & Schmidt, F. L. (1990). *Methods of meta-analysis.* Newbury Park, CA: Sage.

Hyman, R. (1989). The psychology of deception. *Annual Review of Psychology,* 40, 133–154.

Inbau, F. E. (1989). Shoring up eroding options. *Security Management, 33* (6), 53–58.

Janis, I. L. (1972). *Victims of groupthink.* Boston: Houghton Mifflin.

Jansen, E., & Von Glinow, M. A. (1985). Ethical ambivalence and organizational reward systems. *Academy of Management Review, 10,* 814–822.

Jaspan, N. (1974). *Mind your own business.* Englewood Cliffs, NJ: Prentice Hall.

Johnson, E. (1983). *International handbook of contemporary developments in criminology: General issues and the Americas.* Westport, CT: Greenwood Press.

Johnson, K. L. (1987, October). How to interview for the truth. *Manager's Magazine, 62,* 28–29.

Jones, D. A. (1986). *History of criminology: A philosophical perspective.* Westport, CT: Greenwood Press.

Jones, D., & Bennett, P. (1986). *A bibliography of business ethics 1981–1985,* Lewistown, NY: Edwin Mellon Press.

Jones, J. W., Ash, P., & Soto, C. (1990). Employment privacy rights and pre-employment honesty tests. *Employee Relations Law Journal, 15,* 561–575.

Jones, J. W., Joy, D. S., & Rospenda, K. M. (1990). Employee deviance base rates: A summary of empirical research. Unpublished report. Park Ridge, IL: London House, Inc.

Jordan, S. (1988). Analysis and approximation of a JIT production line. *Decision Sciences, 19,* 672–682.

Kahneman, D., & Tversky, A. (1979). Prospect theory: An analysis of decision under risk. *Econometrica, 47,* 263–291.

Kandel, D. B. (1975). Stages in adolescent involvement in drug use. *Science, 190,* 912–914.

Kanter, R. (1968). Commitment and social organization: A study of commitment mechanisms in utopian communities. *American Sociological Review, 33,* 499–517.

Katz, D., & Kahn, R. L. (1978). *The social psychology of organizations* (2nd ed.). New York: Wiley.

Kenrick, D. T., & Funder, D. C. (1988). Profiting from controversy: Lessons from the person-situation debate. *American Psychologist, 43,* 23–34.

Keogh, J. E. (1981). *The small business security handbook.* Englewood Cliffs, NJ: Prentice-Hall.

Kirkpatrick, D. L. (1977). Evaluating training programs: Evidence vs. proof. *Training and Development Journal, 31,* 9–12.

Kirkpatrick, D. L. (1983). Four steps to measuring training effectiveness. *Personnel Administrator, 28* (11), 19–25.

Kirwan, C. (1989). *Augustine.* New York: Routledge.

Kleinmuntz, B. (1985). Lie detectors fail the truth test. *Harvard Business Review, 85,* 36–42.

Kleinmuntz, B., & Szucko, J. (1984). Lie detection in ancient and modern times: A call for contemporary scientific study. *American Psychologist, 39,* 766–776.

Kohlberg, L. (1969). Stage and sequence: The cognitive development approach to socialization. In D. A. Goslin (Ed.), *The handbook of socialization theory and research* (pp. 347–480). Chicago: Rand-McNally.

Kohlberg, L. (1981). *The philosophy of moral development.* New York: Harper & Row.

Kohn, M. L., & Schooler, C. (1978). The reciprocal effects of the substantive complexity of work and intellectual flexibility: A longitudinal assessment. *American Journal of Sociology, 84,* 24–52.

Kohn, M. L., & Schooler, C. (1982). Job conditions and personality: A longitudinal assessment of their reciprocal effects. *American Journal of Sociology, 87,* 1257–1286.

Korchkin, S. (1987). Personality correlates of a measure of honesty. *Journal of Business and Psychology, 1,* 236–247.

Kovach, J. L. (1985). Spies on the payroll. *Industry Week, 225* (4) 75–77.

Kozlowsky, M., & Moaz, O. (1988). Commitment and personality variables as discriminators among sports referees. *Journal of Sport and Exercise Psychology, 10,* 262–269.

Landy, F. J. (1985). *Psychology of work behavior* (3rd ed.). Pacific Grove, CA: Brooks/Cole.

Landy, F. J. (1987). Stamp collecting versus science: Validation as hypothesis testing. *American Psychologist, 41,* 1183–1192.

Lary, B. (1988). Thievery on the inside. *Security Management, 32* (5), 79–84.

Latane, B., & Darley, J. M. (1968). Group inhibition of bystander intervention in emergencies. *Journal of Personality and Social Psychology, 10,* 215–221.

Lawler, E. E. (1986). *High-involvement management: Participative strategies for improving organizational performance.* San Francisco: Jossey-Bass.

Lewicki, R. J. (1983). Lying and deception: A behavioral model. In M. Bazerman & R. Lewicki (Eds.), *Negotiating in organizations.* Newbury Park, CA: Sage.

Lewis, M. (1989). *Liar's poker.* New York: Norton.

Libbin, A. E., Mendelsohn, S. R., & Duffy, D. P. (1988). Employee medical and honesty testing. *Personnel, 65* (11), 38–48.

Lincoln, J. R., & Kalleberg, A. L. (1990). *Culture, control, and commitment: A study of work organization and work values in the United States and Japan.* New York: Cambridge University Press.

Linden, R. C., & Graen, G. (1980). Generalizability of the vertical dyadic linkage model of leadership. *Academy of Management Journal, 23,* 451–465.

Linville, P. W., & Jones, E. J. (1980). Polarized appraisals of out-group members. *Journal of Personality and Social Psychology, 38,* 689–703.

Lipman, M. (1973). *Stealing: How America's employees are stealing their companies blind.* New York: Harper's.

Lippa, R. A. (1990). *Introduction to social psychology.* Belmont, CA: Wadsworth.

Loeb, S. E., & Cory, S. N. (1989). Whistle blowing and management accounting: An approach. *Journal of Business Ethics, 8,* 903–916.

Logan, T. G., Koettel, R. C., & Moore, R. W. (1986). Personality correlated of a test of honesty. *Psychological Reports, 59,* 1015–1018.

Lorber, L. Z., & Kirk, J. R. (1987). *Fear itself: A legal and personnel analysis of drug testing, AIDS, secondary smoke, VDT's.* Alexandria, VA: ASPA Foundation.

Lord, F. M., & Novick, M. (1968). *Statistical theories of mental test scores.* Reading, MA: Addison-Wesley.

Lord, R. G., & Maher, K. J. (1991). Cognitive theory in industrial and organizational psychology. In M. Dunnette & L. Hough (Eds.), *Handbook of industrial and organizational psychology* (2nd ed., vol. 2, pp. 1–62). Palo Alto, CA: Consulting Psychologists Press.

Lowman, R. (1989). *Pre-employment screening for psychopathology: A guide to professional practice.* Sarasota, FL: Professional Resource Exchange.

Lumley, E. (1875). *The art of judging the character of individuals from their handwriting and style.* London: John Russell Smith.

Luthans, F., Baack, D., & Taylor, L. (1987). Organizational commitment: Analysis of antecedents. *Human Relations, 40,* 445–470.

Lykken, D. T. (1981). *A tremor in the blood: Uses and abuses of the lie detector.* New York: McGraw-Hill.

Madia. (1990, September). DRP vs. order point inventory management: New solutions to old problems. *Automation, 37,* 44–47.

Magnusson, D., & Endler, N. S. (Eds.). (1977). *Personality at the crossroads: Current issues in interactional psychology.* Hillsdale, NJ: Erlbaum.

Mahoney, T. (1979). *Compensation and reward perspectives.* Homewood, IL: Irwin.

Manhardt, P. J. (1989). Base rates and tests of deception: Has I/O psychology shot itself in the foot? *The Industrial-Organizational Psychologist, 26* (2), 48–50.

Mangione, T. W., & Quinn, R. F. (1975). Job satisfaction, counterproductive behavior, and drug use at work. *Journal of Applied Psychology, 60,* 114–116.

Manley, W. W. (1991). *Executive's handbook of model business codes of conduct.* Englewood Cliffs, NJ: Prentice-Hall.

March, J., & Simon, H. (1958). *Organizations.* New York: Wiley.

Mars, G. (1973). Chance, punters, and the fiddle: Institutionalized pilferage in a hotel dining room. In M. Warner (Ed.), *The sociology of the workplace: An interdisciplinary approach.* London: Allen & Unwin.

Martin, S. L. (1988). Honesty testing: Estimating and reducing the false positive rate. *Journal of Business and Psychology, 3,* 255–267.

Martin, S. L., & Terris, W. (1990). The four-cell classification table in personnel selection: A heuristic gone awry. *The Industrial-Organizational Psychologist, 27,* 49–55.

Martin, S. L., & Terris, W. (1991). Predicting infrequent behavior: Clarifying the impact of false-positive rates. *Journal of Applied Psychology, 76,* 484–487.

Masuda, B. (1990). Understanding your shrink. *Security Management, 34* (7), 33–34.

Mathews, M. (1988). *Strategic intervention in organizations.* Newbury Park, CA: Sage.

Mathieu, J. E., & Zajac, D. M. (1990). A review and meta-analysis of the anteced-ents, correlates, and consequences of organizational commitment. *Psychological Bulletin, 108*, 171–194.

McCrea, R. R., & Costa, P. T., Jr. (1985). Updating Norman's "adequate taxonomy": Intelligence and personality dimensions in natural language and questionnaires. *Journal of Personality and Social Psychology, 49*, 710–721.

McCrea, R. R., & Costa, P. T., Jr. (1986). Clinical assessment can benefit from recent advances in personality psychology. *American Psychologist, 51*, 1001–1002.

McCrea, R. R., & Costa, P. T., Jr. (1987). Validation of the five-factor model of personality across instruments and observers. *Journal of Personality and Social Psychology, 52*, 81–90.

McCrea, R. R., & Costa, P. T., Jr. (1989). The structure of interpersonal traits: Wiggin's circumplex and the five-factor model. *Journal of Personality and Social Psychology, 56*, 586–595.

McDaniel, M. A. (1988). Does pre-employment drug use predict on-the-job suitability? *Personnel Psychology, 41*, 717–729.

McDaniel, M. A. (1989). Biographical constructs for predicting employee suitability. *Journal of Applied Psychology, 74*, 964–970.

McDaniel, M. A., & Jones, J. W. (1988). Predicting employee theft: A quantitative review of the validity of a standardized measure of dishonesty. *Journal of Business and Psychology, 2*, 327–345.

McDonald, G. M., & Zepp, R. A. (1990). What should be done? A practical approach to business ethics. *Management Decision, 28* (1), 9–14.

McFall, L. (1987). Integrity. *Ethics, 98*, 5–20.

McKee, T. E., & Bayes, P. E. (1987). Why audit background investigations? *Internal Auditor, 44* (5), 53–56.

Meier, R. F., & Short, J. F. (1982). The consequences of white-collar crime. In H. Edelhertz & T. Overcast (Eds.), *White-collar crime: An agenda for research* (pp. 23–49). Lexington, MA: Lexington Books.

Meinsma, G. (1985). Thou shalt not steal. *Security Management, 29*, 35–37.

Mendelsohn, S. R., & Morrison, K. K. (1988). The right to privacy at the workplace: Part 1. Employee searches. *Personnel, 65* (7), 20–27.

Mentkowski, M. (1988). Paths to integrity: Educating for personal growth and professional performance. In S. Srivastva (Ed.), *Executive integrity* (pp. 89–121). San Francisco: Jossey-Bass.

Merriam, D. H. (1977). Employee theft. *Criminal Justice Abstracts, 9*, 375–376.

Merton, R. K. (1964). Anomie, anomia and social interaction: Contexts of deviant behavior. In M. B. Clinard (Ed.), *Anomie and deviant behavior: A discussion and critique* (pp. 213–242). New York: Free Press.

Miceli, M. P., & Near, J. P. (1985). Characteristics of organizational climate and perceived wrongdoing associated with whistle blowing decisions. *Personnel Psychology, 38*, 525–544.

Miceli, M. P., & Near, J. P. (1988). Individual and situational correlates of whistle-blowing. *Personnel Psychology, 41*, 267–281.

Miceli, M. P., & Near, J. P. (1989). The incidence of wrongdoing, whistle-blowing, and retaliation: Results of a naturally occurring field experiment. *Employee Responsibilities and Rights Journal, 2* (2), 91–108.

Miceli, M. P., & Near, J. P. (in press, a). Whistle-blowing as an organizational process. In S. Bacharach and R. Magjuka (Eds.), *Research in the sociology of organizations*. Greenwich, CT: JAI Press.

Miceli, M. P., & Near, J. P. (in press, b). *Whistle blowing in organizations*. New York: Macmillan.

Mischel, W. (1968). *Personality and assessment*. New York: Wiley.

Mischel, W. (1977). On the future of personality measurement. *American Psychologist, 32*, 246–254.

Mischel, W., & Peake, P. K. (1982). Beyond déjà vu in the search for situational consistency. *Psychological Review, 89*, 730–755.

Model guidelines for preemployment testing programs. Washington, DC: Association of Personnel Test Publishers.

Monson, T. C., Hesley, J. W., & Chernick, L. (1982). Specifying when personality traits can and cannot predict behavior: An alternative to abandoning the attempt to predict single-act criteria. *Journal of Personality and Social Psychology, 43*, 385–399.

Moore, R. W. (1988). Unmasking thieves: From polygraph to paper. *Journal of Managerial Psychology, 3*, 17–21.

Moretti, D. M. (1986). The prediction of employee counterproductivity through attitude assessment. *Journal of Business and Psychology, 1*, 134–147.

Morris, J., & Sherman, J. D. (1981). Generalizability of an organizational commitment model. *Academy of Management Journal, 24*, 512–526.

Mottaz, C. J. (1988). Determinants of organizational commitment. *Human Relations, 41*, 467–482.

Mowbray, S. (1988). Trends: Character studies. *Canadian Business, 61* (7), 71–73.

Mowday, R. T., Porter, L. W., & Steers, R. M. (1982). *Employee-organization linkages: The psychology of commitment, absenteeism, and turnover*. New York: Academic Press.

Murphy, K. R. (1987). Detecting infrequent deception. *Journal of Applied Psychology, 72*, 611–614.

Murphy, K. R. (1989). Maybe we *should* shoot ourselves in the foot: Reply to Manhardt. *The Industrial-Organizational Psychologist, 26* (3), 45–46.

Murphy, K. R. (1991). Utility issues in employee drug testing. Presented at Annual Convention of the Society for Industrial and Organizational Psychology, St. Louis.

Murphy, K. R., & Cleveland, J. N. (1991). *Performance appraisal: An organizational perspective*. Boston: Allyn & Bacon.

Murphy, K. R., & Davidshofer, C. O. (1991). *Psychological testing: Principles and applications* (2nd ed.). Englewood Cliffs, NJ: Prentice Hall.

Murphy, K. R., & Lee, S. L. (1991). Explaining the correlation between integrity and job performance: The role of conscientiousness. Unpublished report, Colorado State University.

Murphy, K. R., & Thornton, G. C., III (1992). Characteristics of employee drug testing programs. *Journal of Psychology and Business, 6*, 295–309.

Murphy, K. R., & Thornton, G. C., III (in press, b). Development and validation of a measure of attitudes toward employee drug testing. *Educational and Psychological Measurement*.

Murphy, K. R., Thornton, G. C., III, & Prue, K. (1991). The influence of job characteristics on the acceptability of employee drug testing. *Journal of Applied Psychology, 76*, 447–453.

Murphy, K. R., Thornton, G. C., III, & Reynolds, D. H. (1990). College students' attitudes towards employee drug testing programs. *Personnel Psychology, 43*, 615–631.

Nash, L. L. (1986). Ethics without the sermon. *The business of ethics and business: Harvard Business Review* (pp. 85–96). Reprint No. 11403.

Near, J. P., & Miceli, M. P. (1986). Retaliation against whistle blowers: Predictors and effects. *Journal of Applied Psychology, 71*, 137–145.

Near, J. P., & Miceli, M. P. (1987). Whistle-blowers in organizations: Dissidents or reformers? In B. Staw (Ed.), *Research in organizational behavior* (vol. 9, pp. 321–368). Greenwich, CT: JAI Press.

Newcomb, T. M. (1929). *Consistency of certain extrovert-introvert behavior patterns in 51 problem boys.* New York: Columbia University, Teachers College.

Normand, J., Salyards, S. D., & Mahoney, J. J. (1990). An evaluation of pre-employment drug testing. *Journal of Applied Psychology, 75*, 629–639.

Norris, F. (1991, September 19). Forcing Salomon into Buffett's conservative mold. *New York Times*, vol. 141, sec. 3, p. F8.

Norton, T. W. (1988). Righting resume fraud. *Security Management, 32* (9), 87–90.

Nunnally, J. C. (1982). *Psychometric theory* (2nd ed.). New York: McGraw-Hill.

O'Bannon, R. M., Goldinger, L. A, & Appleby, J. D. (1989). *Honesty and integrity testing: A practical guide.* Atlanta: Applied Information Resources.

O'Boyle, T. F. (1985, August 8). More firms require employee drug tests. *Wall Street Journal*, p. 6.

Office of Technology Assessment (1983). *Scientific validity of polygraph testing: A research review.* Washington, DC: U.S. Congress, Office of Technology Assessment.

Office of Technology Assessment (1990). *The use of integrity tests for pre-employment screening.* Washington, DC: U.S. Congress, Office of Technology Assessment.

O'Hair, D., & Cody, M. J. (1987). Gender and vocal stress differences during truthful and deceptive information sequences. *Human Relations, 40*, 1–13.

Ones, D. S., Viswesvaran, C., & Schmidt, F. L (1992). An examination of validity generalization and moderators of integrity test validity. Presented at Annual Conference of Society for Industrial and Organizational Psychology, Montreal.

O'Reilly, C. A., Chatman, J. A., & Caldwell, D. F. (1991). People and organizational culture: A profile comparison approach to assessing person-organization fit. *Academy of Management Journal, 34*, 487–516.

O'Toole, G. J. A. (1988). *The encyclopedia of American intelligence and espionage from the Revolutionary War to the present.* New York: Facts on File.

Paajanen, G. E. (1988). The prediction of counterproductive behavior by individual and group variables. Doctoral dissertation, University of Minnesota.

Patrick, C. J., & Iacono, W. G. (1991). Validity of the control question polygraph test: The problem of sampling bias. *Journal of Applied Psychology, 76*, 229–238.

Patterson, G. R., DeBaryshe, B. D., & Ramsey, E. A. (1989). A developmental perspective on antisocial behavior. *American Psychologist, 44,* 329–335.

Payne, S. L. (1989). Self-presentation tactics and employee theft. In R. Giacalone & P. Rosenfeld (Eds.), *Impression management in the organization* (pp. 397–408). Hillsdale, NJ: Erlbaum.

Penn, W. Y., & Collier, B. D. (1985). Current research on moral development as a decision support system. *Journal of Business Ethics, 4,* 131–136.

Pervin, L. A. (1985). Personality: Current controversies, issues, and directions. *Annual Review of Psychology, 36,* 83–114.

Pervin, L. A. (1989). Persons, situations, interactions: The history of a controversy and a discussion of theoretical models. *Academy of Management Review, 14,* 350–360.

Peterson, R. T., & Carlson, D. C. (1987). Combating employee dishonesty. *Business, 37* (4), 42–44.

Pocock, P. (1989). Is business ethics a contradiction in terms? *Personnel Management, 21* (1), 60–63.

Price, R. H., & Bouffard, D. L. (1974). Behavioral appropriateness and situational constraint as dimensions of social behavior. *Journal of Personality and Social Psychology, 30,* 579–586.

Pyke, D. F., & Cohen, M. A. (1990). Push and pull in manufacturing and distributing systems. *Journal of Operations Management, 24,* 24–44.

Rafaeli, A., & Klimoski, R. J. (1983). Predicting sales success through handwriting analysis: An evaluation of the effects of training and handwriting sample content. *Journal of Applied Psychology, 68,* 212–217.

Raskin, D. C. (1988). Does science support polygraph testing? In A. Gale (Ed.), *The polygraph test: Lies, truth and science* (pp. 96–110). London: Sage.

Reid, J. E., & Inbau, F. E. (1977). *Truth and deception: The polygraph ("lie detector") technique* (2nd ed.). Baltimore: Williams & Wilkins.

Reid, L. D., Murphy, K. R., & Reynolds, D. H. (1990). Drug abuse and drug testing in the workplace. In K. Murphy and F. Saal (Eds.), *Psychology in organizations: Integrating science and practice* (pp. 241–265). Hillsdale, NJ: Erlbaum.

Risser, D. T. (1989). Punishing corporations: A proposal. *Business and Professional Ethics Journal, 8* (3), 83–92.

Rosenbaum, D. P., & Bauer, T. L. (1982). Measuring and controlling employee theft: A national assessment of the state of the art. *Journal of Security, 5* (2), 67–80.

Rosenbaum, R. W. (1976). Predictability of employee theft using weighted application blanks. *Journal of Applied Psychology, 61,* 94–98.

Rosendale, D. (1987, June 7). A whistle-blower. The *New York Times Magazine, 136,* 56.

Rotter, J. B. (1982). *The development and application of social learning theory.* New York: Praeger.

Ryan, A. M., & Sackett, P. R. (1987). Pre-employment honesty testing: Fakability, reactions of test takers, and company image. *Journal of Business and Psychology, 1,* 248–256.

Rynes, S., & Gerhart, B. (1990). Interviewer assessments of applicant "fit": An empirical investigation. *Personnel Psychology, 43,* 13–35.

Sackett, P. R. (1985). Honesty research and the person-situation debate. In W. Terris (Ed.), *Employee theft* (pp. 51–65). Chicago: London House Press.

Sackett, P. R., Burris, L. R., & Callahan, C. (1989). Integrity testing for personnel selection: An update. *Personnel Psychology, 42,* 491–529.

Sackett, P. R., & Decker, P. J. (1979). Detection of deception in the employment context: A review and critique. *Personnel Psychology, 32,* 487–506.

Sackett, P. R., & Harris, M. M. (1984). Honesty testing for personnel selection: A review and critique. *Personnel Psychology, 37,* 221–245.

Sackett, P. R., & Harris, M. M. (1985). Honesty testing for personnel selection: A review and critique. In H. J. Bernardin & D. A. Bownas (Eds.), *Personality assessment in organizations.* New York: Praeger.

Salancik, G. K. (1977). Commitment and control of organizational behavior. In B. Staw and G. Salancik (Eds.), *New directions in organizational behavior* (pp. 1–54). Chicago: St. Clair.

Sapse, A. M., Shenkin, P., & Sapse, M. (1980). *Computer applications in the private security business.* New York: Praeger.

Saxe, L. (1990). The social significance of lying. Invited address, Annual Convention of the American Psychological Association, Boston.

Saxe, L. (1991). Lying: The thoughts of an applied social psychologist. *American Psychologist, 46,* 409–415.

Schein, E. H. (1968). Organizational socialization and the profession of management. *Industrial Management Review, 9* (2), 1–15.

Schneider, B. (1987). The people make the place. *Personnel Psychology, 40,* 437–453.

Schutt, S. R. (1982, March). White-collar crime: The nation's largest growth industry. *The Accountant's Digest,* pp. 18–20.

Schutte, N. S., Kendrick, D. T., & Sadalla, E. K. (1985). The search for predictable settings: Situational prototypes, constraint, and behavioral variation. *Journal of Personality and Social Psychology, 49,* 121–128.

Schweitzer, J. A. (1987). *Computers, business, and security: The new rule for security.* Boston: Butterworth.

Sculnick, M. W. (1986, Autumn). Disciplining whistle-blowers. *Employee Relations Today, 13,* 189–194.

Serpa, R. (1985). Creating a candid corporate culture. *Journal of Business Ethics, 4,* 425–430.

Sherif, M., & Sherif, C. W. (1969). *Social psychology.* New York: Harper & Row.

Shoplifting in America (1991, January 19). *The Economist, 318,* 65.

Simon, D. R., & Eitzen, D. S. (1986). *Elite deviance* (2nd ed.). Boston: Allyn & Bacon.

Sinai, L. (1988). Employee honesty tests move to new frontiers. *Business Insurance, 22* (38), 3, 14–16.

Singer, M. (1971). The vitality of mythical numbers. *The Public Interest, 23,* 3–9.

Snyder, C. R., Higgins, R. L., & Stucky, R. J. (1983). *Excuses.* New York: Wiley.

Srivastva, S., & Barrett, F. J. (1988). Foundations of executive integrity: Dialogue, diversity, development. In S. Srivastva (Ed.), *Executive integrity* (pp. 290–319). San Francisco: Jossey-Bass.

Standards for educational and psychological testing (1985). Washington, DC: American Psychological Association.

Staub, E. (1978). *Prosocial behavior and morality: Social and personal influences* (vol. 1). New York: Academic Press.

Staw, B. M. (1977). *The two sides of commitment.* Presented at Annual Convention of Academy of Management, Orlando.

Steers, R. M. (1977). *Organizational effectiveness: A behavioral review.* Santa Monica, CA: Goodyear.

Stevens, J. M., Beyer, J., & Trice, H. M. (1978). Assessing personal, role, and organizational predictors of managerial commitment. *Academy of Management Journal, 21,* 380–396.

Stevens, L. N. (1988, April 21). Employee drug testing. Testimony (summary) before the Subcommittee on Employment Opportunities, Committee on Education and Labor, House of Representatives.

Stone, D. L., & Herringshaw, C. (1991). Effects of the purpose of the test, perceived relevance, and use of test results on reactions to honesty testing. Presented at Annual Convention of Society for Industrial and Organizational Psychology, St. Louis.

Stone, D. L., & Kotch, D. A. (1989). Individuals' attitudes toward organizational drug testing policies and practices. *Journal of Applied Psychology, 74,* 518–521.

Stone, E. F., & Stone, D. L. (1990). Privacy in organizations: Theoretical issues, research findings, and protection mechanisms. In G. Ferris & K. Rowland (Eds.), *Research in personnel and human resources management* (vol. 8, pp. 349–411). Greenwich, CT: JAI Press.

Strobl, W. M. (1978). *Crime prevention through physical security.* New York: Marcel Dekker.

Sutherland, E. H., & Cressy, D. R. (1978). *Criminology* (10th ed.). Philadelphia: J. P. Lippincott.

Swaim, R. C. (in press). Childhood risk factors and adolescent drug and alcohol abuse. *Educational Psychology Review.*

Swinyard, W. R., Rinne, H., & Kau, A. K. (1990). The morality of software piracy: A cross-cultural analysis. *Journal of Business Ethics, 9,* 655–664.

Tatham, R. L. (1974, fall). Employee views on theft in retailing. *Journal of Retailing, 50,* 49–55.

Taylor, R. R. (1986). A positive guide to theft deterrence. *Personnel Journal, 65* (8), 36–40.

Teitelman, R. (1989). Through the glass darkly. *Financial World, 158* (13), 46–47.

Terris, W., & Jones, J. (1982). Psychological factors related to employees' theft in the convenience store industry. *Psychological Reports, 51,* 1219–1238.

Terris, W., & Jones, J. (1983). *Attitudinal and personality correlates of theft among supermarket employees* (Tech. Report). Parkview, IL: London House Press.

Thorndike, R. (1949). *Personnel selection.* New York: Wiley.

Trevino, L. K. (1986). Ethical decision making in organizations: A person-situation interactionist model. *Academy of Management Review, 11,* 601–617.

Trevino, L. K., & Youngblood, S. A. (1990). Bad apples in bad barrels: A causal analysis of ethical decision-making behavior. *Journal of Applied Psychology, 75,* 378–385.

Tucker, J., Nook, S. L., & Toscano, D. J. (1989). Employee ownership perceptions at work: The effect of an employee stock ownership plan. *Work and Occupations, 16*, 26–42.

Tuleja, T. (1985). *Beyond the bottom line.* New York: Penguin.

Tweedy, D. B. (1989). *Security program design and management: A guide for security-conscious managers.* New York: Quorum.

Underwood, B. J. (1983). *Attributes of memory.* Glenwood, IL: Scott, Foresman.

U.S. Department of Labor, Bureau of Labor Statistics. (1989). *Survey of employer anti-drug programs.* Washington, DC: U.S. Dept. of Labor.

Van Maanen, J. V., & Schein, E. J. (1979). Toward a theory of organizational socialization. In B. Staw (Ed.), *Research in organizational behavior* (vol. 1, pp. 209–264). Greenwich, CT: JAI Press.

Vaughan, D. (1983). *Controlling unlawful organizational behavior: Social structure and corporate misconduct.* Chicago: University of Chicago Press.

Victor, B., & Cullen, J. B. (1987). A theory and measure of ethical climate in organizations. In W. Frederick (Ed.), *Research in corporate social performance and policy* (vol. 9, pp. 51–71). Greenwich, CT: JAI Press.

Waln, R. F., & Downey, R. G. (1987). Voice stress analysis: Use of telephone recordings. *Journal of Business and Psychology, 1*, 379–389.

Walsh, J. M., & Hawks, R. L. (1988). *Employee drug screening and detection of drug use by urinalysis.* Rockville, MD: National Institute on Drug Abuse.

Walsh, T. J., & Healy, R. J. (1973). *Protecting your business against espionage.* New York: AMACOM.

Wanous, J. P. (1980). *Organizational entry recruitment, selection and socialization of newcomers.* Reading, MA: Addison-Wesley.

Weber, J. (1990). Measuring the impact of teaching ethics to future managers: A review, assessment, and recommendations. *Journal of Business Ethics, 9*, 183–190.

Weiner, Y. (1982). Commitment in organizations: A normative view. *Academy of Management Review, 7*, 24–31.

Weiss, H. M. (1978). Social learning of work values in organizations. *Journal of Applied Psychology, 63*, 711–718.

Weiss, H. M. (1990). Learning theory and industrial and organizational psychology. In M. D. Dunnette & L. M. Hough (Eds.), *Handbook of industrial and organizational psychology* (2nd ed., vol. 1, pp. 171–221). Palo Alto, CA: Consulting Psychologists Press.

Werner, S. H., Jones, J. W., & Steffy, B. D. (1989). The relationship between intelligence, honesty, and theft admissions. *Educational and Psychological Measurement, 64*, 609–626.

White collar crime (1987, September). U.S. Department of Justice, BJS Special Report NJC-106876. Washington, DC: Superintendent of Documents.

White, L. T. (1984). Attitudinal consequences of the preemployment polygraph examination. *Journal of Applied Social Psychology, 14*, 364–374.

Winsdor, S. (1991). The use of audit sampling techniques to test inventory. *Journal of Accountancy; 171* (1), 107–111.

Wright, J. C., & Mischel, W. (1987). A conditional approach to dispositional constructs: The local predictability of social behavior. *Journal of Personality and Social Psychology, 53*, 1159–1177.

Wyer, R., & Srull, T. (1986). Human cognition in its social context. *Psychological Review, 93,* 322–359.

Zaleznik, A., Christensen, C. R., & Roethlisberger, F. J. (1958). *The motivation, productivity, and satisfaction of workers: A production study.* Cambridge, MA: Harvard University Press.

Zeitlin, L. R. (1971). A little larceny can do a lot for employee morale. *Psychology Today, 5* (1), 22–26.

Zemke, R. (1986). Employee theft: How to cut your losses. *Training, 23* (5), 74–78.

Zucker, L. G. (1983). Organizations as institutions. In S. Bacharach (Ed.), *Research in the sociology of organizations* (vol. 2, pp. 1–45). Greenwich, CT: JAI Press.

Name Index

Subject Index

absenteeism, 20–21, 137, 209
absolute decisions (*see* decision strategies)
alternatives to theft, 167–168
animal cognition, 24
anomie, 151
appropriateness indices, 118

bandwidth-fidelity dilemma, 139
base rates:
  and detection, 59
  effects of, 76–77, 81, 98, 121–122
  estimation, 77–78, 86, 200–201
  expertise in detecting deception, 79
  interpretation, 201–204
  production deviance, 78
  theft, 78
behavioral cues (*see also* deception), 79
behavior samples, 69
"big five" theory, 136–137
biographical data (*see also* dishonesty, demographic correlates; employee theft, demographic correlates), 135–136
business ethics, 62, 182, 186–191
  defined, 187
  history, 186
  personal ethics, 187–188
  profits, 188–189
  societies, 186–187
  training, 184–185, 190–191
business failures, 10

change scores, 217–218
classification, 64–65
codes of ethics (*see* ethics)
commitment (*see* organizational commitment)
comparative decisions (*see* decision strategies)
computer crimes, 164
computer monitoring (*see also* surveillance), 63, 164–166
conscientiousness, 137–138
  and honesty, 130–131
consistency of behavior, 26–30
construct validity (*see* validity)

contracts, 16–17
Control Question Technique (*see* polygraph examination)
corporate corruption (*see also* white-collar crime), 12–13, 47–48
  and organizational climate, 157
  punishment of, 150
  situational causes, 149
corporate social responsibility, 51
counterproductive behavior (*see also* production deviance), 130
criminology, 43–44

deception:
  behavioral correlates, 87, 107–108
  early research, 24
  physiological correlates, 87, 102
  recognizing, 61–62
decision errors, 65–68
  costs, 66–68, 81–83
  false positives, 97–98
  minimizing, 82–83
  role of values, 68
  tradeoffs, 66, 80, 81–83
decision groups, 171
decision strategies, 80–81
deviance (*see also* production deviance; property deviance), 17
  and organizational level, 17–18
difference scores (*see* change scores)
diffusion of responsibility, 54
Diogenes, 1, 2
dishonesty (*see also* employee theft; honesty):
  demographic correlates, 83–84
  individual vs. organizational, 148
  motivation, 84–85
  prediction of, 62–63
  types, 18–23
  workplace, 9–18, 200–201

Employee Assistance Programs, 163
employee drug testing, 175
  extent, 14, 109
  policies, 109, 111
  reactions to, 112–113, 206
  validity, 111–112

Also available
from Brooks/Cole

Classics of Organization Theory,
Third Edition
edited by Jay M. Shafritz, University of Pittsburgh, and
J. Steven Ott, University of Utah

Bringing together 49 articles by premier scholars, Shafritz and
Ott highlight the major schools of thought in organization
theory. Reorganized to reflect recent changes in the field, this
edition retains its historically oriented approach, allowing
readers to follow the ebb and flow in the development of organization theory during the
past 20 years.

The most widely quoted and reprinted theorists are represented this reader, including
*Adam Smith, Luther Gulick, Herbert Simon, Richard Cyert, Abraham Maslow, James
March*, and *Henry Mintzberg*. 480 pages. Paperbound. ISBN: 0-534-17304-7. 1992.

Classic Readings in Organizational Behavior
J. Steven Ott, University of Utah

More than 40 representative works by critically important
writers in organizational behavior are compiled in this reader.
Readings explore such key topics as Motivation, Group and
Intergroup Behavior, Leadership, People in Organizations,
Power and Influence, and Organizational Change and
Development.

*Abraham Maslow, Douglas Murray McGregor, Solomon E. Asch, Irving L. Janis, Mary
Parker Follet, Robert K. Merton, Gerald Salanncit, Jeffrey Pfeffer, Warren G. Bennis,
Rosabeth Moss Kanter* are just some of the writers who are represented in this volume of
classics. 638 pages. Paperbound. ISBN: 0-534-11073-8. 1989.

No risk! Order either book under our 30-day money-back guarantee!
Call toll-free 1-800-354-9706 for the latest prices and to place your order.
If you would like to consider either text for classroom adoption, please
write on department letterhead to the address below.

Brooks/Cole Publishing Company
511 Forest Lodge Rd.
Pacific Grove, CA 93950
(408) 373 - 0728   FAX (408) 375 -6414